7-05

A Literary Tour of Wyoming

Compiled and edited by

Michael Shay, David Romtvedt and Linn Rounds

www.pronghornpress.org

Acknowledgements

The editors acknowledge the support of the Wyoming Center for the Book and its board, both past and present. Thanks to Lesley Boughton, state librarian, who dedicated the library's resources and staff, particularly Linn Rounds, to the production of this book. We thank Howard Kaplan, an early reader of the manuscript who made valuable suggestions for revision. Thanks to the Wyoming Arts Council and its director John Coe, who helped establish the WCFB in 1995 and who lent Mike Shay, literature program manager, to the book's cause. Both the Ucross Foundation and the Library of Congress Center for the Book made donations that helped in the publication of this book.

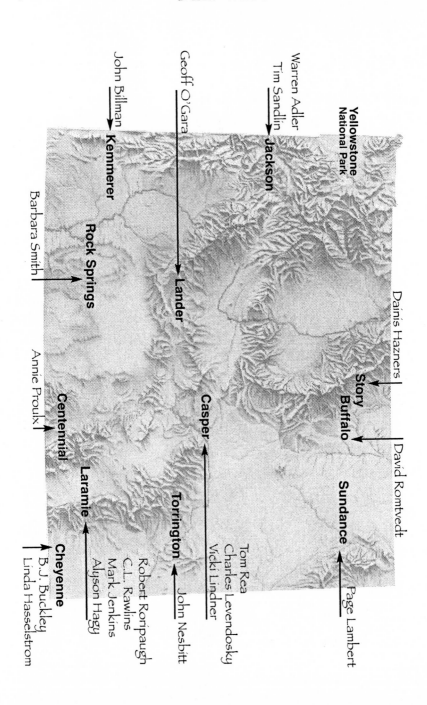

John Billman → **Kemmerer**

Geoff O'Gara

Warren Adler
Tim Sandlin → **Jackson**

Yellowstone National Park

Barbara Smith → **Rock Springs**

Lander

Dainis Hazners

Annie Proulx → **Centennial**

Casper

Story ←
Buffalo ← David Romtvedt

Laramie

Torrington

Sundance ← Page Lambert

Tom Rea
Charles Levendosky
Vicki Lindner

Cheyenne ← B.J. Buckley / Linda Hasselstrom

Robert Roripaugh
C.L. Rawlins
Mark Jenkins
Alyson Hagy

John Nesbitt

Table of Contents

DEEP WEST

A Literary Tour of Wyoming

Foreword

In 1991, when I moved north from Colorado to become the Wyoming Arts Council's literature program manager, I thought I knew a few things about the state. The wind always blew. Cowboys roamed the range. UFOs zipped across the wide night skies, occasionally disgorging intergalactic sadists to mutilate cattle. Owen Wister's *Virginian*, Jack Schaefer's *Shane*, and Mary O'Hara's *Flicka* had pretty much defined Wyoming's literary landscape. In the early 1990s, new books by Gretel Ehrlich, Teresa Jordan, and James Galvin threatened to eclipse the classics.

Now, more than a decade later, I can admit that I was right about some things, wrong about others. I have yet to see a UFO and only rarely do I see a cowboy. But it is true that the wind often blows. Most importantly, Wyoming has a rich, evolving, literary tradition.

I have met most of the state's writers and read a fair number of their books. I have had the privilege to supervise an extensive literary awards program that has given fellowships to more than sixty writers, the majority of whom still live in the state. That surprised me. Wyoming's history was written mostly by "trappers, travelers, traders, transients, tourists, and transplants," according to Wyoming Poet Laureate Robert

Roripaugh. It's a rare bird that is able to survive cradle-to-grave in this place of high drama but few jobs.

I look at these fellowship winners and see Dainis Hazners, a poet who raises goats and, until a few years ago, was half-owner of a bookstore in Sheridan. He recently won a much-deserved NEA creative writing fellowship. Mark Jenkins lives in Laramie within spitting distance of the state's lone university, yet supports his family as a magazine columnist, freelance editor, author of travel-adventure books, and a tester of outdoor survival equipment. Page Lambert is an essayist and fiction writer who lives in the Wyoming Black Hills. She quit her bank teller job in Sundance a few years ago and has never looked back. During the summer, she leads nature-writing workshops down the Babine River in British Columbia and the Colorado River in Utah. Cheyenne's Linda Hasselstrom writes, teaches, edits, and conducts women's writing retreats at her family's ranch in South Dakota. Tim Sandlin has held every job available in the lucrative Jackson Hole service industry, including cook and dishwasher. He now writes screenplays and gets an occasional cell phone call from Hollywood celebs.

All of these writers traveled a long, hard road to get where they are, and sometimes still hang on to their livelihoods by their fingernails. We're all thankful that they continue to tough it out.

I serve on the board of the Wyoming Center for the Book. Founded in 1995, it is one of a network of state-based centers for the book sponsored by the Library of Congress. In 1998, some of us board members began kicking around the idea of an anthology that would also include a literary map, which is one of the suggested programs for Centers for the Book. Wyoming already had literary maps: *Map of the History and Romance of Wyoming,* created in 1928 by University of Wyoming's Grace Raymond Hebard and Paul M. Paine. It was reprinted in 1936 and 1993; this latest version was sold in a limited edition version which went toward UW scholarships. Another literary map was published in 1984 by the Wyoming Association of Teachers of English.

While maps are fine, we knew we needed to feature the actual work by the state's writers. We are, dadgummit, the Wyoming Center for the *Book*. And writers are not tourist destinations, unless you're someone who craves the limelight (but if you were, Wyoming would not be the spot for you). Thus, we embarked on the adventure of this anthology.

The West was a pretty hot literary commodity during the 1990s. Montana writers, especially, seemed to blaze forth in the early '90s with the anthology *The Last Best Place*. Montana's Tom McGuane, Jim Harrison, Jim Welch, and Bill Kittredge lead the list of writers of hard-edged fiction and non-fiction. Native-American writers such as Sherman Alexie, Adrian C. Louis and Linda Hogan have finally received some overdue recognition. Colorado's Pam Houston hit the charts with *Cowboys Are My Weakness*, an irreverent look at the cowboy mystique, and New Mexico's Rudolfo Anaya is now widely acknowledged as "The Grandfather of Chicano Fiction."

Where does Wyoming fit into this trend? All of us would like to see more extensive publishing of the state's writers, but the track record is pretty good. The last few years saw major books by Annie Proulx, Jon Billman, C.L. Rawlins, Lee Ann Roripaugh, C.J. Box, Kathleen and Michael O'Neal Gear, Joe Marshall III, Mark Spragg, and Mark Jenkins, among others. It also saw a number of very good books set in the state: *The Grass Dancer* by Susan Power, Margaret Coel's mystery series set on the Wind River Reservation, and Bill Tremblay's *The June Rise*, to name a few.

These trends bode well for the future. Rich lodes of raw material wait to be mined. Many writers tackle the theme of "The New West" with humor and daring. Landscape continues to be a major theme. Fiction writer Michael Martone, when serving as a literary fellowship judge, remarked that he had learned more than he wanted to know about cottonwoods in the course of reading that year's manuscripts. Cottonwoods, tumbleweeds, antelope — all icons of life on the high prairie. Then there's the weather: the dimensions of a winter white-out can keep you up nights contemplating metaphors for snow and cold.

In this book, writers of the Deep West offer a taste of what it's like to live and work in Wyoming. It's "slick in spots," as the radio announcers say during winter road reports, but also tough and poignant and funny. The Center for the Book at the Wyoming State Library and the Wyoming Arts Council are happy to celebrate Wyoming writing and promote the world of the book through this collection.

Michael Shay
Cheyenne, Wyoming
January 2003

Preface

In *Deep West*, we've tried to give the reader some sense of both the depth and breadth of writers and literature in Wyoming at the beginning of the twenty-first century. The writers who have contributed to this volume were asked to give us a sample of their work — poems, stories, essays, memoirs, whatever they felt would best represent what they do. The writers were to decide what mattered to them, what they wanted to put before readers.

Each writer was also invited to contribute an essay on place. In explaining what we sought for this essay, we asked, "How has your work been influenced or not influenced by life in Wyoming? What are your views on regionalism in literature? Are there issues about place that interest you?" We learned pretty quickly that some writers could give a hoot about place and so we told everyone to, "subvert the assignment if that seems to you more useful or more fun." As with the other contributions, we left it to the writers to decide what matters. "Say what you want," we emphasized. "You're kidding," one writer responded. "No, we mean it. Say what you want."

The order in which these poems, stories, and essays appear is based on both the ways they reflect the place that is Wyoming and the West and the ways they reflect the ideas many have of this region. Of course, one problem or pleasure is that there isn't a single West and so we've divided *Deep West* into three regions — "The West," "Farther West," and "No West." "The boundaries are fluid and murky, though, and many writers live in all three zones.

Among the famous lines attributed to Mark Twain, there is this:

"You ever been to Wyoming?"

"Wyoming? No. I've never been any farther West than California."

There is an Old West — a now largely symbolic and mythological place that never actually existed. For better and worse, this place appears to have been partly invented by a writer named Owen Wister in his novel *The Virginian*. Sometimes I think that if I ever see the name Owen Wister again or the title *The Virginian,* I'm going to throw away my saddle and spurs and move for good to Connecticut or New Jersey or Pennsylvania where Wister himself came from.

Many citizens and writers in the physical geography that is the interior mountains and plains region (including all of Wyoming) identify themselves with this Old West. We've chosen to call it simply "The West." It is a land of cattle ranching (sometimes sheep), of breaking horses, of saddles and spurs, of lone starry nights, and of hard work out of doors. It's also a land of primary resource exploitation — timber, coal, oil, natural gas, uranium, and, now, coal bed methane.

Sometimes this West includes a kind of nature-based spirituality, a magic sense of the oneness of Nature and God and the hope that whether you are American Indian or immigrant from another continent you can do the right thing by your human neighbors and by the plants and animals with whom you also live. Ironically, this West that includes a spiritual connection to the land is often at odds with contemporary movements for environmental protection.

Part real and part fantasy, this West is an appealing place and an appealing idea, one with a strong good heart. It is a place many people long for and love. Notwithstanding my anti-Wister cracks, I long for this place and love it, too. Perhaps its existence in our hearts and minds will have to be enough.

There is also a New West. To turn Twain on his head, maybe we can call this place "Farther West." That would get us away from some of the controversy surrounding the term New West — a name that some hope can be used to create a political climate for changing the way we've always done things in the West — that's the Old West. This New West is sometimes seen as the clear antidote to the Old West. It is a place that is often associated with The Sierra Club, The Nature Conservancy, Earth First. Sometimes it is associated with aluminum and titanium bicycle frames, spandex clothing, hang gliders, and rock climbers. Its homes are said to be in places such as Moab, Utah; Aspen, Colorado; and Jackson, Wyoming.

There is hope that the New West can help us to shake off the nostalgic leanings of our Old West and lead us to face hard questions. How can the West remain the West as it becomes largely urban? How can the land be preserved given the scarcity of water and the demand for that water from an ever growing human population? What inalienable rights do the plants and animals have in this West?

Sometimes the terms Old West and New West come down to being smokescreens for the fight between Old Timers and Newcomers. And truth be told, in both categories there are people who ask the questions listed in the preceding paragraph, people who will give their all to leave this land as beautiful as they found it. We don't really live in the Old West or the New West. Rather, we live *here*. We slowly come toward union with our place. We move Farther West.

An early reader of *Deep West*, whose comments we'd solicited in order to help us clarify our chore in creating a book meant to represent Wyoming's literature, wondered what made a Wyoming writer? Our reader felt puzzled by Laramie native Mark Jenkins' piece on female circumcision in Africa. Does this belong in a literary tour of Wyoming? The inclusion of such a work was seen as evidence of the collection's lack of cohesion and vision.

Oh, God, here we go again, I thought, that problem of defining what a Wyoming writer is. Maybe it's impossible in a world of swirling zip codes and conflicting allegiances. Maybe we ought to give up trying to identify writers by putting them in categories. We are all residents of "No West," that place that owes its existence to the Zenlike sense of *no thing*. But *no thing* is not absence. *No thing* is the emptying of our mind of categories and preconceptions. Stephen Mitchell, in translating Lao Tzu's *Tao Te Ching*, wrote, "First you erase the blackboard; then you can write something new." Put in reverse, it's like what the New York City poet Frank O'Hara said, "Everything is in the poems." We admit that Lao Tzu was not a Wyoming writer and because we can't verify whether or not O'Hara ever visited Wyoming, we haven't been able to include him in this volume either,

Our reader's question about what makes one a Wyoming writer was serious though and I can imagine many readers wondering over this. By including the work that appears in "No West" we have implicitly stated a belief that a Wyoming writer may or may not write about the place.

Geoff O'Gara, who lives in Lander, Wyoming, and whose work is included in this volume, put it this way in mentioning the influences he has felt on his writing: "Only one western writer — if we mean writers who actually live in and write about the West — has had a large influence on me..." O'Gara took no chances — he went ahead and defined "Western writer." For O'Gara, such a creature both lives in and writes about the West.

I've said, though, that that's not how we defined the term for this collection. We agreed that the writers must live in (mostly) and be associated with Wyoming, but we set no subject matter limits. For us, writers who have spent their lives or some goodly portion of their lives in Wyoming and who consider the state their place are Wyoming writers. We are identifying a homeland rather than a style or subject matter.

It's a sticky issue and you can see I'm going around and around it. One year the work of the writer Rick Bass was included in two anthologies — one devoted to the best writing from the American South and the other to the best writing of the American West. At that time, Bass lived in Montana, but he had lived in several southern states. His writing included settings from both regions and dealt with issues that were particular to each region. In art, unlike in life, you can be in two places at once.

Many writers here are deeply connected to the place but not to the label "Wyoming writer." Rather than be in two places, maybe they are comfortably situated in that place we have called No West.

Story poet Dainis Hazners put it this way: "This place, the West if you will, though it matters to me, and affects me, and though I am here to stay, is in some ways clearly incidental to my concerns/efforts as a writer and human being."

And another of the writers in this collection, Tom Rea, while not speaking for Wyoming writing whose subject is not Wyoming at all, has spoken of the importance of not being trapped by our past ideas of what a Wyoming writer and Wyoming literature are. Once, driving the point forcefully home, Rea said in a half-joking, half-serious tone that there will never be a Wyoming literature until that literature includes stories about homeless teenage drug-addicted unwed mothers in Casper. For people outside Wyoming, I should explain that by saying Casper, Rea meant a "city."

Wyoming's literature must be, as all literature must be, larger than our love of the landscape.

What we have striven for and what we hope we can offer in *Deep West* is not a collection of literary artifacts about Wyoming. It is more than that and simpler than that — a collection of work by writers who live in Wyoming.

While it may be interesting that some of our state's writers do not write of the place, to me it's more interesting that so many do. A large number of the writers included in this book — B. J. Buckley, Annie Proulx, Page Lambert, Robert Roripaugh, and others — speak again and again from their feelings and ideas about what it means to live in and be shaped by Wyoming.

But I was telling you about the materials we solicited

from writers for this volume. First were the poems, stories, and essays. Some of this material has been newly written and is being published here for the first time. Some is previously published material that the writer felt was representative of his or her work.

The second thing was the essay on place. Some of the writers leapt to this, excited and pleased to put down their thoughts about the place with which they identify. Others felt uncertain about what they might say or how they might say it. And there was a not negligible number of writers who tried to refuse, telling us they had no interest in such a piece of writing, or that it had no bearing on their writing, or that it had all been said too many times to bear being said again. For some of the writers, then, we have samples of their work and an essay on place while for others there is only the original work — the poems or stories themselves.

Robert Frost, who was as rural as the best of us, is said to have said that, "Poetry is what gets lost in the translation." Wyoming's former poet laureate Charles Levendosky wondered if Frost meant that in explaining or summarizing a poem, the poem gets lost. If Frost meant that, Levendosky said he would agree. But maybe Frost meant something else.

Our relationship to a place is like the poem that way. We risk destroying it when we try to summarize or explain. Still, some of us make the effort. Robert Frost said something else that I think is relevant to writing in Wyoming. I can't remember his exact words but his idea was that writing poems without rhyme and meter was like playing tennis without a net. There's a cussedness in some of us that means we find playing tennis without a net very engaging. And then there's necessity. When people live in the provinces or when the empire crumbles, tennis courts are often left without nets and we have no choice.

One of our contributors, Annie Proulx, notes in her essay that "...because most of my life has been peripatetic, because I have no fixed territory, I have always been in an outsider's position — perhaps the natural stance of a writer..." And in explaining her sense of identification as a Wyoming writer,

Proulx says, "All of my novels and many of my stories have been written in Wyoming, even in the years when I lived in northern New England. For more than a decade Wyoming has been my writing place and sometimes my subject. The long sight-lines and the pull of the horizon, strong weather and the instinct to traverse ground stimulates the making of fiction. I have an intense interest in rough country and the people it makes, and that interest is satisfied here."

In saying this, Proulx tells us a great deal about her personal values, her sense of the source for her writing, and what she thinks goes into making one a Wyoming writer. But there are some things she doesn't reveal. As to what keeps her in Wyoming, she tells us only that she will not tell us. "The private reasons that have to do with night skies, pale grass, wind that falls on you like a load of dirt won't be set down here."

That's a good place to stop, I think, that place where we recognize that there are some things we can't figure out how to say. And others we could say but won't. That's another facet of Wyoming writing — reserve or, perhaps better said, privacy. Its shaping force should not be underestimated.

David Romtvedt
Buffalo, Wyoming
June 2003

Part One

The West

"Growing up on the northern Plains, I thought that all the world was a wide expanse of endless prairies and rolling hills. I couldn't imagine the world being anything but beckoning open spaces, bright sunrises and spectacular sunsets, booming, crackling thunderstorms that petrified the mind and invigorated the spirit. I couldn't picture a world that didn't know the meadowlark's song, a place where the wind didn't dance with the grasses."

Joe Marshall III
from *In the Dance House*

Annie Proulx

Annie Proulx was born in Norwich, Connecticut, in 1935. She received her B.A. at the University of Vermont and then attended Sir George Williams University (now Concordia University) for her M.A.. She has been honored with many literary awards including PEN, Faulkner Award for Fiction, *Chicago Tribune* Heartland Prize for Fiction, National Book Award for Fiction, Pulitzer Prize for Fiction, the 2001 Evil Companions Literary Award, 2000 Willa Award from Women Writing the West and Best American Short Stories award in 1998, 1999 and 2000. Her fiction has been translated into more than twenty languages and includes such titles as *Accordion Crimes, The Shipping News, Postcards, Heart Songs and Other Stories, Close Range, Wyoming Stories. That Old Ace in the Hole* is her latest novel from Scribner.

From "Pair a Spurs," *Close Range, Wyoming Stories*

The Coffeepot

The Coffeepot southeast of Signal had been an o.k. little ranch but it passed down to Car Scrope in bad times — the present time and its near past. The beef-buying states, crying brucellosis which they fancied cattle contracted from Yellowstone bison and elk on the roam, had worked up a fear of Wyoming animals that punched the bottom out of the market. It showed a difference of philosophies, the outsiders ignorant that the state's unwritten motto, *take care a your own damn self,* extended to fauna and livestock and to them. There was a deeper malaise: all over the country men who once ate blood-rare prime, women who once cooked pot roast for Sunday dinner turned to soy curd and greens, warding off hardened arteries, *E. coli*-tainted hamburger, the cold shakes of undulant fever. They shied from overseas reports of "mad cow" disease. And who would display evidence of gross carnivorous appetite in times of heightened vegetarian sensibility? To counteract the anti-meat forces Scrope contributed ten dollars toward the erection of a roadside sign that commanded passersby to EAT BEEF and, at the bottom, bore the names of the seventeen ranchers who paid for the admonition.

It was a bitter winter and a late spring; he was feeding into May waiting for green grass. Every ranch was out of hay and the nearest source was a long day's journey to eastern Nebraska where the overall boys squeezed them hard. Ten days before June a blizzard caromed over the plains drifting house-high on lee slopes, dragging a train of arctic air that froze the wet snow, encased new calves in icy shells. For a week the cold held under glassy sky, snow-scald burning the cows' udders; it broke in minutes under a chinook's hot breath. Melt water streamed over the frozen ground. The bodies of dead stock emerged from fading drifts, now you don't, now you see em, a painful counting game for ranchers flying over in single-engines. Scrope's yard flooded, a mile of highway disappeared under a foot of water while they held his mail at the post office, but before it ebbed another storm staggered in from the west and shucked out six inches of pea hail, a roaring burst that metamorphosed into a downpour, switched back to hail and finally made a foot of coarse-grained snow. Two days later the first tornado of the season unscrewed a few grain elevators from the ground.

"I never seen so goddamn much weather packed into two weeks," said Scrope to his neighbor, Sutton Muddyman, the two mud-speckled pickups abreast on the chewed-up road, tailpipes rattling. The dogs in the truck beds ran back and forth in parallel tracks and grinned at each other.

"Spanked us around pretty good," said Muddyman. "What worries me is the snowpack. There's still the bulk a snowpack up in the mountains and when she starts to melt we'll see some real water. That EAT BEEF sign puttin you in the money yet?"

"The only people see it is the ones live on Pick It Up. All two a them. I suppose we should a put it on a blacktop highway where there's some traffic." He scratched the rashy hollow of his throat. Blonde stubble glinted on his cheeks. "Hell," he said, "it's all hard times in this business. You was smart to get out."

"Car," said Muddyman. "Don't think for one minute that I got it easy. I get the rough end a the pineapple ever day. I guess I better get goin. Inez's ice cream's meltin outta the bag."

"Take it on home, Sutton," said Scrope stepping gingerly on the gas prong, the pedal gone for months, while Muddyman eased south in his gravelly ruts.

Scrope, 40 years old, had lived on the Coffeepot all his life and suffered homesickness when he went to the feed store in Signal. He'd acquired a morbid passion for the ranch as a child when he believed he could hear its grass mocking him. This ability had come the year Train, his older brother, died in some terrible and private way in the bathroom where their mother found him, an event he had never understood and still did not. In that time he couldn't grasp what was going on or might happen next, for his parents said nothing to him but stayed close to each other whispering and weeping. He would hear them in the kitchen, their low voices trickling on and on like two water seeps, but when he stepped in, boots squeaking, they fell silent. Train's name could not be mentioned, that much he knew. Later they lied to him about such inconsequentialities as the names of weeds, the freshness of the butter on the saucer, how much school a ranch boy needed — not much, his father said, then complained years later that Car had not become a banker or insurance man. After his father's funeral he asked his mother straight out, "What was all that stuff you and Da used to talk about? Was it about Train? What happened to him, anyway?" But she looked away from him and through the window, her gaze traveling out to the red hoodoos and the crumpled sky beyond and she said nothing at all.

The grass, on the other hand, never shut up, making a kind of hissing snicker like sawed-off John Wrench in high school days in the last row of the movies when he asked a girl to have some of his popcorn, his penis thrust through the bottom of the box up into the greasy kernels. Scrope's ex-wife Jeri had had some of that popcorn. *Best one lost, worst one stays*, hissed the grass.

The Coffeepot was small but well-balanced, eight

sections of mixed range, some irrigated hay ground (not enough), grazing rights to BLM land. Bad Girl Creek watered the ranch, in low ground twisted into a slough improved by beaver to three small ponds. A dusty driveway, intersected by a line of power poles slung with a single wire, wandered in from the main road, numerous side-branches cutting toward the far parts of the ranch. Eighty yards west of the ranch house Mrs. Gressley's house trailer rested on cinder blocks in the shade of a cottonwood. An arrangement of corrals and fences led to a mild slope and at the height of the rise Scrope had put up a calving barn.

Scrope's old man had built the log ranch house after World War Two, and the son had changed nothing, not the faulty plumbing with its mineral-clogged pipes, nor the rusty porch swing that had stained Jeri's flowery skirts. The entryway was as much dog kennel, opened into the kitchen. A photograph of the ranch taken in 1911 hung above the table, gaunt Scrope ancestors grinning in front of their dugout, the shadow of the photographer touching their feet. It had been there so long Scrope couldn't see it, yet was aware of it in the same way he was aware of oxygen and daylight — he'd notice if it was gone.

The southeast corner of the ranch was high bony ground populated by a pair of bobcats, a few rattlesnakes; the distinctive features were a big wash and red crumbling hoodoos that sprouted fossils after heavy rain. Once a desperate runaway from the juvenile detention home hid out beneath an overhang for a week. In the rags-and-blood sunset Car had caught him sneaking burned carrots and beef tallow out of the dog's dish, invited him in, learned his name was Benny Horn, slid him a plate of beans, candy bar for dessert, pointed out a tick on his neck and talked him into giving himself up, promised a below-minimum-wage, part-time, seasonal job when he got out.

"I knew your daddy," he said, remembering a shiftless loudmouth. When the kid left, so did a stack of change on the windowsill and two mismatched socks from the back of a chair.

For twenty years the Coffeepot's foreman had been a

woman, Mrs. Gressley, a crusty old whipcord who looked like a man, dressed like a man, talked like a man and swore like a man, but carried a bosom shelf, an irritation to her as it got in the way of her roping. The old man had hired her a few months before he crossed the divide and at first local talk was that he'd lost his mind.

The terrain of Scrope himself consisted of a big, close-cropped head, platinum-blond mustache, a ruined back from a pneumatic drill ride on the back of a sunfishing, fence-cornering, tatter-eared pinto that John Wrench, two decades earlier, had correctly bet he couldn't stay on, feet wrecked from a lifetime in tight cowboy boots, and simian arms whose wrists no shirt cuffs would ever kiss. His features — a chiseled small mouth, water-colored eyes — had a pinched look, but the muscled shoulders and deep chest advertised a masculine strength that had, over the years, attracted not a few women. His marriage, brief and childless, fell apart in half an hour. Then he looked at the moon through a bottle every night, watched pornographic videos, ate, in addition to large quantities of beef and pork, junk food from plastic sacks which set off itchy rashes and produced bowel movements containing long orange strands as though he had swallowed and digested a fox.

The Box Hammerhandle

Directly south of the Coffeepot lay the Box Hammerhandle — Sutton and Inez Muddyman's place. Sutton Muddyman, of bunchy muscle and oily black curl, claimed dude ranching was hard work made harder by the need for intense and unremitting cheeriness, and although he and Inez weren't suited to the constant company of urban strangers, it paid the bills and brought them more Christmas cards than they could open. Their daughter Kerri was a pastry chef in Oregon and living with a reformed gambler of whom they wanted no news. They kept thirty or so horses on the ranch, a small band of sheep, pack llamas and a pirate's crew of dogs constantly in trouble with skunks and porcupines, once with the bobcats who gave them lasting memories of a trespass in the hoodoos.

Scrawny and red-headed, a little savage with an early change of life, Inez Muddyman had been one of the Bibby girls and raised, as she said, on a horse from breakfast to bed; it was she who took the dudes up into the mountains where tilted slopes of wild iris aroused in them emotional displays and some altitude sickness. She had been a good barrel racer and roper as a girl, made a few points and a little cash on the weekend circuit but hung that up when she married Muddyman. Off a horse she was awkward and stave-legged, dressed always in jeans and plain round-collared cotton blouses stained light brown from the iron water. Her elbows were rough, and above her amorphous face frizzed bright hair. She didn't own a pair of sunglasses, squinted through faded eyelashes. In the bathroom cabinet next to Sutton's kidney pills stood a single tube of lipstick desiccated to chalk in the arid climate

Three routes connected the Coffeepot and the Hammerhandle: a plank bridge over Bad Girl Creek — the joint property line — but that way involved opening and closing fourteen gates; a water crossing useable only in early spring and late summer, and the five mile highway trip, one that Scrope avoided because of bad memories as it was at the highway bridge he had nearly killed his wife and broken so many of his own bones that he was now held together with dozens of steel pins, metal plates and lag screws.

Writing in Wyoming

All of my novels and many of my stories have been written in Wyoming, even in the years when I lived in northern New England. For more than a decade Wyoming has been my writing place and sometimes my subject. The long sight-lines and the pull of horizon, strong weather and the instinct to traverse ground stimulates the making of fiction. I have an intense interest in rough country and the people it makes, and that interest is satisfied here. The private reasons that have to do with night skies, pale grass, wind that falls on you like a load of dirt won't be set down here.

And I have slender but old ties to this place. One of my ancestors, Joseph Marie La Barge, born in L'Assomption, Quebec in 1787, paddled a single birch-bark canoe from Quebec to St. Louis when he was twenty-one and worked in the fur trade for William Ashley's Rocky Mountain Fur Company. His name was attached to La Barge Creek where he was scalped or wounded though not killed, some time before 1830, and later to the town of La Barge in the western part of the state.

Because I come from a mixed Franco and New England Yankee background, because most of my life has been peripatetic, because I have no fixed territory, I have always been in an outsider's position — perhaps the natural stance of a writer, though the outsider's eye is common to all humans. When we step on new shores, enter unknown country or strange rooms we cannot stare hard enough. All that we see is fresh, fascinating and important. The early impressions of a new place, color, sunlight, food, common plants, mannerisms, language, accents, stance, street scenes, glimpsed argument or affection, strike us as extraordinarily vivid and forever representative of the place.

An outsider's eye can be the writer's most valuable tool, a highly developed, persistent and grasping perception of place and event. How accurate are such observations and the novels based, not on lifelong and intimate knowledge of place, people or language, but on sharp, early impressions? Is a piece of fiction constructed on such quick-read ground worth anything or merely a caricature, a clichéd précis of the subtler undercurrents of lives in a particular place? Or does the outsider's eye more clearly see the habits and traits, the shape of rock and gully that have become invisible through long association to one raised in the place? Does one see virtues and the other vices? Does one see brilliant possibilities and the other sad history? There are no surveyor's lines. The outsider writer is keenly aware of the danger of cliché and surface impression, even, to some extent, its unavoidability; the corrective is an understanding of human behavior and the driving necessity to write well. The native writer knows how difficult it is to see the swamp for the frogs; the corrective is the same. Both proceed because serious literature is written by risk-takers. Every writer is a professional observer who strains gathered information through the screens of imagination. Those two qualities, power of observation and imagination, are basic to story telling and the writing of fiction.

The writer's choice of subject matter is immense. The vast possibilities, as the character Jorge puts it in William Gass's powerful short story, "The Pedersen Kid," of "all that could happen" is truly astounding. Why then is so much of our contemporary fiction limited in scope, tiresomely narrow and boringly self-centered? I think two or three pernicious influences are at work here, and they have to do with the outsider's eye and the imagination, the writer's two most critical powers.

The writer Bob Shacochis, in a speech at a University of Nevada conference a few years ago, described an incident in which the Indian-American writer Bharati Mukherjee, born into a high-caste Calcutta family, was berated by the author of a doctoral thesis, another Indian woman, for writing about "lower-class Indian and Pakistani immigrants," people of whom, said the critic, Mukherjee could know nothing as she was born into a different class. Mukherjee replied that "what she seeks to do is assassinate my imagination." Shacochis commented:

If we, for political reasons, are not allowed to write about a place we've never been, or write about people whose lives we can understand only through the imagination, then literature and art will be stuck in the self-reflective light of the here and now, a solitary place inhabited only by the solipsistic me, a landscape from which the collective us has been exiled. In this view the ultimate goal of literature is either narcissism or self-loathing, the writer a rapacious beast who is better off boxed within a cage of mirrors.

He continued by pointing out that many American writers have "already, of their own volition, put themselves in that cage....[T]he modern writer favors the present tense and the first person, ...exercising an imagination that never leaves home, or worse, never leaves the self."

Another wall of this mirrored box is the gendered fiction that some feel women should write — fiction based on the supposed concerns and sensibilities of women — children, motherhood, nurturing, the putative war between the sexes, lesbian affections — though at least one critic, Mark Shechner, in the winter 1997 issue of *Salmagundi*, remarks that women writers have finally escaped from the need to please by writing on pre-ordained subject matter; they may write now, as men do, about anything they damn well please.

A pernicious second influence on the novels published today and on the approach of novelists to the world and human nature is the extraordinarily bad advice given to hundreds of thousands of writers through all stages of their development, with particularly virulent effect in the formative period of their work. That tiresome and harmful advice is to "write about what you know." What do any of us know? Not much. But it is the stuff of euphoria to learn and understand, to satisfy, to explore. This silly dictum closes all doors but one, cuts the writer off from the larger aspects of life, encourages navel-gazing and glorification of the self, denies the writer the excitement of learning about and observing others, the study of human behavior, the fine work in understanding strange landscapes and how place will drive a story and its characters. The advice discourages cultural comparisons, discourages venturing out of one's own street into another part of town. It fails to spark an interest in words or languages or turn of phrase. And if you don't think this narrow view of life, the meager possibilities of the journey from cradle to grave has any effect on our literature, pick out fifty new novels at random and read them. What is important in writing, as in life, is what excites the curiosity and intellect, the acquiring of knowledge and the development of compassion for the human condition.

I live at an altitude of 8,200 feet in the Medicine Bows in southeast Wyoming. The town has a population under a hundred people. Although I have lived briefly in cities — New York, Tokyo and Montreal among them — I am by upbringing, inclination and long habit a person of rural sensibilities. I also spend time in a small cabin *sans* electricity or plumbing in the Powder River Breaks at 4,000 feet, and for a little while each year make it to sea level on the Great Northern Peninsula of Newfoundland, to a tiny outpost and an old house leaning over the sea. These places are tremendously different from one another, yet alike in isolation and rural character.

For the facts of life in rural places all over the world are similar; high unemployment; lack of public transportation; life dominated by weather and climate; poor communications; poor medical and dental care; first-hand experience with danger and risk-taking; fear of strangers; bigotry; intolerance; pride in the difficulty of life; conservatism; belief in physical strength; cooperation; friendliness; low crime rate; generosity; advanced sense of humor; easy-going pace; inventiveness; practicality; familiarity with bodily functions and the rhythms of life in humans, livestock and wildlife. A strong sense of religious values seems connected to perceived landscape aesthetics; there is a disinclination to change things. Often a can-do, want-to attitude makes impossible situations possible. There is security in knowing oneself, one's physical and psychological abilities and limits. Competence in making things work is everyday business. The bull-headed refusal to deal with failure, to keep going past the point of rationality, to last and withstand adversity is the bedrock of rural character.

Although I am not blind to their faults or to mine, I

respect and like and feel at home with rural people whether they live on the rocky edge of the North Atlantic, or on isolated high plains ranches. And I take it as a given that Wyoming landscape — any landscape — shapes characters and stories as it does real people in real life.

David Romtvedt

David Romtvedt was born in Portland, Oregon, and raised in southern Arizona. He first came to Wyoming in 1968 to work in Yellowstone Park. He left after one summer and didn't return until 1984 when he came again, this time as a Ucross resident. While at Ucross, he met his future wife Margo Brown, a potter from Buffalo, and has lived in Wyoming ever since. He is the author of nine books of poetry and prose, including *A Flower Whose Name I Do Not Know*, which won the National Poetry Series Book Award in 1991 and *Windmill: Essays from Four Mile Ranch*, in 1997. He has won fellowships from the Wyoming Arts Council and the National Endowment for the Arts, including an NEA international exchange fellowship that allowed him to study and teach in Mexico in 1996. He is co-founder of the musical group The Fireants, which has performed at schools, libraries, and community centers throughout the state. For the past five years, Romtvedt has directed the Worlds of Music program, which has brought world-renowned musicians to Buffalo for free classes and performances. He also teaches in the creative writing program at the University of Wyoming.

From *How Many Horses*

Where the Deer Have Slept

I love stumbling upon the places
where the deer have slept
the night before, the room-sized
circle of flattened grass.
And when I get off, the horse
noses there but does not eat.
I lie down on my back.
My eyes close and I tuck
my arms tightly to my sides
then roll until within that circle
I come to the edge.

Something Inside

Dear Belem:
Daily we have to wash the bitter taste
from our mouths, and no matter
the soap that taste comes back.
For several letters I haven't been able
to tell you this story — our mare Marthe,
the four-year-old, kept going into Cyprien's pasture.
I think she was in love with his old bay Tom.
Cyprien would lead Marthe back and all leather
voiced say, "You keep that mare outa my field.
You don't, I'm gonna do something." I didn't
know. What would Cyprien do? He threatens
everyone. And Marthe wanted to go over there.

One day Cyprien comes walking up leading Marthe.
Her eyelids are shut kind of crumpled
and there's blood on her face. Cyprien
walks straight up to the house and he throws
two eyeballs down in front of me — Marthe's eyes.

You can't believe, Belem, how big
a horse's eyes are. Cyprien shows me
his knife and how he took the pointed end
of the blade, slipped it gently in the corner
of both sockets and popped her eyes out.
Like that. And he walks away. "She never
gonna find her way into my field again,"
Cyprien says over his shoulder.

How can there be such a wicked balance,
Belem? I could not make out which way
to turn, Marthe just standing there,
her big bones beautiful as ever, quiet
and still. I bent over and threw up,
couldn't shoot her, went to the vet
and he killed her with an injection.

Maybe a cat or a dog you can put to sleep
when it's old but a horse does not go to sleep,
a horse dies. And I tell you, Belem,
I think I might kill Cyprien myself
and not care if it's clean or right.
The nights are dark enough
to make us all blind and the stars
are bullet holes on the windshield
of my old truck.

Firecracker

Dear Belem:
They say the dead remain
inside us when they are gone. Maybe
that's true but still they are gone.
Forgive me my continuing insistence
on writing of the horses as if they
were people or as important as people.
Perhaps it is self-indulgent in these days
of nuclear bombs and people's present pain
in South Africa, in Salvador, in the Middle East,
in our own rich countries, Belem,
and I won't try to deceive you
with talk of animals as metaphors
for universal human values.
The simple truth is I have come to care
for the horses and maybe I do believe
they are as important as we are.

Strangely, Belem, sharing our lives with us,
they come to share our ailments and deaths.
Did you know horses get cancer?
It is not even rare. The most common
is malignant melanoma — in all horses,
though mostly grays. Appaloosas and white horses
suffer squamous cell carcinoma, a skin cancer.
All these words — soon there will be horse oncologists.
Even to me that feels somehow frivolous, oncologists
with their words — *sonogram*
nuclear scanner, gamma scanner, hard radiation machine,
lymphoma, and lymphocyte — and their diagnoses —
equal parts biochemistry, voodoo and intuition.

See how I'm wound up on this subject.
You know, Belem, the story I'm leading toward,
the way I lead a horse toward a trailer
inside which he'll ride to the vet's.
It was eighty-year-old Jean Irigaray's racer
Firecracker, who was twenty-six himself
and hadn't been on a track in years.
Firecracker's cancer was the melanoma.
Jean knew nothing of what went on inside
his horse's body. Dr. Tom explained that
most likely the bad cells filled Firecracker,
that they had entered the lymphatic system,
maybe the kidney and liver. Little could be done
though Tom explained how he could destroy lumps
along the skin — cut them out, or burn them,
or freeze them with nitrogen. Jean was heartbroken,
Belem, a true breaking of his heart.
Horse or human, Jean didn't think.
He asked could nothing else be done?
Dr. Tom said he would call the CSU vet school
and get back to us in a few days.

I drove Jean home and, though it was cold,
we walked in the pasture. The wind was wailing
so the dried leaves spun and danced
like a brain storm. "Twenty-six years,"
Jean said, and I think he meant everything —
the pasture, the irrigation ditch and dams,
the battered fenceposts and worn barbed wire,
the way the clouds boil so thick layers
shift and fly, opening and closing
windows onto the blue. This
is not sentimental bullshit, Belem.
For some, these horses are their only
union with another world.

On Wednesday I drove Jean back to the vet's.
Dr. Tom felt all over Firecracker's body.
He ran both hands together along the horse's neck,
hard questioning fingers, warm.
He told Jean there were small bumps everywhere,
cancer all through the body. I kept quiet, Belem,
seeing Firecracker's insides as a garden
of foul flowers all blossoming at once —
inky bloody blooms, poisonous pollen, barbs and ash.

At the base of the neck Tom used an electric knife
to cut out a lump — sizzle of hair and flesh —
and, though the horse was anaesthetized,
he could smell it and in terror bashed against
the padded walls of the squeeze chute. Exposed,
the lump was a dull rubbery blob, somnolent
and benign. Quick-frozen, sliced and dyed,
it was analyzed. Later there were core samples
of bone marrow — hollow needles drilled into
Firecracker's pelvis, then blood and urine analysis.
Into the loose soft skin between his front legs
dyes were injected. All this went on
at the university down in Colorado.
"Just like a human," they told Jean,
"We can do radiation, chemotherapy, treatment
just like a human..."

But you can talk to a human, Belem,
and nowadays, on humans even, the plug
is pulled and people go home to die
in their living rooms, the busy world
at the window, friends and family passing
in and out. And wouldn't a horse rather
stand in the shade of a cottonwood
or lean against the south wall of a shed
in a winter wind than die in a building
smelling of antiseptic and soap and human?

We just don't let go, do we?
As part of an experiment, CSU paid
for most of it, still Jean spent $3000.
He told me money doesn't matter.
For a horse, Belem. I shut up
knowing he'd been for fifty years
one of the stingiest of the carefully stingy
Basque ranchers. He even went down there
and stayed in a motel — a characterless room
with a copy of a western landscape
above the bed, a plastic drinking cup
sealed in a plastic bag by the sink,
a TV with cable and HBO.

I pictured Jean rising alone each day,
dressing carefully for a good day.
I wanted to go down with him
but didn't ask, thinking I was ghoulish.
I remembered Jean's wife, dead three years,
and wondered if this attention was connected,
another way Jean mourned that loss.
It was a cheap thought, for what mattered
to Jean, as strongly as his wife had mattered,
was the horse, the integrity of its life.

It's another thing these people, these animals,
this place has taught me. I don't have to
tell you what, you know. And, Belem,
I promise you, I'll never forget.

"Oh, If You Could Know"

Down there, that's where we rode
through the greasewood, in the field
about a mile that way, I called those
the Lizard Rocks cause I'd go there
and hunt lizards, all day, loved lizards,
and snakes, and horned toads who pushed
against my hand when I'd pet them.
I thought they liked it
so I'd turn them over and stroke
their bellies. They seemed hypnotized.
Later I learned that upside down
horned toads passed out.

I kept chameleons in the houseplants
and turtles in the bathtub. In winter
I'd get so excited when I found a fly.
You know how flies freeze
then if it gets warm they wake up
but they're woozy and easy to catch.
I'd grab them and feed them to my lizards.

I climbed over every rock
poking a stick into each crack and hole,
wiggling the stick in the sand
looking for Swifts hiding from the heat.
But you had to be careful
cause there might be a rattlesnake
and scorpions sleep in the sand, too.
I never took water or food —
too busy for that — but when I got back,
covered with dust, I was starving,
dying of thirst, and late.

This dry ranch and these horses
are my state of grace.
I don't forget any of it, even what I hate,
like when Simon made me help kill prairie dogs.
I caught a baby one and wanted to save it,
but Simon made me put it back in the hole
and pour in the poison oats. I cried
and he never made me do it again.

We used to trail sheep from Four Mile
to Wormwood because there weren't any scales
at Four Mile then. All day we'd ride
following the sheep. At night
we'd sleep on the ground
next to the animals and the stars.

I was afraid I'd screw up
but I loved it anyway. I'd try to keep the sheep
together. Simon would say to other ranchers,
"This is Margo; she's my top hand."
And look proud. But alone, he'd yell at me
for my mistakes, and once I did lose
an entire band of sheep Simon had to find.

Then there was docking —
we'd get up at 3 a.m. day after day
and cut tails and testicles off lambs
until everyone and even the earth
was blood-soaked and sticky
and we were standing in blood-mud.

Long summer days, my cousin Brad and I
would ride to Powder River, seven miles
from the cabin at the end of the ranch.
We'd pick up fallen branches and pretend

to be knights in armor, aim our cottonwood lances
at each other's hearts, galloping
as fast as we could, at the last minute
veering away so we never hit each other.
We'd just run and run and run.

That's it — I've been happiest with horses.
I can't tell you how it feels inside
or what horses mean or why childhood
in this dry empty spot, more barren
and desolate, you know that's what people
think about Wyoming, especially here,
this dry ugly desert of cactus and cold,
no trees, a little yellow grass.

But I look around and everything's
alive — the greasewood field, the Lizard Rocks,
Brad and me with our cottonwood lances,
the horses and the long ride to the river
and for all of it, I never wanted to go home,
just wanted to be there, be here. Come on,
today we'll ride, you and me, and you'll see.

Birds Too Fat To Fly

John tells Margo she is placid.
She worries he secretly means bland.
But one bright fall day she saw
a group of eagles — Golden and Bald —
feeding on a carcass. They
were like vultures, so full
they couldn't leave the ground.
They lurched up and down
the hillside relearning the lessons
of their youth. They were,
Margo told me, "Birds too fat to fly."
And laughed, "What a great phrase —
think of Trouble, Harold and Penelope
alone together on winter range
and when we go to get them,
we have to coax them in, shake
cans of oats and promise them endless
warm barns and clear fresh water
and no saddles." Then she makes up
their phrase — "They're horses
too quick to catch." It's a game.
I say the sky is the sky
too blue to believe. "Come on,"
Margo sweetly taunts, "You can
do better than that." And throws me.
Cold too bitter to breathe.
Draws too deep to defend.
Erosion too aged to erase.
Grass too gone to green.
She really laughs at that last
and names the whole: "Ranching
too disastrous to deny."

But who cares —
happiness too holy to humble
and life too lovely to lose.
She puts her arms around me
and stands placidly, motionless,
whispers in my ear, "Birds
too fat to fly..."

History

Dear Belem:
Wormwood and Four Mile — two big ranches,
thousands of acres and Harriets' place even bigger,
in winter all slate gray and bone empty, steely
low sky, only a few people roaming over the emptiness,
dragging a living out of it, pushing sheep and cows.

I remember the ghosts, Belem, the old ones
who came before us, who never stood in the glare
of a halogen yard lamp, never rode across a field,
electricity whirring in wires overhead.

Luke, a Wind River Shoshone, appeared drunk,
knocked on my door, didn't speak, left.
Next morning, he crawled out from under the porch.

All the smashed pickups — the Fords upside down
in ditches, slid off the sides of frozen mountains,
mashed head-on into walls, fences, somebody's new house
or barn, other pickups. Smashed, they come to a stop
and, inside, one more dial on a blinded bloody heart
refuses to turn. I am ashamed, Belem,

of what we've made of the land and of those
once who lived with it. From the Interstate
you see miles of grassland, mountains, trees
high on the slopes. In spring the creeks
come ripping down new courses. From a distance
the surface looks fine but you can't see shit
from the window of a car driving the Interstate.

This was our only home, this
arid heaving body that is nearly dead.
Oh, hell, Belem, if Wyoming were a K-Mart,
the damned state would be a blue-light special
on disaster.

The fights — Fort Fetterman, Fort Phil Kearny
the Wagon Box, the Little Bighorn. Even the mosses
and lichens quiver in fear of us. The screams of the dead
refuse to fade as they rise to Heaven, and the sins
of the fathers are visited upon the sons.

Look, Belem, I'm a white American alive
in the last years of the twentieth century.
It took my people two generations to unravel
another people's way of life, to unravel biology.
Not even Wyoming stays the same — Cheyenne,
Shoshone, Sioux, Blackfoot, Crow, gone,
artifacts stolen, seeds scattered. I can't
get too close to this, I'm no Indian.

Just say I'm wrong — the people are alive
and will come back. Leave all this behind
and wander, eyes caressing the hills.
Ignore the fences and signs, the nomads in airplanes,
the buffalo buried in a park, and the bear,
who when they roam are shot or drugged, tagged
and flown up on the last narrow ridge,
the backbone of the world, broken back.
There are no wolves and mountain lions retreat
higher and higher. The coyote find their way
so we've hired a bounty hunter who killed
4,000 last year. I lie down in dream and try
to greet my animal brother. I'm sorry, Belem,

I rant and preach and condemn, but it's because
I feel stupid and weak. Even the life under the earth,
the roots, we know how to kill — drilling rigs,
open pit mines, pipelines. Geology can teach us
to peel back any part of the planet's face, strip it
to the bone. I leave out my part, my car and truck,
my natural gas heated house and steel fence,
the grapefruit I eat shipped from Texas to my table.

I'm part of it, Belem. I know that but don't know
what to do. It's like being so drunk that when
the music stops I don't hear the change, or so tired
I drive straight off the roof of the world
and come down, my face and forehead smashing
through the windshield, blood and glass and bone
but I feel no pain. I'm afraid, Belem, afraid
nothing we know will save us, and nothing
we do will change what we've made. There,
a message that, for once
I'm happy to know you'll never read.

Looking for Horses

I first came to Wyoming in the summer of 1968 to work as a cook's assistant at the Mammoth Motor Inn in Yellowstone National Park. During that summer I broke my nose while fleeing from a moose. I'd shown an inordinate amount of interest in the moose's calf. In addition to learning a little something about moose and their offspring that summer, I spent many late nights swimming in the Firehole River, and in mid-July, I got snowed in at Yellowstone Lake. After three months, I left Wyoming, not having really known I'd ever been here.

In the fall of 1984, I returned to Wyoming as a resident at the Ucross Foundation. The Foundation provided me with two months time to pursue my writing — no interruptions and no responsibilities beyond writing. I wrote. And I made a good friend, a Ucross staff member with whom I often went running in the late afternoon. Sometimes we ran cross country and watched the slanting light slip behind the hills surrounding Ucross. Other times we ran along the state highway toward Clearmont, or toward Buffalo, or toward Sheridan. One afternoon it was about ten degrees and snowing. There was a driving wind from the north. We ran into the storm until we thought we couldn't bear it any longer then we turned and ran back.

Also while at Ucross I met the woman I later married. My wife was born and raised in Buffalo, Wyoming. Her parents were born and raised in Buffalo and her grandparents immigrated to Buffalo from Russia and the Basque Country. Since my second arrival in Wyoming, eighteen years have passed. It seems a long time to me but to those who have been here for generations, it's a very short time indeed. I remain a newcomer to Wyoming. It is largely thanks to my wife and her family that I have come to whatever understanding I have of what it means to belong to a place. It is also through them that I'm beginning to see how strongly a place shapes one's personal life and one's work.

I say this and feel a certain irony. The two essential features of a landscape that rise again and again in my thoughts and feelings are water and trees. If asked to draw a landscape, or to imagine the place I most wanted to live, I'd offer water and trees, two natural features which are strikingly absent from much of Wyoming.

When I first arrived here, I didn't find the open landscape inviting. It was so bare. A person standing in one spot on the plains could be seen for miles in every direction. I felt naked and unprotected. And yet without being inviting to me, the landscape was beautiful. Austere and imposing. Neutral. "It's your life," the landscape seemed to say.

After marrying, I began to spend time on my wife's family's ranch. Then I began to do a few little chores on the ranch. One summer I helped doctor a sick cow. Later, there was doctoring a young horse who'd cut herself badly on a fence. Through a good portion of a long slow fall, the horse needed twice daily penicillin injections and irrigating of her wounds. More ordinary work included shearing sheep and moving cows, repairing gates, fixing fence.

Finally, I found my way to windmill maintenance and repair. As the years went by, I did more and more of this work, becoming a kind of specialist in sheared off bolts and broken sticks, worn leathers and snapped brake cables. I came to love the empty and bare landscape of the land around Powder River — the imposing breaks and eroded draws, the stunted cactus and ragged cottonwood trees. When I got down close to it, the land was neither empty nor bare.

Before living in Wyoming, I'd spent much of my life on the coast in Oregon, Washington, and Southeast Alaska. As a new Wyomingite, I found myself dreaming about water and trees, listening for the ocean. I wanted to walk an expanse of beach, feeling the salt air crinkle my skin, staring aimlessly out to the west, into the Pacific's immensity and toward Japan.

All that longing for a place I wasn't! It made me look more closely at Wyoming. I needed to understand it, to enter into an understanding with it. I began to write about Wyoming, both its history and its nature. I'd lived for many years in the Pacific Northwest and believed I felt most at home in that place. Yet I'd never felt moved to write about it. The irony of my situation was not lost on me.

One day after about four years in Wyoming, deep in winter, I found myself adrift. I was at the ranch with no chore. There was nothing I knew anything about that needed fixing or checking. I decided I would go hunt up the ranch horses, just to see that they were O.K. I'd found it astounding that the horses were left almost entirely to their own devices during the winter. They could shelter up on the lee side of a steel building, or hunker down low in a cottonwood grove that lined a dry wash, but other than that they were at the mercy of the weather.

Maybe my desire to check on the horses was caused by a letter I'd received from the New England poet Maxine Kumin. As a horse lover, trainer, and rider as well as a writer, Maxine had told me in her letter how offensive and cruel it seemed to her that many western farmers and ranchers leave their horses out over the winter with no protection. "No barn, no heat, no feed. It's abusive," she wrote, "Criminal."

I looked through the window of the ranch house, a two room cabin with neither electricity nor running water. The thin winter light was slate colored. It would be a good thing if I simply got up and went outside, did look for those horses. It was maybe ten below zero. Could have been five or fifteen. Bright sun. Almost no wind. That means it was fairly comfortable.

I hiked up the road away from the ranch buildings to a rise where I could look down into both the Bridge Pasture and the western edge of the River Pasture. Each of these pastures is several thousand acres in size so unless the horses happened to be quite close, I wasn't going to see them. The ground was alternately bare of snow and drifted deep. In one spot, the earth was scoured by the wind, in another the same wind had piled up huge walls of snow.

I bent down at a patch of earth and pressed my ear to the cold ground, interested in what vibrations might come to me. I tried to let my heartbeat slow to that of the planet, tried to let my breath settle and ease. That was one of the things the openness had done for me — reminded me not to hurry so, not to worry so.

There being no sign of horses, I walked back to the tack shed at the buildings. I wrapped a bag of oats in a strong nylon halter and then slung that over my shoulder somewhat like a bedroll, or like an emotional compass. I didn't take any tools, no knives, no guns, no high powered binoculars to see into the distance, no special whistles beyond the range of human hearing. If I found the horses and one was hurt or sick, I had nothing but the oats, the halter, and my romantic neither-here-nor-there self.

So I set off walking the way I'd gone a half an hour earlier to the same rise looking down into the Bridge and River Pastures. From there I walked mostly to the west along the southern spine of the Bridge Pasture. All the way to the western edge I went along this fairly level high ground. From the high point the land fell away in a series of steep draws running mostly north and south. Standing on the high point at the top of a ridgeline I could look down into two draws. But that was all. If the horses were in the low area of land a draw or two over, I'd see nothing. I had to walk up and down every other draw. Of course, if I were in the bottom of a draw and the horses came up out of the top of a draw away from me, there would be no way I'd know where they were going. I certainly wouldn't see them if they chose to avoid me. I could walk up and down these draws forever, the horses always staying a draw away. I began looking for clouds of breath that might mark their recent passage. I looked for hoofprints in the snow.

As the short winter day went on, I found myself waving my arms to keep them warm and shading my eyes to look into sun-driven shadow, into air shimmering with cold. I saw an eagle's nest without any sign of a bird. I saw leafless cottonwood trees. The sky was intensely blue above the white snow and the almost straw-colored earth. There were no clouds. At every hoofprint, I stopped, paused, and made my informal inspection. I knew nothing about how to gauge the age of the print. It ought to look well-defined if it's new, I said to myself. I began to check crusty patchy snow thinking that such would hold a print better. Why would a horse walk up on a pile of patchy crusty snow? Sometimes I squatted on my heels and waited, trying to make no noise, listening hard for the clatter of rocks or the rumbling sigh that is characteristic of horses. I wanted to find the horses, to know for myself that all was well. But if I never saw the horses or even if there hadn't been any horses, I hoped I would have the sense to go out walking like this on a winter's day. For no reason, it pleased me to shove the side of my head against the frozen earth, to squat and listen while watching my breath hover before me, to inspect each draw and cutbank. I would be my county's official inspector of emptiness.

There came a moment when I had to begin thinking about going back to the cabin, about getting in out of the dark and cold. The lengthening shadows seemed to be tugging at the hills as if to drag them away or as if to detach themselves from the hills and fly. The shadows stayed attached to the hills. I began to walk in spiraling circles, crossing the draws and ridges, going up and down, up and down as I paced around and around. There were so many motions it became dizzying.

I thought of the story of a man walking on the deck of a boat. The man walked in the opposite direction the boat was going. The river's current hurtled the boat toward the sea but as the boat reached the mouth of the river, the tide came in and the water began to move against the direction of the boat. Meanwhile the wind blew from the side, giving the illusion that no matter which way the man walked, he was being nudged in an entirely new direction. The gray cloud from the boat's smokestack flew away from the boat on the side opposite the wind. All these motions. Not to mention the turn of the earth.

Feeling dizzy, I squatted one more time and sat, scanning the horizon for the still silhouette of horse. I thrust my face upward and sniffed, seeking traces, something I could taste on the wind, something redolent of horse.

Slightly before dusk the moon began to rise. It came so rapidly over the horizon that I believed I could feel the turning of the earth. I stood and found that it was impossible to walk without dancing a little, whether or not I'd planned to. There they were. Nine horses, four-footed and sure, in a line, slowly climbing one of the ridges with the moon behind them so I saw only dark shapes hesitating above the line of the earth. I began to run toward them and, as I got closer, the lead horse lifted its head and stared, then bolted. Soon all of the horses were running, trailing out in a long line.

I knew there was some narrow channel I could enter and run with them. I cut across an expanse of open ground — a prairie dog town. I ran faster, my mouth and nostrils opened wide, gulping down the frozen air, feeling its bite. Some sound came calling and I wondered if it was a bird. Not paying attention to my feet, I stepped in a hole and fell hard on my right side. My shoulder landed in a clump of frozen cactus. I must have hit my head on a small rock.

I don't know how long I lay there. It couldn't have been more than a few minutes, maybe only a few seconds. Any longer and I would have had frostbitten hands and feet, a blackened nose. I opened my eyes and sat up. I stood and was pleased to find I hadn't twisted my ankle or knee. I felt fine. Then I reached up and felt a sticky spot of blood behind my right ear. It was odd that it could be sticky while being so cold. I rubbed my hand over the spot and came away with a smear of blood on the palm of my glove. I wiped the glove on a patch of snow, leaving a crimson stroke on the sparkling white surface. Then I pulled the glove off and touched my head again. There was a bump but it wasn't that big and I didn't have a headache. Couldn't be too bad. I pulled a handkerchief out of my pocket and gingerly wiped the wound. The moon had risen a little more above the horizon line and seemed to be slowing down. The horses were gone. There was nothing to do but walk back to the buildings.

As I walked, I kept turning quickly behind, convinced that if I was fast enough, I'd find tracks behind me that weren't my own. Back at the cabin, I started a fire. While the cabin warmed, I went to the cistern and got two buckets of water. Seated once again by the stove, I wiped my head with a wet washcloth and rinsed the red out into a dishpan.

Water and trees. Earth and sky. Slowly I begin to bring my experiences together, to see how, as the pieces of a jigsaw puzzle, two landscapes are one. And there is no irony left in either. Only the many faces of the land on which we walk.

Linda M. Hasselstrom

Linda Hasselstrom has, for nearly forty years, earned her living by working on the family cattle ranch in South Dakota, from freelance writing, and from teaching workshops in writing and publishing. She holds an M.A. in American Literature from the University of Missouri and her work has been widely published in periodicals and anthologies. Her nonfiction titles include *Windbreak, Going Over East, Land Circle, Bison: Monarch of the Plains, The Roadside History of South Dakota*, and *Feels Like Far*. Her most recent nonfiction book is *Between Grass and Sky: Where I Live and Work*, published by the University of Nevada Press, 2002. Collections of poems include *Dakota Bones*, and most recently, *Bitter Creek Junction*, published by High Plains Press of Glendo, Wyoming. She is co-editor, with Nancy Curtis and Gaydell Collier, of *Leaning into the Wind* and *Woven on the Wind* (Houghton Mifflin). Since 1992, Hasselstrom has lived in Cheyenne, Wyoming, but her writing still centers on the South Dakota ranch she now owns.

Becoming a Broken-In Writer

"I always wanted to be somebody, but I should have been more specific."
                                        –Lily Tomlin

I became a rancher on the arid western South Dakota prairie at nine years old when my mother married the only father I ever knew and we moved to the ranch. Riding a fat old sorrel mare, I learned about the grasslands from a father I adored, and dreamed of spending my life there with a cowboy in a white hat.

By 1987, I was forty-four, riding the bronze prairie of the same ranch on an elderly gray gelding beside my second husband, George R. Snell. I loved this man who accepted both my need to write and my compulsion to stay on the ranch, and I didn't know anyone who owned a white hat. Learning ranching, George listened patiently to my father's orders. With four books in print, I was working on another and knew at last where my life was headed.

Five years later, my father booted me off the ranch, a widow with no steady job and no income. My horses were all dead and my only souvenirs were a few boxes of books and photographs.

I learned about ranching so early I thought it was fun.

On horseback beside my father, fencing pliers and staples jingling in our saddlebags, I learned to evaluate the condition of water holes and cattle, to respect bovine instincts and intelligence. I always carried a notebook so writing grew naturally from our work. I read books to learn, as I learned to distinguish the old whiteface cow whose teats got sore when she calved from the one who licked my ear when I milked her. Eyeball to nostril, I could calculate which way to jump by a cow's body language. Seasoned by labor, I looked to my father for information about the prairie.

My mother's work — cooking and cleaning, mending and gardening — seemed insignificant. A bird-boned, blue-eyed belle, she made me feel huge and awkward. All my life, even when she was ninety, men who met her whispered, "Your mother's beautiful!" I was middle-aged before I recognized the courage of her acts in leaving a ranch for the big city, then moving back to her own country after two divorces to marry again and dedicate herself to home-making and domesticating me.

My father decreed that I would go to college and believed a woman working outside was proof her man couldn't support her. After several hired men demanded higher wages or drank up a week's wages, or vanished on payday, he put me to work, paying me in cash and cows. I registered my own brand when most of my friends were buying their first pair of nylons. When I was fourteen, he bought a new John Deere tractor, my "birthday present," he said. During long hot days in the hayfield, I watched buzzards and studied coyotes and took pride in being "as good as a man."

Both my parents, true to their own upbringing, reacted to pain or grief in the same manner. If I got kicked shoving a cow through a gate, my father said, "Don't think about it and it won't hurt." When I doubled up with headaches after a day sorting cattle in dusty corrals, mother gave me an aspirin, saying, "Think of something else. Go to sleep and it will stop."

As college loomed, mother encouraged me to date the sons of town businessmen by negotiating with my father so I could stay out later — she didn't want me to marry a rancher. When I talked of coming back to run the ranch myself, my mother shuddered and my father shrugged. After college, I married and planned a life of college teaching. Divorced at thirty, I skedaddled back to the ranch to work for my father at wages that barely covered subsistence. Relatives and neighbors opined I'd wasted time and money in school only to pitch hay. They approved when I taught part-time and shook their heads when I turned down full-time jobs.

I'd discovered my subject matter and a *need* to write. Considering the region's environmental problems, I recognized that living and working on a ranch gave me a perspective different from those of city and college friends. I talked with my neighbors about their lives, read western history, and observed the land, learning some of my father's deep knowledge of our small ecosystem. While George committed himself to ranching, I wrote about the conflicts between earning a living from the land and "saving the environment." We both worked for my father as hired labor.

Observing the strong women in my neighborhood added a new theme to my writing. Some, like my mother, shaped their lives to fit a man's, while others might appear to conform but found considerable freedom within a rigid framework. My neighbor, Margaret, ten years younger, might agree with me on practical ways to conserve local resources but she disliked the Equal Rights Amendment. My Aunt Josephine, was married to my father's older brother, Harold, who sneered at my fat old horse and gave me an Arab mare and colt. Jo was one of our community's most visible — and audible — women, gathering and relating news of all kinds. She hated "women's lib" and insisted the ERA would require women to use men's bathrooms. But she kept her own cattle and sheep, her own brand, and a separate checking account. When Harold hired help during calving season, Jo slipped out at two a.m. to be sure he was checking the heifers. Even when she helped brand two hundred calves, she'd have dinner ready when Harold wanted it. After Jo died hard and slow from a brain tumor,

Margaret planted a tree in her memory. Later, after a car accident in which her back was broken, she planted five hundred windbreak trees. Eventually diagnosed with the HIV virus, contracted in blood transfusions, Margaret spent her last months warning our isolated community about AIDS.

Jo and Margaret, representing generations preceding and following mine, epitomized the western woman, as Margaret's daughter Bonnie epitomizes our future. All embraced contradiction. Growing up with men who habitually belittled women, they quietly proved the men wrong but refused to identify themselves as liberated. Margaret once noted that I did not mention the ERA when her brother was digging my four-wheel-drive truck out of a snowdrift. Cooperation, I'd decided, allowed partners to accomplish more than competition.

Like other ranch women, I learned to smile and wash potatoes real fast when six unexpected guests showed up at mealtime, but I broke tradition by asking George to wash dishes and help clean the house. Outside, he and I worked together, caring for cows and fixing fences, branding and shoveling snow. Far from the liberation battle, I wrote about the prairie's freedom, applying what I'd learned from neighboring women to writing, as well as to living.

I read my father's agricultural papers to supplement my particular knowledge with the views of agricultural experts. But experts in "agri-business," who lived in college towns in farming regions, urged ranchers to study world markets, and modernize their operations with machinery. The family ranch, they said, would be replaced by efficient corporate ranches. Environmental publications scolded ranchers for overgrazing, and said beef killed consumers by plugging arteries and causing cancer. I even listened politely when animal rights activists yelped about ranchers torturing calves, and vocal vegetarians suggested I grow artichokes.

My father grumbled as he folded each paper and headed for the garage to put new spark plugs in his 1950 John Deere tractor. He grew angrier each year, insisting that the only way to do things was his way. At last George began to study for a degree in counseling, unwilling to remain on the ranch. When he was ready, I promised, we'd leave the ranch together.

Meanwhile, I wrote, doubting my realities would ever appear in print, though I imagined my journals might provide clues to subsistence on the plains after "agri-business" destroyed our economy and the health of the plains grasslands. A stubborn streak, possibly inherited from my grandmother Cora, who killed rattlesnakes and skunks with her hoe, inspired me to send samples from a year's journal of ranch life to twenty-six publishers with rural interests. After I collected twenty-six rejection letters, Barn Owl Books published *Windbreak: A Woman Rancher on the Northern Plains*, in 1987. *Going Over East: Reflections of a Woman Rancher* was published late that year by a different press.

Soon, letters encouraging me to keep writing filled my mailbox by the highway, where Margaret once caught me sobbing over a touching note. "If you're gonna cry that hard," she said, "Go out in our alfalfa field. We need moisture." Ranchers, men and women, young and old, scrawled their thanks for my chronicle of their lives. Teenagers who yearned to raise goats headed west to become my apprentices. Neighbors, allowing as how this writing business wasn't so hard, wanted me to publish their diaries so they could be rich and famous, too. Old friends who'd always wondered what happened when I dropped Ph.D. studies wrote to invite themselves to the ranch. Inspired by these confirmations, I wrote and submitted essays about my ranch work and observations to publications all over the country. In credits, editors often referred to me as a "nature writer," a choice I found intriguing.

In September of 1988, doctors discovered a malignant tumor in George's spinal cord, caused by radiation that treated his Hodgkin's disease. Ten days later, at forty-two, he was buried in the cemetery a few miles from the ranch. My father began behaving as if I were ten years old. When I asked my father to make me a partner or sell me part of the ranch, he ordered me to give up writing and work as his hired hand, or leave. In May of 1992, I took refuge with a friend in Cheyenne,

Wyoming, close enough to return quickly in the emergency I expected. Later that summer, short of money, I rented my house to strangers. After years of fastening my roots in prairie sod, I'd become a nomad.

My father died on August 7, 1992. A week after his funeral, my mother learned from his lawyer how many acres he owned. We sold my father's cattle herd to pay probate costs, and put tenants in the house. Investments kept mother in a nursing home, happily revising her memories until her death. I inherited nothing. After four years of sorting out the estate, I sold my cows and borrowed money to pay property taxes and buy the land. With no cows and dozens of repairs to make, I leased the land to a neighbor. With my companion, I bought a house in Cheyenne, Wyoming, where I've learned a great deal about country life by observing the city's center. In my ranch house, I conduct writing workshops and retreats for women.

I continue to write about the lessons I'm learning from this prairie land and its people. My favorite comment from a reader might describe the grasslands as well. I'd given a reading from my work at an agricultural college in the eastern farming region of South Dakota, and a teacher asked students to comment on the program. She forwarded a comment from a young man:

She seemed to be like the boots she had on, worn and broken-in to hardship but, because of that, soft, supple, and beautiful.

Everything I Need to Know I Learned from My Horse

When I was nine years old, my mother married a rancher and I found myself — I mean that literally — living in the country. My real life began then and preceding years vanished from my memory. I'd fantasized about horses for years, but my dreams grew solid when I bought an old mare. Besides learning to ride, I learned everything I needed to know for the rest of my life.

The plump Blaze was much more solid — O.K., fat — than I'd hoped, as is typical of illusions. When Uncle Harold tried to badger his brother into buying me a better horse, my new father replied, "I'm not paying big money for some nag!" So when I turned eleven, Harold gave me an unbroken Arab mare with her yearling filly. I named the filly Rebel because she reared, screaming, flaring her tail like a flag when the lariat settled around her neck. Then she shook her mane, snapped her big white teeth together, pawed with her front feet and kicked as we led her home between our older horses.

"We'll have to gentle her to ride," said my father. I now realize that we got acquainted while he trained me the same way. But "gentle" didn't mean "easy." He figured you learned best by doing and doing again and again, over and over until you got it right. So I rode a horse every day until my middle teens because every day my father made it his business to find a chore requiring a rider. Without a youngster and a green horse to teach, he'd have driven a pickup to check the cows or mend fences. But he took fatherhood so seriously he didn't mind that creating educational toil for me required labor for himself.

By the time I trained Rebel to ride, her brother Yankee was ready to school. Until I turned fifty, I seldom rode a horse I hadn't trained. As I reluctantly moved into city chaos, sure it would drive me crazy, my last horse died.

Reflecting that I'd rather be among horses than people, I recognized how much I'd learned from them about living. Some horse-taught lessons apply literally while unfolding into greater meanings. I learned, for example, how to stay in a saddle, and how to remount if I fell or was thrown off. Inherent in that lesson were tactics I used to raise myself from figurative dust as well, and to climb back onto whatever problem I've chosen to ride. Living in a city, I naturally spend less time pitching hay and more time thinking. Rules I learned at the bony knees of my horses, I've concluded, can apply equally well to folks who never go anywhere near a horse.

Trust your horse was the first important rule Rebel taught me after she learned about being a trustworthy cow horse. One day our Angus bull climbed out of our pasture full of adoring heifers into an adjoining empty pasture — defeating his entire procreative purpose. He was switching flies in celibate splendor on a hilltop until my mare and I arrived. Then he jumped up, bawling low and flinging snot in all directions, and ran toward the Cheyenne River, about forty miles away.

My father followed him in the pickup, occasionally disappearing from view for fifteen minutes as he detoured around washouts. Rebel followed the bull up slopes and across gullies as if she was being towed. Occasionally I'd ride up beside the bull and try to turn him. He'd lower his blunt head and shake it while Rebel sidestepped and tossed her head. We followed him around that pasture for three hours, keeping him in a trot until he got tired enough to turn toward home. Rebel stretched her neck out, bit the bull's tail and dropped into her smooth running walk. He jogged straight into a neighbor's corral and up the loading chute into the pickup.

My father got in the pickup, grinned tightly and said, "You ought to be able to find your way home from here." He drove away as the sun dropped behind the Black Hills and the prairie turned black in all directions. I couldn't see a thing. But I heard a little voice straight out of one of my books about girls and black stallions: "*Trust your horse.*"

I loosened the reins in my hand, trying to forget my

father's advice to keep them tight. I brushed my heels softly against Rebel's side and said, voice wobbling, "Let's go home, girl."

She bobbed her head, jingling the bit, and walked fast, slinging green foam back on my face. At first, I flinched from every gust of air. As the mare slowed, leaning into a hill, I caught a whiff of sage and clay. Instantly I remembered the long slope we'd run down that afternoon and knew where I was. Rebel slowed to a walk on the downhill grade. Then her hooves splashed water and I smelled spearmint: we were passing the spring beside the ruined homestead cabin. That yowl was the rusty windmill in a shifting wind. Turning my head, I glimpsed a blade flash against a last wisp of sunset.

Trust your horse. I had no choice but to ride forward in the dark, believing. The longer I stared about me, the better my own senses functioned. Eventually, emulating the horse, I learned to walk confidently in darkness, seeing where my footsteps would fall in the glow of starlight, scenting the fear of cattle just spooked by a mountain lion.

On that night ride, Rebel headed for the barn. Obedient to instinct, she wanted to get to her feed rack, to the place where I pulled off the saddle and brushed her down. Reflecting on her behavior later, I realized her desire to go where she was fed and cared for signified more than answering physical need. Knowing how to find her way *home* in the dark was a natural part of being a horse, of recognizing a particular place in her bones and sinews. She knew the countryside around us that night in relation to the center of her world. At Rebel's home, she was able to sleep and eat in comfort, and drink clean water. There, we cared about her in more than one sense.

People often say, "Home is where the heart is," but these days many of us rush to leave home as soon as possible and train ourselves to stay away. The horse already knew what I've only recently discovered: No matter how far and fast I may run, *no experience is as satisfying, as restful, as coming home.* Even though I call my house in a city my home, I find renewal in each return to the ranch where I matured as my horses trained me for adulthood.

Through the years, I thought about that first night ride and understood why my father wouldn't let me gallop after the bull waving my whip and yelling. Before the bull was winded, the horse would be exhausted. "We don't handle cattle the way they do in the movies," he said.

Once I'd taught for a few years, I added my own corollary to this rule: yelling and whipping doesn't work with children, either. By trailing the bull, slowly but persistently, I wore him down physically and mentally. The same technique worked for teaching schoolchildren of any age, for observing wild animals, and to approach a prospective husband. *Take your time. If you can't outrun your opponent, wear him down.*

As I grow older and the chance of my outrunning anything or anyone diminishes, I relish this truth even more. All voters, I opine, should remember it each time we face another slate of politicians making promises they don't intend to keep.

To put this technique into practice, I cultivated patience, discerning that even a winning race horse spends a lot of time standing around. Most humans who work for a living find themselves in the same position: bound to something heavy. Tied, some horses fret, shaking their heads, chewing the bit, gnawing on corral posts. They froth at the mouth and paw the ground until they've dug themselves into a hole. Likewise, humans who drum their fingers on steering wheels or slam drawers and yell at everybody may get ulcers but they seldom improve their lives or escape. After all that stewing, they haven't got enough energy left for the next job, or for pleasure either. A horse standing quietly, switching flies, may be reciting Shakespeare, or verses from the Equine Bible. Perhaps she dreams and conserves her strength. Either way, she's in better mental and physical shape than the average human at the end of the day.

Horses may also use their waiting time to recall every occasion when a human has abused them, and to plan the appropriate revenge. So another horse-inspired rule is: *A horse never forgets.* Whip a horse or use sharp spurs and the horse will get even. No matter how long it takes. From horses, I learned that the consequences of my actions will catch up with me, inspiration to calculate results in advance. A horse who always runs from the bridle, for example, may get a one-way ticket to a French restaurant with horse meat on the menu. Humans generally can avoid this fate, but don't count on it.

Hanging around horses also taught me: *Don't fight the bit.* Once you wrap your lips around that piece of iron and clamp it between your jaws, behave yourself. My horse Oliver was a biter. He liked to extend his lips and nuzzle my arm, especially if it was bare. Some days, he fondled me with his lips and then bit me. He also bit tree branches and the top wire on fences until my dad put an electric wire across his pen. The juice flowed intermittently, so he had time to wrap his lips all the way around the wire before the shock hit him. He had a hard time letting go, but he seldom bit wire again.

Still, when we tied him to the pickup and headed for the pasture, he snapped his teeth on the tailgate until I smeared it with hot sauce. But I couldn't electrify or season my jeans and he later bit my backside so hard I wore a purple and green impression of his teeth for weeks. Nearing the end of a long day, he turned his head and chewed on the toes of my boots. My folks could never understand why the toes vanished before the soles were even worn.

No, the moral of the story isn't that he gave up biting or we sold him to the glue factory. We needed him — we owned worse horses — but we seldom turned our backs on him. Another horse-taught policy: *Don't trust a critter, human or otherwise, who munches on you.*

A related horse principle is ancient and metaphorically reliable: *Don't complain about your job.* If you hate the work or the conditions, quit. Old-timers called it Riding for the Brand.

Once I rode a rented Arab mare along a high, narrow trail in the Rocky Mountains. She bucked hard for the first five miles, on rocky ground. Then she began to lurch and stagger as we negotiated a foot-wide path along a three-hundred-foot drop to the Shoshone River. Thinking she'd pulled a muscle or worn herself into exhaustion, I got off several times to lead her.

A professional wrangler in our group noticed the mare's trouble, and showed me a way to fasten my cinch so I could release it quickly. "That way," he said cheerily, "if that mare goes over the edge, you can fall the other way and jerk your saddle off so you don't have to hike down and get it."

I looked over the edge, a loooooooong way down, and decided if I didn't end up in the river with a dead horse, I'd be happy to buy another saddle.

Later, the wrangler pointed out that the horse had no idea how dangerous the trail was, or she wouldn't have walked it. So I adopted another equine edict: *Ignore the risks.* You might survive and you might not, but you'll sure enjoy yourself more than if you worry.

Later that night, we decided the mare had colic. She'd been eating dry hay all winter. The first night of the trip, the wrangler picketed her in a boggy meadow where she gorged on green grass. We applied the best first aid we knew and walked the mare half the night to encourage her intestines to empty, but she died.

Bingo! another equine rule: *When you find rich forage, don't be greedy.* Most horses will graze whenever the reins are loose enough, snatching nourishment at every opportunity, even if it's beneath their standards. Applying this axiom in my own life, I reason that I never know how long I might have to wait for my next nourishing conversation or satisfying work, let alone dessert. And I'm often surprised to find something tasty where I didn't expect it. From these doctrines and the unfortunate mare comes another familiar law: *Whatever goes into a system must emerge.* In the mare's case, it didn't emerge naturally. The day we left, a ranger shoved sticks of dynamite in the natural apertures on either end of the horse and lit the fuses. This bizarre wilderness policy evolved from experience: if carcasses weren't scattered, the smell of decomposing flesh attracted grizzlies who might start snacking on hikers after they finished the horse.

This knowledge led me to concoct new policies. First, whether a substance is "waste" or "post-consumer" products or "recycled materials" may depend largely on your attitude. We tried to treat the mare kindly and doctor her ailment but she died anyway. Perhaps she went on to a higher purpose — feeding an endangered grizzly or fertilizing wild flowers. I always hated shoveling out the barn, but loved the effect on my garden.

Thinking about waste led me to another principle: *Relieve yourself whenever possible.* If you're a wandering female, especially in my neighborhood, bushes tall enough to hide behind may be miles apart and covered with thorns or ants. I've also noticed that no matter how lonely the country seems, if I park my car beside a road to relieve myself, within seconds I hear a polite male voice inquiring if I need help.

When I first began to ride, my father gave me another decree: *Don't ever run a horse downhill.* Since as usual he didn't explain, I tried it to learn for myself. Deep in some fantasy of chasing rustlers, I was riding Rebel downhill at a gallop when she stepped in a hole. Luckily, it wasn't deep enough to break her leg. She only tripped and rolled — head over tail, brain over buttocks, mind over hind — all the way down. I stayed in the saddle, too scared to let go, being mashed a little more every time the horse rolled over. When we hit bottom, she stood and shook herself, gave me a look of disgust and started grazing. Her knees were scraped raw. As soon as I could move, I started crawling around on the hillside looking for my glasses and mumbling to myself. Since then, I take my foot off the gas on a downhill run so I have time to look for prairie dog holes and other dangers. Works driving a horseless carriage or planning an essay, too.

Being around horses, I soon noticed how they informed themselves, nostrils flared and both ears swiveling. For humans, I translate this guideline as: *Pay attention.* If you listen to everything, you'll be better able to sort out what's really useful before you decide how to act.

When Rebel discovered something truly dangerous, like bison in the neighbor's pasture, she spun around on her hind feet. *Face danger,* she figured. She looked it over with first one eye, then the other, making a considered judgment about what to do.

On the other hand, Rebel's son Oliver was terrified of big white rocks. If he saw a white rock within a mile, he ignored me and the cows he was supposed to be driving. Closer to the rock, he'd honk air and spring from one hoof to another. When we passed it, he'd roll his eyes and bend his neck, trying to gawk over his shoulder. Busy watching the rock, he once stepped on something squishy. When he dropped his nose to investigate, a rattlesnake bit him.

So I stopped watching the horizon for Big Scary Stuff. I don't care if Nostradamus said a meteor is going to hit the earth, because I'm worried about cow prices and wondering if the neighbor's buffalo have busted the fence again. *Concentrate on local problems* is the phrase I use to myself.

Oliver recovered from the snakebite, but his nose was the size of his rear end all summer. While he forgot white rocks, a rattling weed made him do somersaults. Naturally, I formulated another creed: *To discover truth, stick your nose in it.* You may get bitten. You may discover you can survive events some folks consider fatal, like snakebite, marriage, divorce, and probate.

Facing danger is a good axiom, but its reverse is occasionally the best course. Oliver was tied in the corral once when we unloaded a new Angus bull, grouchy from being in the trailer for half a day. The bull stepped out of the trailer, saw the horse and blamed him for a lifetime of afflictions. Dropping his head, he slammed Oliver's belly so hard the barn shook. Then he backed off bawling and pawed the ground while he decided what to hit next. My husband and I scrambled up the fence, so the bull snorted and went for the horse.

But that horse learned fast: *Turn your back to danger.* When the bull got close enough, Oliver pounded him three times in the center of the forehead with both hind hooves. The bull backed off, shook his head and charged again. The horse popped him in the eye a couple of times before hammering on his chest. After awhile, the bull decided to look over the corral, maybe get a drink.

I interpret this flexible law to mean *I face trouble unless that doesn't work. Then I spin around and kick it.* But I find that turning my back on risk also multiplies my options. Instead of kicking, I can run, if I'm not tied up — certainly one reason I avoid having a regular job. When Oliver met the new bull, he was tied to the fence, a situation I've tried to avoid. Besides, if you turn your back on a crisis and never see it again, it wasn't a serious problem and you've saved yourself trouble.

Another maxim my horses originated was: *Walk up hills.* Save the powerful sprint for real emergencies; you'll encounter plenty. A horse will run from danger if she can. My husband voiced his own version of this belief. At six foot two, he weighed 250 pounds, knew kung fu, wore a belt knife, and carried a pistol when he didn't have a rifle. His favorite saying was, "Your best defense is your feet: putting one in front of the other as fast as possible."

Most of my horses were cooperative most of the time, so the habits they taught me are generally positive. But I learned from the lazy, obstinate, rowdy nags, too. My first horse, the fat mare I called Blaze, must have led a rough life before she met me, because she'd sworn off work. She taught precepts by example. When I tried to tighten the cinch on the saddle, she'd inhale, expanding her belly. Until we got acquainted, I couldn't understand why every time she shook herself — roughly every fifteen steps — the saddle turned and I slid out. When I dismounted, my dad advised me to, "Kick her in the belly," thumping the extra air out. A new rule evolved: *After you've been in the saddle awhile, test the cinch.*

Perhaps the saddle made Blaze's back itch, so she rolled to relieve it. I learned to ride with only the tips of my toes in the stirrups so I could kick loose in a hurry. This lesson probably saved my life when I was trying to work with a horse who'd learned nasty habits from the first few folks who tried to ride him. His favorite exercise was to rear and throw himself backwards. You didn't want to be underneath when he lit. So when I get myself in a location I don't know well — whether it's in a political party, or an environmental group, or a marriage — I follow this rule: *Ride loose enough in any saddle so you can get off in a hurry.* If nobody's looking, I ride with one hand on the saddle horn: *Hold on if the trip gets rough.* I swear by both practices, no matter what I'm riding.

Hearsay has taught me a few more horse-inspired procedures. My Uncle Harold related a tale about Art Shoemaker, a neighbor who broke horses to be sold as remounts for the Army. He didn't have much time for each horse, so he developed an effective method to stop bucking. He reached down along the horse's neck to grab the bridle beside the bit. When the horse bucked, he yanked hard, leaning the opposite way to throw the horse on its side. The trick required strength as well as enough coordination to get his leg out of the stirrup on the side that hit the ground. My uncle swore most of Art's horses only bucked once. Other horse-breakers have told me they slam a plastic jug of warm water down on the horse's head as he begins to buck. They speculate that the horse decides bucking makes his head bleed, so he stops. People using either method swore the technique worked and was humane, putting me in mind of my father's advice: *It helps to be smarter than the horse.*

No matter what you think of the horse-inspired training, keep the day's first scripture in mind: *Trust your horse.* If you don't have a horse handy, trust folks who know more than you do, even if they're animals. I've learned a lot by following another injunction from the days when my father taught me about horses. When I find somebody who knows what he or she is doing, I shut up and pay attention.

Jon Billman

Jon Billman was born in Rapid City, South Dakota and now lives in Kemmerer, Wyoming. He is the author of the short story collection *When We Were Wolves*. The title story from this collection earned Billman a 1998 literary fellowship from the Wyoming Arts Council. The story, "Calcutta," won the Zoetrope/ Sam Adams Short Story Contest.

Calcutta

Hubert de Sablettes hunted rabbits, on foot, with only a knife and a basset hound in tow. He was a runner. He ran every day — an addiction — even on the coldest winter mornings — twenty, thirty below zero, — leaving at dawn his home on Klondike Street that was once the Methodist Church, knit watch cap, a water bottle belted to his waist next to the knife, and a buffalo horn cornet to sound the *trompe de chasse*, calling Perch, the hound that ran behind, who could barely keep up. Hubert, gaunt and sinewy, ran up hills, over snowdrifts, into the sagebrush desert until he flushed a snowshoe hare. Then he would chase the white animal, sometimes for hours, until it became too exhausted to go on and just lay there waiting for the knife, or died of an exploding heart.

That was the hunt, the run, as described by the children who claimed they had seen it themselves. Everyone wanted to have seen it, but the hunts took place well away from town, on the vast wastelands good only for gas wells and sheep grazing. Hubert would sometimes run for five or six hours until his workout ended with the kill. Then he would dogtrot back to town, Klondike Street, carrying the limp hare by its hind legs, grimacing from the pain in his own bramble-scarred legs. Some days he would stop in the Hams Fork River and wade in the cold water until the swelling in his legs subsided. This even in winter.

Rumor around Hams Fork, Wyoming, is treated with the courtesy of truth, and rumor here had it that Hubert was a rich count and that he was holing-up in town, hiding in the high desert, a refugee from Europe — France, where he had killed his wife by running her through with a well-honed bayonet after hunting her in a frantic chase in the forest. He was known in Hams Fork as *the Count*. It had become a childhood act of bravery to creep down Klondike Street, into the churchyard at night, friends watching in the bushes across the street, and peer into the lighted stained-glass windows, pretending to be able to see more than vague shadows inside. The metallic kitchen sounds were real: knives on sharpening steels and stones, the basset howling, and the tinny buzz of late-night a.m. radio. And the smell was real, certainly, the smell of garlic and hot goose fat and wild game frying.

Lizabeth Tanner lived next door. Sometimes at night she could see the shadows of children chasing through the yard. The window-peeking was childish, but she too could smell the food and hear the hound and wondered what life in the church was like. Some days she would see the Count walking and would notice the color of his hair in the sunlight: grayish-white, like a summer coyote's. Perch knew Lizabeth and liked her because she would sometimes lean over her fence and treat him with a raw hot dog.

She was a carpenter. Thirty-four and single, she had made her living following the ski-town booms. Now, settled in Hams Fork, she was a contractor, mostly doing remodeling work on the older homes in town, though the mine had recently laid off a hundred or so and work was slow. She had time to remodel her own home, do some fishing, read some of the books she had always promised herself she would, and build a dog sled. The sled she donated to the charity auction that followed the Calcutta.

The Calcutta had become Hams Fork's winter version of the Kentucky Derby. Residents would eat from a prime rib buffet, then bid on their favorite sled teams. Winners would receive a thirty percent cut of the money raised. The bulk of the money went to pay immunization costs for poor children. Chances of winning weren't great, but in a state with fewer than half a million residents and no lottery, the Calcutta was still the social event of the winter. Following the auction was the dance.

Except to run, the Count rarely went out in public, but now he leaned nervously against the paneled wall of the Eagles Club and sipped his blush Chablis from a plastic cup as townspeople tried not to stare, and the auctioneer, an overweight man with a brushy mustache and 20x silverbelly Stetson, rattled off bids. *Hunerd dolla, hunerd dolla, I've a hunerd, do I hear two, two hunerd, hunerd dolla, I need two . . .* Box wine and Budweiser, the Calcutta was not fancy, but the building was warm and folks could catch up on gossip with friends from the other end of the county, people they saw maybe once or twice a year.

Like the gypsy circus in the days when Hams Fork had been merely an ashen coal camp, the International Tour Of Wyoming Stage Stop Sled Dog Race came to town each February. The day before the Hams Fork leg of the race, pickup trucks with mobile kennels containing the yelping Spitz dogs paraded into town, sleds on top, straw and muzzles poking out of the whiffled boxes. Some of the lesser-known teams would go for a mere hundred or two apiece. The Count, awkward yet privileged in carriage, wore his hair oiled down, navy blazer, white oxford shirt, Levis, and handmade Luchese boots. The lobes of his ears and the very tip of his nose were purplish from multiple frostbite. His face was weathered, but he was extraordinarily fit. His leg muscles pressed like a horse's through his pantlegs. His supposed age around town sometimes varied by thirty years. The Count cupped his wine close to his chest and endured the hearty bids of several Reno-wise ranchers and miners who had pooled their money in order to afford the big names in the sport. He made his bids in regal gestures with his right forefinger.

The race director, a tan, former musher out of Jackson Hole named Hunter, stood in the back wearing a long red musher's parka with coyote-fur trim and dogwood company logos emblazoned on the back. His job was to raise the anemic bids, show enthusiasm in the hopes that the bidders would think he knew something they didn't. At times he would interrupt the auctioneer by walking down the aisle between the bingo tables in his arctic ringleader's coat and take the microphone. "Now Dale's team has been training at altitude all winter long!" he might say with steely enthusiasm, or "Terry is especially hungry this race. He led through Dubois last year and he's not coming to town with the idea of losing again." Hunter's tactics worked for the most part, though he was forced to sit on several teams running a gangline of roadkill-fed curs. Hunter wanted to recoup his losses with the favorite, Guy de Calvaire, a French-Canadian musher training on the provincial tundra out of St. Louis, Saskatchewan. *Fifteen, fifteen, yow, sixteen-hunerd, yow, seventeen, seventeen . . .*

The Count kept Hunter and the ranchers at bay and took the rights of the favorite. De Calvaire's team went for $3,500, the highest bid in the brief history of the Calcutta. *Sold. To the man in the navy-blue blazer and the big checkbook. Hope you've got you a rabbit's foot.*

"Les chiens," the Count said softly. "Thank you. Marchez."

"This sled is race-ready," said the race director, looking straight at Lizabeth, "and I admire the construction. Solid ash driving handle, cross pieces, brush bow, rear stanchions. Teflon runners. Everything welded together with rawhide joints. Some of our mushers are gonna wish they were driving this baby come a week from now."

The sled was beautiful, in the same linear way that antique gun stocks, oak letter desks, old saddles, bamboo fly rods, handmade cowboy boots, beavertail snowshoes, and wooden skis are beautiful. *We're gonna start the bidding on this fine piece of craftsmanship at three hundred dollars. Now who'll open the bidding at three hundred dollars?* Hunter's hand went up like the tail of the lead dog in the gangline as the crowd counts down the beginning of the race. *Three now four, four hunerd, four hunerd, yow!* Hubert's hand went up at four. *Four, now five, five hunerd, need five, five*! A glass of cheap wine later, the Count owned an expensive handmade dog sled. Lizabeth watched Hubert run his hands along the lines of the sled.

The next item up for auction was a rust-colored Alaskan Husky puppy, a cross between a Siberian and an American pointer, which had been bred by Hunter. Timber, the blue-eyed puppy, had stumbled over to the Count halfway through the Calcutta to gnaw at the Count's cowhide boots. Every once in a while the Count reached down and scratched the dog's head. As the crowd watched him, Hubert slowly raised his finger and owned the puppy.

They stacked the metal folding chairs in the corner and the rest of the evening was the dance. Hunter, who had honed his dancing skills as part of a set of instinctive traits for Rocky Mountain survival, fared the best at the dance, dancing with every single woman and a few not single. A whistling cowboy dusted the floor with talcum powder, which covered the asbestos tiles like snow. A band called the Noble Hussy Orchestra struck up a western swing. Hunter led Lizabeth through spaghetti turns and athletic dips.

By the third or fourth song the Count left his place against the paneled wall, pushing the sled across the talced floor toward the back door. Timber ran behind the Count until they passed Hunter and Lizabeth and hesitated as Hunter squatted to call him, but the puppy didn't stop until he reached the Count.

In the heavy snow and halo of light from the parking lot, with the mid-tempo "Smokin' Cigarettes and Drinkin' Coffee Blues" at his back, the Count looked over his shoulder and saw Hunter dancing closely with Lizabeth. He kicked the sled through eight inches of newly-fallen champagne, all the way home, the other side of town.

That week KHAM broadcast special hourly dog racing trail condition weather reports and updates on how the racers were faring on the legs prior to Hams Fork — Jackson to Moran, Moran to Dubois, Dubois to Pinedale, Pinedale to Lander, Lander to Hams Fork. From Hams Fork they would race to Afton, then on to the neon finish in Jackson. The map of the course was drawn on a Wyoming highway map in thick black marker and resembled, ten feet and a glass of blush away, an outline of France. Guy de Calvaire and a pack of Europeans stayed tight on the leader, an American dog food tycoon. The course would become more hilly, the dogs more tired. They would get a day of rest in Hams Fork.

The morning of the day before the Hams Fork leg of the race, a howling dawn, Lizabeth awoke to a knock at her door. She tied on her robe and answered it, holding tight to the storm door in the wind. "Oh, Mr. de Sablettes, what a surprise. I'm flattered at what you paid for the sled." She, like everyone, had heard the rumors and didn't invite him inside, out of the sideways-blowing snow. The Count had never knocked on her door, never been to Lizabeth's home.

"It's beautiful," Hubert said. "I thought you might like to drive it."

"I didn't know you had a kennel."

"No, just Perch and Timbre." He pointed to the basset hound sitting by the sled and the puppy in the cargo bag, "and myself."

"Well, I — " But Hubert had turned toward the sled and began linking himself to the gangline with a carabiner. Perch ran to Lizabeth and sat, eyes pleading for a hot dog. Hubert, in harness, looked back to the door, which Lizabeth held tight against herself. He looked down to his feet. Then back to Lizabeth. Hubert wore track shoes, distance flats, with quarter-inch spikes screwed into the soles. No socks. "Won't you come for a ride? I have a beautiful new sled and now I need a driver." His voice blew away on the wind, but his English was careful and Lizabeth could read his lips in the early-morning porch light. Hubert stood facing forward, concentrating, waiting for Lizabeth but no longer acknowledging her. She reached down to Perch and rubbed behind his floppy ears.

Mumbling to herself that this was crazy, Lizabeth went inside to dress. She found her hat and mittens, and stepped outside into the snow where she could see each breath come nervous and fast. She led Perch back to the sled and wrapped him in the sled's red cargo bag with the puppy. Hubert stepped forward, pulling the slack out of the gangline. " 'Gee', I turn right, 'haw', I turn left. 'Whoa', I stop, and you stand on the brake."

Lizabeth stood on the runners and lifted the ice hook. "Mush," she said softly, her breath rising upward.

"Sorry," Hubert said, "It's difficult to hear you in this wind."

"Mush!"

The brush bow lifted, then the sled tracked straight behind Hubert and leveled like a boat on-plane. "Hike!" They ran down Klondike Street in the low, muted light of the early-morning snowstorm, the crystals of snow the shape of tiny arrowheads. Hubert moved slowly, awkwardly at first, but smoothed out and picked up the pace as his joints and muscles warmed and flexed. "Gee!" There were no cars on the streets, but the team set the racing dogs howling as they passed the parked mobile-kennel trucks awaiting the next day's competition. It was feeding time, and the dog handlers stopped chopping frozen salmon and beef roasts, set their axes down, and gawked as the little team slid by. A dream? "Trail!" yelled Hubert as they passed the dog trucks, "Trail!" The hundreds of dogs in town began howling at the event, drowning the steady pattern of Hubert's breathing.

Hubert had long ago become addicted to endorphins, the natural form of morphine his body produced through hard running. But as his running progressed, he needed more and more miles of it to produce the same effect, and the rush wore off faster. He ran harder and longer, running himself deeper into oxygen debt. Without a run he became dogged or edgy, enough that he had to avoid contact with anyone. So without running, he was convinced, he couldn't survive. Running had become his habitat, and if that habitat shrank, like a constricted heart, he would no longer be wild inside, and he would die. He could not explain this to anyone. Only the rabbits knew. The hares. The coyotes. Perch.

They ran the streets of town, a line of quick color in the

storm, Lizabeth keeping one foot on the runners and pedaling the uphills. "Haw!" yelled Lizabeth and they turned left and started up the steep hill of Canyon Road. The sled tracked true in the fresh snow that covered the sooty streets, though she found herself thinking about the design, about modifications she would build into the next Calcutta's sled, mostly slimming it down, making it lighter. Most of all the sled felt heavy, the Count straining alone on the gangline. Next year she would slim the stanchions, cross pieces, and slats. The foot pads would be made of something lighter than strips of old snow tires. Guilty for the weight, she tried to pedal when she could, but Hubert kept the pace fast enough that her kicks did little to propel them forward. Perch and Timber pointed their muzzles out of opposite sides of the cargo bag. Perch still looked back at Lizabeth with hot dog eyes. Timber had fallen asleep to the rhythm of the run.

"Haw!" yelled Hubert. They shot down Elk Street, Lizabeth standing on the brake as not to let the sled run over the runner on the long downhill. "Gee!" he yelled again and they swung onto the Union Pacific service road that paralleled the railroad tracks. A yellow and black locomotive engine with a chevron snowplow over the cow catcher blew its air horn as it slowly gathered momentum from a dead stop and finally passed the sled team at the other edge of town, on its way to the power plants of Utah with a load of coal. Lizabeth, warm in her down parka, lost track of time, but thought the Count must be exhausted. Crystalline rime formed on Hubert's fleece hat and wind shell jacket.

"You've got to rest!" she yelled, "Let's have coffee!"

Hubert looked back, surprised. "Yes, all right," he said. "Gee!" she commanded, and Hubert made a right onto Antelope. "Gee!" another right onto Third West, and "Gee!" across Moose, back to Klondike.

Hubert was skittish in public. People avoided him and he avoided them when he could. He shopped for groceries at night, bundled in winter clothes, just before the I.G.A. closed, though people still studied him and speculated what he must be eating based on the basket full of ingredients he bought. Green onions and bulk garlic by the pound. Fresh spinach and Anaheim peppers. Potatoes, carrots, parsley, avocados no matter what the season and their price. Dried beans. Rye flour. Brown rice. Tabasco and balsamic vinegar. Port wine. Apples. "How do you marinate rabbit?" they asked each other, or "What on earth could he be doing with all that garlic?" Hubert held Timber on his lap, stroking his ears. Lizabeth set the cup and saucer before him on the kitchen table.

"Cream? Sugar?"

"Black, thank you."

The house now smelled musky, acerbic, hard sweat and garlic. Sawdust and wood glue. It had belonged to a mine foreman in Hams Fork's early days. Lizabeth had taken out some of the interior walls and now it was light and spacious. Most of the furniture was hardwood that she had designed and built herself. "You must be training for something. The Boston Marathon? The Beargrease? Iditarod?" Her question echoed against the hardwood floors of the house.

"No, I run for myself mostly," Hubert said softly. There was a long silence as they sipped coffee and crunched chocolate biscotti cookies Lizabeth had made. The wind whistled in the power lines outside. Pellets of snow rapped at the windows. They could hear each other chewing and sipping. Under the table Perch grunted in his sleep.

"I'm sorry," Lizabeth said, "but I have to ask. What about the rabbits?"

"There are many of them. I marinate them, yes, in cheap red wine, then saute them in much garlic, a little onion."

"But why do you hunt them that way?"

"It's the only way I can hunt them. Without insulting them." There was a long silence, sipping sounds, a clock ticking. "Enough of me. Tell me, why did you become a carpenter?"

She paused, digesting what he said. "When I was little, my father said to me, 'There are only two respectable occupations. One's a bootmaker, the other, a carpenter.' I never really saw myself as a bootmaker. I worked out of Telluride for awhile. Jackson. Ketchum, Idaho. Just the summer months. I skied all winter, fished all fall. But it got so building saunas and adjoining bathrooms with 14-karat bidets and flush handles in condominiums with names like the 'Bear Foot' just put me off my feed. One morning I found myself two stories up, hammering a Swiss-style molding on a K-Mart Alpenhaus in Red Lodge, Montana. I set my hammer down, took the nails out of my mouth, turned and looked behind me, at the landscape I was helping to exploit and ruin. I collected my pay and moved to the high desert. Hams Fork. My father always used to say that people were breeding like rabbits. It'll be a long time before many of them follow me here."

"I agree with your father. A carpenter is a very respectable profession."

"Yes. I've just decided to improve what's already here. I don't live life on a postcard anymore."

Hubert stood awkwardly, signaling his need to go. "I have something for you," he said, "Because you know." He let himself out into the snowstorm and ran to the sled, with Perch and Timber chasing after him. The Count reached into the foot of the same bag and produced a cloth flour sack. He ran back to the door and handed it to Lizabeth. "You understand," he said, "you can do something good with these." Lizabeth opened the sack. Inside were a dozen or so hare pelts. She was puzzled, but she reached into the sack and felt the fur with her fingertips as if pinching salt, then rubbing the pinch into a roux. When she looked up again, Hubert, his dogs, and his dog sled were gone.

So the myth had been merely borrowed for two hundred years. The mineral rights had been stolen from the Indians, who came from somewhere else and stole hunting rights from each other. It had all been wildness, before the polar ice caps began their melt. Now Hubert de Sablettes ran. Under the power lines held high with silver towers like giant spatulas, and the cellular towers like church steeples on the ridgetops. Over the buried phone cables that allow the Californios to live in Teton County and commute daily to L.A. via their modems. The big bears were gone. The wolves. This place had become Europe, the only wilderness inside the hearts of a few.

The first mushers were French fur trappers who used the dogs to run their traplines. *Marchez! Hike! Marchez!* Now the top mushers in America are gaunt and hungry Europeans: Scandinavians, Austrians, Germans, and Frenchmen training out of Canada. They eschew heavy pack boots for running shoes that they duct tape to their Gore-Tex pants to keep the snow out as they run, pushing their sleds up hills. The Americans have become thick and complacent, and though they can still afford the best of dogs, grow heavy on the sleds.

One musher that afternoon, an American from Grand Marais, Minnesota, told Hunter at the checkpoint midway between Hams Fork and Afton, that he had seen a man near the ridge, on foot, running by himself in the snow and rabbitbrush, twenty-five miles from town. The race director radioed in that they needed to call out Search and Rescue, that no one could survive up there, unaided in that wild country, the snow, wind, and cold, alone.

Living in a Church

I live in a church. It was built and christened a Methodist church in 1900. Later on it was baptized an Assembly of God church; the sign is still downstairs in the furnace room. After that it sat empty for a few years before Joannie, the painter who lived here before us, turned it into a studio and home. One of her old canvases serves as a curtain. A mural of moose, trout, and coyotes decorates the outside brick south wall, making us appear suspect, hippies maybe. Joannie used to see ghosts. She moved to Texas to run a restaurant; we moved in because the rent is only $200 a month. Old Joe our landlord misses Joannie, and if he knew it was such a bargain he'd raise our rent to $215. The belfry houses a handsome working bell and the neighborhood kids are always knocking on the door to ring it. Pull the bell rope after ten p.m. and the police show up.

The front doors swing wide, making it easy to garage my wide-beamed canoe. I kick snow out of the way and roll the barbecue onto the walkway in front and grill peppers all year long. Good store ice stays clean and hard all winter in the drift along the driveway. When the snow melts or it rains hard the roof leaks. In summer, sip a beer and watch bats feed in the streetlights.

The chapel is open — no walls — and gives the feeling of a ski lodge. There is a chaste kitchen that makes the whole place smell of garlic. To the left of the sink is — luxury of luxuries! — a new Whirlpool Super Capacity *Plus* washing machine. The bottom element in the oven is burned out. Dried chili peppers and garlic hang from nails in the paneling. A five-pound bag of red beans. A gallon of Frank's Original Red Hot that Mick and Pam brought back from Sam's Club in Salt Lake City, hoping we'd make them buffalo wings. Three couches that I'm quite certain once housed mice nests. My wife wishes there were more doors to slam when she's angry at me. A sign with the old-school

Smokey says PREVENT RANGE FIRES. I set up a card table and wax touring skis in the living room. In the northwest corner is my office, hidden by a bookshelf, with my prized writing tool, a steel Korean-era Army clerk's desk. Ron, who helped me move it, says they just melted down an old jeep to make it. When we have our next earthquake I'll hide under it. For paperweights I have several fist-sized chunks of kimberlite — the host-rock of diamonds! — I picked up near Iron Mountain. We don't have an electric dryer or cable TV. In summer, sheets, socks, and underwear dry on the front railing in ten minutes; in winter, clothes dry overnight strung over an old pew in the basement and breezed with a fan.

On the altar wall is a huge masonite painting of Custer, arms folded, that my father painted and gave me for Christmas; in the dark, alley light coming through the window, it looks like an acrylic Jesus. Left of Custer is a brilliant watercolor in an ornate gold frame, painted by my buddy Mick, called "How The West Was Won." It shows a puncher in buffalo chaps, neat mustache, arms crossed, while a vague but pretty woman in a purple dress hangs fresh laundry in the background. The painting was a wedding gift, and when the church catches fire it's the first thing I'll grab on my way out the window.

I have a Sony shortwave radio. At night I surf the world's airwaves. I get shipping forecasts and angry evangelists telling me the end is near. There is a woman who leads eerie chants and strums "Satan, Your Kingdom Must Come Down" on an electric guitar. I'm pretty sure there is radon in the basement.

The place smells musty, just like an old church, and brings back memories of childhood Christmas services in the basement of the Congregational church I grew up in — traditionally-scalding hot chocolate and sweet mouse poison. Pretzels dipped white with carob. Peanuts in the shell. Dead bats in the back stairwell the girls were afraid to look at. By Easter, Mary, Joseph, three wise men, Jesus, plywood sheep and camels had come inside to collect another year's dust in the furnace room that smelled like my furnace room now: cobwebs and old insulation. Our furnace room used to be a rectory and it had to have been some sort of penance to live there. I need to remember to change the furnace filter in the fall. At dinner we light candles stuck in Chianti bottles and drink red wine to Mose Allison and Van Morrison. Spinach salad with garlic and Nauvoo bleu cheese. Grilled chicken with black beans on whole wheat tortillas. Hot peppers.

The paint is solid, but we desperately need a new roof. Joe is hesitant. He's much more worried about me watering the lawn and mowing once every few days. Weeds in the driveway. I envision a shiny metal job, blue or green maybe, and in winter when the outside temperature hits thirty above, wham, the snow slides off with a small avalanche. The toilet lid is possessed and will not stay up and sometimes crashes down halfway through my business, three a.m.; it's unnatural and causes me to do a little jig I would rather not do but know by heart.

We have church mice. The cat keeps them in check, but sometimes late at night I hear them climbing the walls from the inside. One night last winter I awoke at two a.m. to a mad chase in the sanctuary, down the stairs. I clicked on my reading light and saw a field mouse the size of a prairie dog run under the bed, out the other side, and into the closet where he apparently escaped to the inside of the wall. The cat accordioned into the wall but did not catch the mouse. Ants in the cupboard where we keep the honey.

There are real bats in our belfry, little browns. Just two inches long, each summer night they eat up to five hundred mosquitoes an hour. Our attic is probably full of valuable guano. I've never seen a mosquito in our yard.

Last evening a crop duster flew a grid over town, a Revelatory locust, dropping a fog of Dibrom 14 to control mosquitoes, never mind that they are controlling with them frogs, toads, caddis flies, grasshoppers, earthworms, trout, birds, bats, human livers and on up the food chain. Poison is poison. Better living through chemicals. For most here in Kemmerer, it's about making this saxicolous coal camp their version of livable — if you have to live in hell, better bring a window unit. That night I didn't get to sit in the plastic chair and sip my summer bourbon (of which I like the smell as much as the taste) over the ice that chimes against the glass. My Wyoming had been poisoned. Best to run when you hear the throttled growl of a Super Cub, engine wound like a weed eater. Cover the sugar bowl, as the old waddie says.

We were married in the church on a snowy October day by a Zen cowboy judge named Mike. The ceremony was heavy with Indian folklore and beautiful. My wife Hilary's parents are British and they were there, and afterward we called a few friends to come over for champagne. For luck, according to some English tradition, I ate a chunk of pickled herring the size of my wrist, fin still attached. My luck has been good.

We had a Christmas party and many people we didn't know showed up out of curiosity. I had won a turkey in a raffle and we baked it. Outside I grilled hot peppers with olive oil, lime juice, and margarita salt. Some guys with Pabst Blue Ribbons asked me what it's like to make love in a church. Many people left food and drinks and no one slipped on the ice out front and broke anything, so the party was a success; beer cans and turkey bones.

In February seventeen dogs come. Racing dogs, Alaskan Huskies, sled dogs and their trainers. The International Rocky Mountain Stage Stop Sled Dog Race paws through Kemmerer on its way to Afton, and the air is carnival-like. We host a mushing team from Colorado. They spread straw in the driveway, string chains, mix hot water with fatty beef and Tuffy's kibble, and feed and water the athletes. Inside they wash dog booties in our new washer and string them like Christmas lights to dry. Two years ago it was forty degrees below zero at the start of the race. Last year a bitch named Rocky bit me, requiring a tetanus shot at Public Health in the basement of the courthouse.

Just a few hundred yards from my front door is the Wyoming high desert, Old Testament in its xerophilous scale. And though the Big Wonderful is shrinking with every new septic tank sunk in the ground, more pronghorn live here than anywhere in the world. There is a Byzantine network of roads that lead to gas wells. A pipeline ships more gas to Wyoming from Canada. We have Canada thistle too. Thousands of sheep eat the bluebunch wheatgrass and Idaho fescue down to where a grasshopper will starve. Once in a while a moose wanders from the willows along the Hams Fork River and into town to eat fertilized bluegrass from the overwatered lawns, where citizens cheat back the desert with sprinkler systems and herbicide. I wish we had more dandelions. Out there in the desert there are diamonds and Canadian geologists hunting for them.

Ron comes over many evenings to drink whiskey from a shot glass that says LEADVILLE COLORADO ELEVATION 10,152 and tell stories of hunters and cowboys and mules and ballplayers and bears. He is a horse packer and a Game and Fish biologist, and he is horse and kid poor. He wears sandals even in winter, plaid shorts, and a t-shirt that reads *Bad Spellers of the World Untie!* Ron is the real deal. I go horse packing with him, scouting for elk calves. He rides a spirited paint pony and races along the trail in his red Game and Fish shirt, suspenders, leather chinks, and a beaten Resistol hat called a "Saddler" pulled low over his eyes. Ron looks like a cavalry scout. He was born in Japan. "Admire a big horse and saddle a small one," he says, and does. His favorite thing, next to whiskey, is a nap on the dirt in the high outback, horses eating forbs through their hackamores. "A fartin' horse'll never tire . . . Fartin' man's the man to hire," says Ron.

Beware of   Wyoming's Old Testament possibilities: God will take back Wyoming, and He'll do it with His big stick: weather.   Global warming promises to birth a whole Armageddon of hyperthyroid El Niños. On June 17th, we had six inches of snow. Is it a sin that a little part of my spirit does the Cotton-Eyed Joe when an avalanche takes out a vacant summer home? As a writer, I need to be here to report from the front, to record the paroxysm of elements and their effect on the Wyoming condition

Last week a shirtless guy in a rusty pickup stopped in front of the church. He was sipping a beer from a can. "Say buddy, where's the courthouse?" This guy looked like the type who might require the services of a courthouse. I told him how to find it, two blocks that way. "Hey, is this some kind of pawn shop or something?" He was referring to the bicycles, gas grill, patio chairs, spade, rake, laundry on the railing. The front doors were swung wide. Inside: bell rope, canoe, nearly-new Whirlpool Super Capacity *Plus*, many skis, broken range, float tube, office chairs, cookware, candles, couches, fly rods, backpacks, beer bottles to be recycled, cat, Frank's Original Red Hot, many books, bags of catfood, jeep-desk, fire shovel, Christmas tree stand, computer, Coleman camp stove, Coleman camp fuel, sleeping bags, coolers, blue coffee table, a tent, Christopher Columbus' globe (with electric light), oars, Custer/Jesus, and *"How The West Was Won."*

"No," I told him. "It's home."

Today a slow-moving Pacific system has warranted a flash flood watch for Lincoln County. I'm listening to Townes Van Zandt's "Heavenly Houseboat." The cat is watching birds from the 100-year-old windowsill that frames my jeep-desk to the north. I have coffee. James Agee or one of his contemporaries — I don't remember who — once said, with respect, *All God's earth is a toilet.* I live by the mantra that a man ought to take a long piss on the ground each and every day. Look up at the contrails or stars. This side of the Continental Divide, your stream flows through Utah and toward the Pacific. Whistle "Why Don't You Love Me Like You Used To Do." Wyoming is the best place to do it.

If Joe knew I took nightly leaks in the alley out back, he'd evict me.

John D. Nesbitt

John D. Nesbitt grew up in the farm and ranch country of northern California, where he worked in the fields for many years as he went through school. He earned a bachelor's degree at U.C.L.A. and then a master's and a doctorate at U.C. Davis. He now lives in the plains country of Wyoming, where he teaches English and Spanish at Eastern Wyoming College in Torrington. His western stories and modern west stories have appeared in many magazines and anthologies. Nine traditional western novels, *One-Eyed Cowboy Wild, Twin Rivers, Wild Rose of Ruby Canyon, Black Diamond Rendezvous, Coyote Trail, North of Cheyenne, Man from Wolf River, For the Norden Boys* and *Black Hat Butte* have been published in hardbound, large print and paperback; another traditional western, *Red Wind Crossing,* is forthcoming.

Two contemporary western novels, *Keep the Wind in Your Face,* and *A Good Man to Have in Camp,* keep company with *Antelope Sky* and *Seasons in the Fields,* two collections of contemporary western short stories. Nesbitt has also brought out a collection of traditional western short stories, *One Foot in the Stirrup*; a collection of humorous short stories, *I'll Tell You What,* and *Adventures of the Ramrod Rider,* a medley of parody, satire, poetry and pristine romance. His fiction, nonfiction, book reviews, and poetry have been widely published. He has won many prizes and awards for his works, including a Wyoming Arts Council literary fellowship for his fiction writing, two awards from Wyoming Writers, Inc. for encouragement and service to other writers, and two awards for western novels from the Wyoming State Historical Society.

Cowboy Heart

The long shadows of morning lay on the snow as Ryan led the two horses from the stable to the cabin. It was a cold, crisp morning, and the boy could feel the energy of the horses as he saw their breath rise in clouds. Glancing again at the cabin, he saw Vance standing in the doorway. The older man stood with his right arm elevated as he smoked on the stub of a cigarette. The interior of the cabin was dark, so Ryan imagined Vance had turned off the lamp and was pausing with the warmth at his back as he finished his smoke.

As Ryan came to a stop with the two horses, Vance tossed the butt of his cigarette into the snow on his right, then stepped forward to take one of the halter ropes. He moved with the smooth, automatic motion of an old ranch hand as he tied the horse to the hitching rail, patted its neck, ran his hand down the horse's shoulder, and took a brush out of his chore coat pocket and started brushing.

Ryan tied off his horse, went to the open doorway, and reached inside to find his brush. The warm air carried the mixed smell of bacon, coffee, tobacco smoke, horse blanket, and saddle leather. The stable was really no more than a lean-to, so the ranch hands kept all the tack inside the cabin. Vance said it was just as well that way, as it kept the raccoons from chewing on the salty leather, and a fellow didn't have to shove a freezing cold bit into a horse's mouth.

Ryan liked the whole set-up. He liked the idea of spending most of his Christmas vacation this way — sleeping in a bunk next to a wood stove, whiling away the evening in lantern light, living in the midst of saddles and bridles and ropes and spurs. He liked being away from cars and television. He knew his friends would be going to the mall in Cheyenne or playing basketball in the gym, and he was sure some of them thought he was pretty lucky to make a little money at the same time he was off on an adventure. At least Ryan thought it was a good plan.

Vance apparently thought so, too, in his own terms. The night before, as he had laid his cigarette in the ashtray next to his tumbler of whiskey, he had said, "This is a good way to be, I'll tell ya. Up and away from it all, far from the tents of the wicked."

Ryan was amused by the older man's version of worldly wisdom. Even frying the bacon for breakfast had the quality of a good joke waiting to happen, with a punch line about as funny as being thrown from a horse and breaking a leg. Vance had told a story about working on a ranch where the bunkhouse cook had salted all the food pretty heavily.

"Everyone was mad all the time, and no one knew why. Then the cook blew up and quit, so we took turns cookin' for about a month, and after a while everyone got back to normal. Then we figured out it was all that extra salt that had us wound up so tight." He lifted all six slices of bacon out of the skillet and laid them on Ryan's plate. "I don't even eat this stuff any more. The doctors told me to lay off the salt and fat both." Creases came to the corners of his eyes, and the ends of his grey mustache went up. "Course, they tell you to lay off a lot of things. Mainly the things you like the best and can get your hands on real easy."

Ryan brushed his horse and appreciated the warm animal smell on the cold air. He glanced across the horse's back and saw that Vance was gone; then he saw the older man coming out of the cabin and carrying his saddle, blanket, and pad. Vance smiled as if there was another good joke on the way.

Ryan was just getting his saddle in place on the horse's

back when Vance came out with the two bridles. Ryan took his and looped it on the saddle horn, then cinched his rig. As he put the bit into his horse's mouth he saw Vance lead his horse away from the hitching rail. Ryan watched the man check the cinch, turn out the stirrup, raise his boot up into place, and pull himself aboard.

"I'll tell ya, kid. You wanta ride every day, 'cause even when you do, the stirrups just seem to get higher and higher."

Their ride took them west through hilly country, where the black cattle were easy to spot against the white snow and pale grass. Nearly all of the cattle were grazing on southern exposures, where the sun was warmer and where more of the snow had melted. Vance said the cows were in good shape; he said that was what they were working on right now. The cows had had their calves weaned and had been bred, and now they were putting on a good feed. As long as the good weather held out, there wasn't much to do but ride around and take a look.

"Work's too easy right now," Vance said. "You get your guard down. Next thing you know, a big storm can come up, and you wanta have an idea where all these gals are hangin' out." He glanced sideways. "Come a good storm, you'll earn your pay and then some."

Ryan nodded. Come a good storm, and he might wish he had stayed down in the valley. But right now he liked it.

At mid-morning they jumped a big mule deer buck, a four-pointer that looked almost as big as a horse as it bounded across the sidehill above the trail. Both riders came to a stop.

Vance motioned with his hat brim and said, "He's a good 'un. He made it through the season."

Ryan watched as the husky deer came to a stop and looked around. "Did you hunt?"

Vance laughed. "When you're this far from town you don't really hunt. You just go out and get camp meat when you need it."

"Oh."

"A nice deer like that one, you like to leave him be. Let him live a little longer and improve the species."

"Uh-huh." Ryan focused on the spot behind the deer's right front shoulder, the spot where he would put the crosshairs if the chance came to him. Then he looked at Vance.

The old cowboy sat with both hands on the saddle horn. "Those deer have a lot of heart."

"Uh-huh."

The deer went back into a trot, and Vance put his horse into motion. Ryan let his horse fall in as before, and the two ranch hands, one young and one old, continued their ride across the calm, cold country.

They made it back to the cabin at noontime, with a plan to change horses after lunch. Vance heated up a stew of dark meat, carrots, and potatoes. Ryan tasted it and shook some salt onto it. He imagined the meat was venison, and he recalled the big deer they had seen.

"I'd bet if we get a deep snow, those deer'll feel it too." He looked at Vance. "Won't they?"

"You bet they will. They've got more freedom to migrate than a cow does, but they can get stuck."

"I bet."

Vance paused as he cut a chunk of meat in two. "I heard a story one time about a guy who roped a deer off a snowmobile."

"Really?"

"Yeah. This was probably about the time you were born, or a little later."

"Uh-huh."

"The way I heard the story, he rode up to the deer in deep snow, and roped it plumb easy. Then he tied it to his machine and started draggin' it."

"Really?"

"Yeah. Nice guy. He wanted to feed it to his coyote dogs, and he thought he'd have it strangled by the time he got back."

"Wow."

"But when he got there, the deer still had some fight left in him, and he stood up on all four."

"So what did the guy do? Did he shoot it?"

"Nah. He just let a few of his coyote-huntin' dogs loose, and they tore it up." Vance looked straight at Ryan. "A real sport, you know."

"I guess." Ryan imagined the deer making its last stand, choking on a tight rope as it fought off the dogs. He recalled Vance's earlier remark that deer had a lot of heart. "Who'd you hear that story from?"

Vance pushed his plate away. "From the guy's wife."

"Really?"

"Yeah. I was interested in her, and for a while there I thought she might leave him."

Ryan waited and then spoke. "Not a good idea?"

"Damn poor one. Wasted a couple years of my life, just hangin' on the ropes and waitin'." Vance got up from the table and came back with the coffee pot in his right hand. "Damn poor idea. Just tears your guts up, is all. If you think ridin' a horse is hard on your ass, try a no-win love affair." He poured two cups of coffee and sat down. "Or better yet, don't."

"I 'magine. Is she still with him?"

"Last I heard, or wanted to hear." The older man reached his right arm across his chest and held the upper part of his left arm.

Ryan saw the wince of pain. "Are you all right?"

"Oh, yeah. This sonofabitch just hurts once in a while. That's all." Vance moved his hand to the left shirt pocket, raised the flap, and drew out the red-and-white pack of cigarettes. He was smiling again, as if there were a good punch line coming up.

Ryan waited, but the older man said nothing as he shook out a cigarette and lit it. Ryan went back to eating.

Vance set his cigarette in the ashtray and took a drink of coffee. "You know what I think?"

"What?"

"I think we ought to get you in a little ropin' practice when there's not a hell of a lot else to do."

Ryan perked up. "That would be fine."

Vance nodded. "Just practice on a few loose head. No

harm in that."

When lunch was done, the older man said he wanted to lie down for a while, so Ryan hauled in firewood and washed the dishes. It was nearly two in the afternoon by the wind-up alarm clock when Ryan sat down at the table to wait.

Vance looked over at him and got up from the bunk. As he came to the table, Ryan thought he looked tired. The skin was pale below his brown eyes.

"Well, I guess we'd better get going," Vance said. "I'll go with you to get the horses. I want to get up and move around."

They went to the corral together and caught their afternoon mounts, a bay and a sorrel. Vance was sure-handed as always, but after he tied the sorrel to the hitching rail he went and sat in the doorway of the cabin.

After a few minutes, Ryan asked, "Are you all right?"

"Oh, yeah. I've just got a stomach ache." Vance pushed himself up onto his feet and went back to his horse.

Ryan thought Vance was still moving around all right as they saddled their horses, but then he noticed the man had stopped and was just leaning with his forearms against the saddled horse. Ryan went around his horse and stood at Vance's left.

The older man turned toward the boy, and his face looked grey and drawn. "Jerry's not comin' back till the day before Christmas, is he?"

Ryan felt a pang of worry as he shook his head. He had an image of Jerry's pickup, the big white Dodge with four-wheel drive and extended cab. Even in dry weather a two-wheel-drive outfit was lucky to make it to the cabin, so Ryan had left his pickup at the ranch. Jerry had driven him up to the camp the day before, along with a supply of grub, and he had said he would be back to bring both the hired hands down for Christmas. In the evening Ryan had learned that Vance's pickup was at the shop in town getting the clutch replaced. He had thought it was real cowboy stuff to be stranded out here with just horses to get around on; now it didn't look like so much fun.

"Do you think we should ride down to the ranch?"

Vance shook his head. "I don't know if I could make it. I feel like a poisoned pup."

Ryan looked at the older man but did not see anything he could understand. "I mean, I'll be right there with you."

"Kid, if I fall out of that saddle, you'll never get me up. And that's how I feel. Weak."

Ryan bit his lip and nodded. "Do you want me to put the horses away, then?"

Vance held the brown eyes steady on him. "No. I want you to ride down to the ranch yourself, and get Jerry to come up here."

Ryan felt his eyes widen. "You mean, just leave you here?"

"That's what I mean."

"I can't do that."

"The hell you can't. And the sooner the better."

Ryan looked at his horse and back at the old man. "Well, what if something happens while I'm gone?"

Vance took a quick breath through his nose. "You mean, what if I die? Don't be a fool. Everyone's got to die sooner or later anyway."

"But you'd be all by yourself."

Vance turned his head down and to the right as he winced. Then he looked up and said, "Everyone's got to die alone. Even those twins that died in the car wreck a couple years back, each of them had to die on his own. Now get the hell gone."

"Isn't there-"

"Don't make me mad, kid. Why do you think Jerry brought you up here, anyway? He thinks I need someone to keep me company and look out for me. I guess maybe he's right on the second part. Now you get the hell down to the valley and not waste any more time."

Ryan felt the sting of realization. Jerry had hired him to keep an eye on the old man, with any cowboy adventures being secondary. Now the moment had come for him to earn his wages, and he could see there wasn't any point in arguing about whether he should go or stay. "Do you want me to put your horse away, then?"

"No, I can do that. You just git."

By the time Ryan had a bridle on the bay and had swung aboard, Vance was carrying his saddle into the cabin.

All the way down the foothills, Ryan felt the fear of something going wrong and his not being able to help it. He made himself think of his mother and father and sister, and his friends who lived in town, and the girls he knew, but always he came back to the same strong sense of dread.

He knew he wasn't supposed to run a horse downhill, especially in snow and ice, but wherever it looked like a clear stretch he let the horse out. When he got down to the flat he turned back and looked at the ridge of hills to the west. The sun was going down in a sky of crimson and gold, and the hillsides lay dark in their own shadows. He turned the horse towards the ranch and kicked it into a lope.

The pickup cab was warm and comfortable, with colored lights on the instrument panel and warm air coming out of the dashboard. Ryan could feel himself relaxing from the long ride on horseback, but he felt anxious for the old man. Although the digital clock on the dashboard read 5:48, it seemed much later.

The headlights swept across the snow and sagebrush as Jerry braked and accelerated at every turn. Ryan looked out the side window and up at the sky. The night was dark and clear, and the window glass was cold as he touched it.

"I hope the old man's all right," he said.

Jerry answered without taking his eyes from the road. "He's not that old. He's only fifty or so."

Ryan looked at Jerry. He saw the dark mustache and full cheeks, the husky shoulders and barrel chest. He figured Jerry was somewhere between thirty-five and forty–all grown up and still in his prime. He was like the deer Ryan had seen that morning, full of strength and power.

If Vance was only fifty or so, he wasn't much older than Ryan's father. Still, he seemed like an old man.

Finally the pickup pulled into the camp, and the headlights swept the stable and cabin. Vance had put the horse away all right, but the cabin was dark.

Jerry parked in front of the hitching rail and reached for the flashlight that lay beside him on the pickup seat. He shut off the lights and engine and said, "You can wait here for a few minutes if you want."

Ryan sat in the warm cab, looking out at the dark night. He had no doubts now that the old man had died, and he imagined the man's spirit floating up into the clear, cold sky. A bright star was shining in the southwest, and Ryan could imagine Vance's spirit making a passage to that star. It would be a cold, lonely flight, but Ryan took comfort in knowing that the old man had not been afraid to die alone.

He imagined Vance had gone in to lie down on his bunk and wait. He wondered if the old man had been mad at him, and then he realized Vance must have sent him away so he wouldn't have to see the man die. If Ryan had waited through to the end, he would have had to ride to the ranch anyway, but in a worse state of mind. Vance had made it easy on him.

The realization made Ryan feel like a kid twice over. He had been sent up to the camp to keep an eye on the old man, and then he had been sent away so he wouldn't have to see the worst of it. Vance had lightened things for the kid, even if it meant dying alone.

Ryan felt a wave of emotion as he thought of the old man, game to the end. It didn't matter that he himself was a kid; what mattered was how a man faced up to things. The old cowboy had a lot of heart. That would be the thing to remember. Even as he thought it, Ryan realized that this moment would stay with him, this moment in which the older man's actions gave their meaning to him.

The cabin door opened, and Jerry's flashlight sent a beam outside. Jerry walked to the driver's side and opened the door. The lights in the cab came on, lighting up the red interior.

"I could use a hand if you think you're up to it."

"Okay." Ryan opened the door and stepped out into the

cold night.

Jerry waited at the cabin door with his flashlight beam pointed at the ground. Ryan could see the shadow of the door jamb on the somber grey wood of the closed door.

"This might be kind of hard," Jerry said.

"I can do it," Ryan answered. He thought to himself, Vance did the hard part. He had been brave for someone else's sake. That could be an encouragement for Ryan to do his part now.

Things of the World

When I first came to Wyoming in 1981, I knew I would not be able to write about this place right away. I knew also that I would want to write about it, because I knew myself as a person who needed to be rooted to a place and who wrote about things in relation to their setting.

As I was growing up in rural California, my sense of place was growing on me without my being aware of it. I observed plants and animals, I paid attention in school, and I listened to the family stories. I grew up with a farming and ranching heritage, and my sense of where I lived, like my sense of history, was western. Mine was the country where the Spanish missionaries had come, and the first vaqueros. It was the destination for gold miners, wagon train emigrants, and Pony Express riders. It was the golden state, the culmination of westward expansion. I stored up all the little bits I had learned on my own, in school, and in all the anecdotes of my early years. Together they defined for me the place where I lived, the center of the world. When I began to write, I wrote about the things I knew.

When I moved to Wyoming, the center moved. I still wrote, and do write, about the other place as I knew it, but I also had to find out about the new center. In many respects, this world was like the one I had left. I moved to a small town with a J.C. Penney, a post office, banks, bars, churches, stockyards, farm implement dealers, and greasy-spoon restaurants. The local farmers raised sugar beets, corn, alfalfa, beans, and wheat. I knew those crops, just as I knew sheep and cattle and horses, which dotted the new landscape with their familiar shapes.

But despite some similarities, enough to help me feel grounded, I began to process the new things. I had already told myself I needed to take this country on its own terms, and I was open to them. I sensed right away that the air was different, and after I had been here through a winter and spring, I realized the greens were of a different hue. I am still conscious of this difference, because I have not lost my earlier sense of place. Maybe the lilac bushes and the ash trees and the corn stalks have the same greens I knew before, but it seems as if even those greens have a different tone. Perhaps it is a function of a different sunlight, due to a different latitude and elevation. But certainly the native greens of the countryside are different, especially the grasses and sagebrush.

Furthermore, variation in color is more subtle here than in the place where I used to work as a farm laborer, gardener, and landscaper. The native plants had a broader range of green, I believe — or at least brighter — and the domestic crops and yard plants certainly had a greater variety. I can recall seeing, close together, a windbreak of silver-green eucalyptus trees, a grove of dark green orange trees, and an orchard of pale green peach trees — all with dramatically different leaves as well. The climate was hospitable to these immigrants from Australia, Spain, and the Middle East.

The color green is just one way of describing what I have come to understand as an ascetic, spare way of life. I was already familiar with the crops raised here, and I had worked in all of them; but I had also worked in dozens of other crops, from chives to boysenberries to oranges. I had tons of apricots and fresh prunes pass through my hands, and I hauled hundreds of tons of peaches with an orchard tractor and a four-wheeled trailer. I hauled cannery tomatoes in huge gondola trailers, with watery juice running out of the tail end like a fat cow pissing. In contrast with such lavish diversity, and marked with fewer trees, the landscape of Wyoming stretches out in what seems to be simplicity. Again, the climate (including the latitude and the elevation) favors less diversity.

In some ways, the simplicity is an illusion, or a superficial perception, for the ecosystem is complex. I just have to look closer. But in other ways, the perception is valid. When I first came here I had more trouble than before at learning students' names — especially the young women. It seemed, at least, as if most of them had the same color of hair (cut and combed the same), the same complexion, and the same clothes. These students were all named Kim and Kelly and Tammy. A few years later they became Shelly and Lisa, then Jennifer and Jessica, then Amber and Crystal. With less diversity in the economy, we naturally have less diversity in population.

To some extent, there is a same-mindedness. Many of the people in this part of the country have eaten very few meats other than beef, pork, chicken, and turkey. Many have never tasted lamb or venison, much less domestic goat or rabbit, and they will scowl at the mention of food they have not tried. Many of them do not know what an abalone is, much less what it tastes like. "This is cow country," they say. "Eat beef." But even in that credo there is some narrowness; many of these people would not touch beef tongue or tripe.

In a land where so many people share a taste for chicken-fried steak with catsup, one is likely to find similarities in thought as well. One encounters widely held beliefs such as the federal government needs to stay away, Californians are weird, road construction is beneficial, and tourism is desirable. The latter two opinions prevail in the face of the previous two because of a widespread assumption that economic gain (in a world of low economic influx and diversity) justifies a lot of inconveniences, indignities, and "hard choices." People who hate the idea of a store selling girlie magazines or of a bar being open on Sunday fight a losing battle against the argument that it's hard to make a living here and we need every chance we can get.

This argument is based, among other things, on two major facts of life in Wyoming: low population and inclement weather. People are spread out at liberal distances, and the distances are emphasized by the weather. These facts pervade every facet of our lives here, even unto the sale of girlie magazines–we have a low population of resident buyers, and our non-residents are seasonal, so we need every chance we can get.

I came to Wyoming because of the low population. I declared that I wanted to live in a place where the cows out-numbered the people, and I was heartily assured that this was such a place. I learned soon afterwards that the antelope came in as a close third, and that made me even happier.

Low population is important to me. I don't care for large towns, tall buildings, and heavy traffic. I don't like crowds or machines. I like to live and write in a world of things, and I like those things to be in their natural state as much as possible. I always wanted to own my own place in the country, where I could observe life close up and unbothered, where I could write in peace.

Low population makes it all possible for me. I can (if only barely) afford to live on a small acreage with a horse outside my window, geese in the winter skies, and wild plum trees in the gully. If more people lived here, I would not have deer and pheasants wandering through my horse pasture, nor would I be at liberty to shoot the jackrabbits and gophers when they ravage the trees and flowers and vegetables I have planted. (It all fits together. Step aside from the main topic for a moment and ask, why shoot jackrabbits and gophers? The answers: it's hard enough to grow anything in this climate, it's good practice for hunting, and I've got the freedom to do it.) Low population makes it possible for me to hunt antelope, deer, and elk with some sense of original purpose, just as it allows me to go camping without making a reservation.

As for the weather, it conditions everything we do. It reminds us that we live in nature. It makes us take all of life seriously, and it makes us pay close attention. Because of low population a person can leave the keys in the car (and a gun in the gun rack), but because of unpredictable weather, she won't leave the window rolled down if she's going to be away from the vehicle for very long. One bad hailstorm or one bad blizzard will put all the pleasant days into perspective. Bad weather reminds us of our own mortality and the need to write when we can, and it also gives us plenty to write about.

Coming from a temperate climate, I was worried about the weather. I learned soon enough, however, that it was part of the whole scheme, inseparable and interesting. I came here because I wanted to live in nature, and the weather was part of what I came for. Once I had my own place in the country (even though I lived in a mobile home on a wind-buffeted hilltop), I was sure I wanted to stay here.

When I got my own place I had been here three years, and I felt I had taken in enough to be able to write about this world. On my own place I continued in earnest, observing the hawks, the geese, the deer, the rabbits, the toads. I took special interest in the wild flowers. I wrote a poem entitled "Wild Rose of Wyoming" and later developed the image more fully in a western novel entitled *Wild Rose of Ruby Canyon*. My love of the blue flax, the wild rose, and the pincushion cactus found its way into a story called "Flowers for Rebecca." It has been the most praised story of *One Foot in the Stirrup*, a collection of Old West stories. Also during my first fifteen years in Wyoming, I wrote several contemporary short stories that I brought together in a collection called *Antelope Sky*. These stories reflect the world around me as I have taken it in.

Where I live is so closely integrated into what I write that I abhor the idea of moving somewhere else, losing what I have here, and starting over. Although it might seem tedious to live in a world in which the children all have names like Jason and Jessica and parents with names like Mike and Cathy, and who all together do not read many books or bother to learn things that aren't required, these people are real. They know, as I have come to know, that we are all in it together. There aren't many of us, we're far apart, and we share the same problems of dealing with the weather and trying to make a living. And, despite the gossip of small towns and rural areas, people pretty much leave each other alone.

Such an environment leaves me free to study what is below the surface appearance of similarity. I do not have to be overpowered by majestic splendor. I am interested in the coming and going of the meadowlarks, the bloom of the cactus, the slow change of color as cold weather sets upon the land. I am interested in how people haul their saddles or transport their coyote-hunting dogs. I am fascinated by the intensity of a dedicated cowgirl, the trust of the cottontails that eat dandelions on my lawn.

This place has grown into me, and I have grown into it. After I had lived on my place in the country for a few years, I found myself preferring the nature tones of the surrounding world — not only for my house but also for my clothes. I quit buying checkered and striped shirts. Even a solid maroon shirt, as I see it, is the color of chokecherry juice; and my increasing inventory of tan, grey, and sage green shirts is a conscious response to my wanting to be in the landscape and not just on it. I know this shift in taste is apparent in my writing, also, because I am a fairly visual writer.

Sometimes I still miss the quail and the oak trees, but I have been able to transfer some of my interest to the meadowlark and the cottonwood. I am glad this place has grown into me, and I am glad I did not try to write about it too soon. I remember the example of a professor from the dreaded East who took a teaching job at UC Davis not long before I left that country. After he had been there a little while he wrote a detective novel in which he implied an understanding of the Sacramento Valley and the Bay Area. I didn't care for the smug tone or for the errors in detail. I came here with that lesson fresh in my head, and I have been content to take things in slowly, over and over.

I am inescapably a regional writer because I write about the common details of my immediate world. I hope to write more about my earlier region, rural California, because I am not done with some of the feelings that correspond to things there. Similarly, I hope to write about a part of Mexico I have become familiar with, and I hope to get a chance to let it grow on me a little more. For the present, thanks to low population and bad weather, this is the center of my world — the plains country of Wyoming. Here I can ponder the world as I cook the deer steak I brought home myself, dip into a jar of chokecherry jelly I made, and pause to listen to the yapping of the coyotes, my closest neighbors.

Robert Roripaugh

Robert Roripaugh was appointed Poet Laureate of Wyoming in 1995. He grew up in California, West Texas, and Wyoming, where he has lived since 1949. Roripaugh attended the University of Texas, completed B.A. and M.A. degrees at the University of Wyoming, and following Army service in the Far East, did further graduate work at the University of New Mexico. Between periods of study, he ranched with his parents along the Wind River Mountains. For thirty-five years, he taught Creative Writing and Western American Literature at the University of Wyoming. Some eighty of Roripaugh's poems and short stories have appeared in a variety of magazines, journals, and anthologies. His books include *A Fever for Living*, a novel set in postwar Japan, and *Honor Thy Father*, an early-day ranching novel that received a Western Heritage Award from the National Cowboy Hall of Fame. He has written two collections of poetry — *Learn to Love the Haze* and a recently published volume, *The Ranch: Wyoming Poetry*.

His recollection of "Wyoming Ranch Life Thirty Years Ago" is included, along with an historical essay by T.A. Larson, as part of the text for Judith Sandoval's *Historic Ranches of Wyoming*. In 1996, a "Main Street, Wyoming" program on Roripaugh and his poetry, filmed on the Baldwin Creek where his family ranched, and at the Pioneer Museum in Lander, was first presented on Wyoming Public Television. Robert Roripaugh is a member of the Western Literature Association, Western Writers of America, and The Authors Guild.

To Owen Wister

When West was West you came into the crystal air
To discover cowboys working cattle,
The smell of sage, empty plains distant in sunlight.

From East to West you came each year, riding trails
Where vision opens into space
And freedom: Wind River, Crowheart Butte, Bull Lake,
The Yellowstone . . . hunting elk,
Stories, fishing the Snake, sweating off the manners
Of Philadelphia until the grizzly
You and Tigie killed in Jackson Hole seemed to you
A man, and each cool prairie morning
You knew the sharpened light, mountains "smoking blue,"
Antelope running tan and white
Against the yellow grass.

Back East you wrote . . . and shaped a myth from life
Which vanished through your fingers.
Living with ghosts of Medicine Bow, the Virginian,
Drybone, Chalkeye, Deer Creek,
Dick Washakie, and Scipio Le Moyne, you framed within
A distant eye a world all gone . . .
Aged . . . transformed into dusty towns, the graveyard

At Fort Fetterman, a country
Overrun with tourists,
The stagecoach route a road.

The books remain, a reputation, a cowboy you idealized.
But coming West or staying East,
You knew the way to love this lonely, changing land.

Yellow Willow: For Yoshiko

October is a time
Of yellow willow,
After green of aspen turns away.
We must wait through
Cooler days
When alders harden into red
Or brown, falling
Towards eons as willows yellow
Wyoming foothills.

I think your fingers
Have the shape
Of willow, like your eyes.
Perhaps it's just
The slowness
Of the way you turn
In quiet fire still. . . .
Or something yellow as the leaf
That holds to green skin darkening
Into brown and gray.

Above Brush Creek,
Watching willow burn,
I return to days in yellow-matted
Rooms, the rainy season mist,
Snowy blossoms
Never touched by yellow.
I could tell you all
Of this and more. I won't.

My eyes are filled with fall —
And willows slow to yellow.

Skull

Archaeologists commit such dusty loves for science,
Rooting in highway fill,
Sifting excavations with the mind's fine screen
As though knowing
The death of basketmakers, the sun's children, hunters,
Denied our faithless egotism.

So imperceptibly we evolve into counters of skulls,
No more . . . much less,
Delineate ourselves into numbers left, these
Announcements of disappearance,
Enumerating without purpose — necromantic lovers
Of those gone, those going.

There must exist a hollowness to bone defying
Resolution: Teeth so lightly
Socketed in heavy jaw, shadows of eyes, splinters
Where nostrils wore away
In melting springs — features not shaped by appearance
But absence. Even so

I feel stricken with a mania for skull, becoming
A collector of extinction,
Shards of life, defining this stitched intricacy
Of badger cranial crack,
This brachycephalic Mongoloid, a bison overlooked
By bone-pickers:

These are skulls, and this is the thighbone
Of a cyanided coyote,
The great bear's hide, knuckle of winter-killed elk
A Crow burial site broken. . . .
This piece of eagle wing once made a whistle
Fluting for a holy man.

The Ranch

There are cattails in the wet borrow pit,
Then a crooked shed sinking
Into alkali where a neighbor's cattle
Ate swamp grass among the thistle.
The road climbs past other ranches
With sheep, hay meadows where the girls
Drove tractors all summer,
And you loved the one who rode a mower.
There are beehives the Mormon owned.
The hills are weathered shale, sagebrush
And thin grass. The fences sag.
Bud's place is a quarter-mile
Off the road below the one-eyed sorrel
And a bay mare who spooks at cars.
The fields are yellow, last winter's
Haystacks have rotted into brown,
And through the window drifts the smell
Of warm earth, weeds, wild roses
Lacing barbed wire.

There is a final curve before the valley
Opens to one side, dropping into
Cottonwoods, the small white house,
A corral with elk horns
Above the gate, the red barn
You repainted waiting for the draft,
A saddle shed smelling of oats
And sweat-soaked leather.
There is an apple orchard above the house,
A Ford tractor, rusting implements.
The pickup is dark green,
A '49 Chevy, and horses are grazing

In the pasture beyond the barn.
Hearing a car at the gate,
The black-and-white dog should bark
And you will drive over the cattle-guard,
Cross two irrigation ditches,
Making the planks thump twice, and tell
Yourself you have found —
Again — the ranch.

The Old Horseshoer

In late spring the horseshoer navigates
Our soggy road, his Studebaker truck
Clanging an anvil, tools of the trade,
Iron shoes in a barrel. Stooped, Day's Work
Mixed with mustache, he sets up under
Cottonwoods, keeping one eye on the corral
Where Sugar, PeeWee, wary Shorty are waiting.
Their coats are patchy, winter hair
Shedding unevenly, "bellies a little gant."

He hasn't come for small talk. Remembering
The last time, he picks out Shorty first,
Ties him high by a heavy halter-rope.
Wearing leather apron with pouches for nails,
The old man lifts a foot, swears, wields
His curved hoof-knife — spits — neatly clips
The edge with rusty pinchers, rasps it level.
He bends the calked shoe by a squint,
Pounds, fits, refits, gauging the ellipses

Against soft blue and Shorty's cautious eye.
His mouth bristling with nails, he works
Under the raised front leg, a circus
Act, gray cap on backwards, hammers near
The quick, twisting and clinching nails down,
Mutters to himself, the light
Green morning opening to sun. Shod in muddy
Boots, he limps around Shorty, picks up
One hind foot easily as a tired lover,
Asks if we've heard the first meadowlark.

Sleeping Out on Sulphur Creek in Autumn: For John R. Milton

West of Coyote Lake the sun meets granite hills. Light
Sharpens over snakeweed and sagebrush
In the flats. . . . Cattle wandering off the water lazily
Inspect my Jeep, bedroll in a grassy draw.
Behind Mitten Spring the rock turns red — after thirty years
A weathered hump familiar as my aging hand.

All afternoon I've hiked alone through gramma grass and sage.
Sheep summered here. The herder's trailing
Them home to the Sweetwater, his lead ewe black, drifting
North ahead of fall. Now Benny Iturrian's out
Of sheep, running cows and calves. I remember his house
On Alkali, bringing him apples from our orchard,

The way flocks of sage grouse strutted up from the water,
Headed for feeding grounds in morning light,
And the sign he made for his front door —
                        WELCOME HUNTERS!
MAKE YOURSELVES AT HOME
                        AND PLEASE CLOSE GATES!
I hope he's well, friendly as ever, gates stretched tight.
All things seem possible here on Sulphur Creek.

The lone hawk hunts a sagebrush draw, drops . . . rising
Empty-handed. Do older eyes see more loss,
Or does the mind, like evening sun, heighten memory before
It's all we are? What matters, I hear you say,
Is how lost family, friends . . . the solitary hawk remain
In remembered lives, images, words we share.

Tonight in a higher sky the stars will be hard. Already
Horned larks are still, quiet has fallen
Down in shadows, the last heavy truck from a drilling rig
Spreads dust along the road to Pickett Lake.
Sage grouse have moved up brushy draws to roost and eagles
Silently make their final sweep across the flats.

It should be easy to sleep. An early snow kept hunters home,
Though now it's melted except for patches
On Beaver Rim. One old antelope buck watched me at dusk
From a distant ridge . . . then went to water
Below the spring, drilling rigs are too far away to hear,
And with a moon coyotes will be calling if I wake up.

Regionalism, Place, and Wyoming Literature

"Regionalism" is a slippery term in literary discussions, used both to praise and damn writing from certain locales and time periods. When American Literature of a century ago was strongly dominated by its Eastern and English roots, regional works could be set aside as an inferior strain of provincial expression and local color, sometimes interesting in customs, speech, characters, and locale but hardly in the mainstream of American culture and refinement.

No sooner was the frontier experience ended in actuality than a long struggle for recognition of serious Western Literature took clearer shape. One part of this involved a growing dissatisfaction with the extremely limited acceptance of regional writing about the West into "American Literature" as defined by major publishers, traditional academic scholars, editors of anthologies, and critical commentary reflecting taste in the East. While many regional fiction writers and poets in New England, the Midwest, the South, and even the West Coast had been accepted, prized, and anthologized by the 1950s, writing from most of the West continued to be treated with critical complaints that the material was too popular and stereotyped to be literary, the books too concerned with landscape and nature to be relevant, and the authors and their characters too innocent and morally uncomplicated, or isolated in time and geography, to match the literary art produced elsewhere in a supposedly more sophisticated nation of the 1960s and 1970s. In his preface to *A River Runs Through It* (1976), Montana's Norman Maclean tells of a literary handicap he learned his stories had from being Western when one publisher rejected them and said, "These stories have trees in them."

In the last quarter-century, the recognition of the quality

and significance of this region's literature has improved through a spreading out across the country of dedicated smaller publishers, knowledgeable reviewers, and librarians and booksellers who understand the work produced in their areas. A new interest in literary diversity has greatly increased the publication of books written by or concerned with people in the West of Native American, Hispanic, Asian, and African descent. The popularity of college creative writing and Western literature courses has increased the number of writers in the region and created more interest in regional literature. And a generation of older, well-established authors — among them Walter Clark, H. L. Davis, Thomas Hornsby Ferril, Vardis Fisher, A. B. Guthrie, Dorothy Johnson, Frederick Manfred, John Neihardt, Mari Sandoz, Virginia Sorensen, Wallace Stegner, William Stafford, and Frank Waters — produced so much excellent work that distinctions between "Western" or "regional" and "American" literature are even more indefensible. Ironically, the movement of Western writing toward equality may be achieved just as much of the region's uniqueness is disappearing. This loss of older customs, attitudes, and ways of life under pressure from population growth, settlement, and development has been an increasingly powerful theme in Western Literature from the time of James Fenimore Cooper's *The Prairie* (1827) to that of A. B. Guthrie's *The Big Sky* (1947), the novels and nonfiction of Edward Abbey, such as *The Brave Cowboy* (1956) and *Desert Solitaire* (1968), and James Galvin's *The Meadow* (1992), set in Southeastern Wyoming, where the losses are personal and very close to home. As historian T. A. Larson writes in *Wyoming: A Bicentennial History* (1977), "Wyoming still has enough of the old magic to stir the blood of visitor and native alike. But surely it is time to reflect . . . and ponder whether what the world wants from Wyoming is worth more than what Wyoming already offers the world."

Since to many outsiders Wyoming has seemed since frontier times to be about as regional as any place could be, it isn't surprising that except for a few well-known authors such as Francis Parkman and Mark Twain who wrote about their experiences passing through the area, or like Owen Wister and

Mary Roberts Rinehart who made extended visits in the summer and fall, Wyoming's writers usually have been labeled as regionalists. A great deal of important writing about the area has been done by explorers, trappers, travelers, emigrants, and transients, people who have come in from somewhere else to form fresh impressions and moved away with memories to which they later give shape. Historically the region was country to pass through on the way farther west or experience while seeking furs, minerals, wild game, a taste of primitive life, or simply adventure, before returning east. As a young state, Wyoming's literature has developed over a short period of time and has been regional in the best sense of the term — writers working in varied ways with aspects of the state's history, natural features and climate, wildlife, and the attitudes, conflicts, character, and ways of life of its human inhabitants.

Wyoming Literature has been less well-known and publicized than that of many neighboring states, and the quality of the state's literary history may be surprising to some. One of the characteristics of Wyoming's literature is the equality of men and women in contributing to its growth. Another is the versatility many writers have shown in the genres in which they have worked. Peggy Simson Curry, the state's first Poet Laureate, published short stories and novels for both adults and younger readers, a forty-page dramatic poem on the Johnson County Cattle War along with her lyric poems collected in *Red Wind of Wyoming and Other Poems* (1977) and *Summer Range* (1981), and a very successful textbook, *Creating Fiction From Experience* (1964).

For me, the concept of "place," the sense writers may have of being shaped by or drawing strength in their writing from a particular part of the earth whether or not they continue to live there, is of more significance than some of the arguments over regionalism, which for the most part are connected with literary history and critical bias. A sense of place has much to do with how writers perceive their geographical environments and the extent to which their writing is influenced by land, nature, climate, and the shaping of human life which has taken place there. In Native American literature we can see the influence of place in the relationship between a people and the Earth. Two books by residents of the Wind River Reservation — *The Sky People* (1971) by Tom Shakespeare, an Arapahoe leader, and *Pachee Goyo* (1981) by Rupert Weeks, a Shoshone storyteller, — show this. Western American literature has always been deeply concerned with landscape and nature as a force which affects the lives of men and women and can even change their characters with positive or negative results.

Life in Wyoming and the West *has* been influenced by space, terrain, weather, and closer contact with nature to a larger degree than many urban publishers and reviewers could appreciate. In evaluations of literature from the South, a strong sense of place has been more readily accepted as strength and quality, as have a number of stereotypical aspects of the environment and life there, while work from the West, especially in fiction, has been considered less relevant because it draws from a place and ways of life supposedly too isolated and out-of-touch with contemporary problems and values to be universal. In recent years such complaints are heard much less frequently, possibly because Americans feel more nostalgic about the West and are interested in a seemingly freer, cleaner, safer, and less crowded life. And presently many talented writers are living in or writing about the region. Good literature usually conveys a sense of place, and what matters ultimately is not where that place is but how skillfully and with what depth the author uses the locale, its ways and people, to express something significant and true about human life and experience that will engage thoughtful readers anywhere.

I came to Wyoming along with the big blizzard in the winter of 1948-49, when my father and mother bought a ranch outside of Lander near the Wind River Mountains. My family had always lived in the West, usually in cattle and oil country, and many of my close relatives were ranchers in California. But Wyoming was different. It was linked more closely to its past, a region of hard and soft rock formations with colors ranging from earth tones to deep shades of ocher, country sometimes broken with folded and tilted land forms or opening out so you could see very far away, across the space and distance, darker shapes of mountains outlined against the sky. But with harsh winters and wind, suddenly changing weather, isolated areas a long way from help in emergencies, it wasn't an easy country to live with, unforgiving of mistakes in judgment. Wyoming was far less developed than other places I had known and seemed ancient in geological time, young in people's attitudes, and intriguing in its human history.

In coming here I slowly began to think of writing stories about the new experiences I was having on the ranch and in the small town and mountains nearby, the people — neighboring ranchers, Scotch families my parents knew, Shoshones and Arapahoes from the reservation, sheepherders and cowhands, and townspeople of all sorts and persuasions — and the country itself, the place becoming home and its past. After a year I enrolled at the University of Wyoming as a transfer student who had majored in journalism and geology. While completing a geology degree, I took a strong English minor. Summers and during breaks from school I worked on our ranch, where we raised cattle, sheep, and hay, not far from the Wind River Reservation. Altogether our place contained about a thousand acres which formed the center of our life as a family for some fourteen years, and was a source for several of my stories and work in poetry that I am still doing now, as well as a long piece on "Wyoming Ranch Life Thirty Years Ago" that is part of the text for Judith Sandoval's *Historic Ranches of Wyoming* (1986).

In Laramie I began taking classes in creative writing taught by the poet Joseph Langland and a variety of literature courses, including one of the earliest college courses in Western American Literature given by Ruth Hudson. Her knowledge of the region's literature gave me a background I would draw upon heavily as a teacher and writer. My interest in writing went back a long way. An elementary teacher before marriage, my mother had written poetry and encouraged me to read good books while I was growing up. My father, who had been raised on ranches and worked many years as a petroleum engineer, was a good storyteller. As soon as we were old enough he took my brother and me hunting and fishing, often with the whole family camping out or renting a cabin on vacations. Before I even started high school in Texas, my father had driven us through much of the West, including Wyoming.

In the early 1950s several of my stories and a couple of poems were published in the literary magazine for student work which was started by Joe Langland and sponsored by the English Department. One issue was also distributed around the state, and a rodeo story I had written about a troubled saddle-bronc contestant created a small stir in Lander, in part because I had somehow given the main character the same name as one of the town's favorite, middle-aged barbers. A reader in Jackson wrote to the president of the university to complain about the frankness of the same story. At least I was no longer a totally unknown writer. After finishing my M.A. and putting up hay on the ranch that summer, I was drafted into the Army as the Korean War was ending and stationed in Missouri and Maryland before being sent to Japan for a year. Back in Wyoming I returned to Laramie as a Coe Fellow in American Studies, again taught freshman English, made two trips to Japan, where I was married, and later brought my wife to America.

In 1958, while I was doing further graduate work at the University of New Mexico, my first story to be published nationally was accepted by the *Atlantic Monthly*. Its setting was in Japan and Wyoming, where a soldier was returning home to his family's ranch after his discharge. I'd finally done a story strong enough to reach a wide audience and convey something of the way the place where I became a writer would affect much of my future writing. My first novel, *A Fever for Living* (1961), was set in Japan as the military occupation was ending. That book draws heavily on a sense of place developed from my being at an army camp in a country totally foreign to anything I had known before. The impressions and memories remained vivid long after the four years I spent writing the book, which was started and finished in Wyoming.

The setting for *Honor Thy Father* (1963) is the Sweetwater

River country between Lander and Rawlins during the late 1880s. Although the novel required a great deal of research on ranch life and history of this period, I knew the country from driving through it over many years, making hunting trips each fall, and helping a friend break horses for an old-time stockman whose family ran cattle on a large ranch east of Beaver Rim. The Sweetwater area and Lander Valley where my family was ranching form a sweep of grass-and-sage rangeland — marked with granite hogbacks, then dropping off into broken foothills below the Wind River Mountains — which has always intrigued me and influenced much of my writing. Laramie, where I've lived for many years, has a different history, geological setting, climate, and lifestyle, but along with being another place important to me as a writer, it is also where I've done almost all of my writing.

For me, a sense of place is essential to both the writing process and the work itself. My short stories and poetry have consistently made use of Wyoming. I don't mind being called a regional writer, because I am and believe that regionalism in another sense — the values of diverse areas keeping their distinct character and culture — is usually a strength in life and literature. But writers work in varied ways and hold a wide range of views about regionalism and the significance of place. Americans have long been a mobile people, increasingly so in recent times. Some writers feel this rootlessness has undermined any deep sense of place, or believe most of us now live in a media-driven culture and human-transformed environment which possess few real differences worth writing about.

As long as distinctions we value and hold onto still remain between Wyoming and the interior West and other regions, discussions about regionalism, place, and their importance to writers and literature will produce disagreements. As an old ranching neighbor told me once when we were branding and castrating calves, "Son, there's no only damn way to do anything. There may be my way and your way, but if one of those bull calves we just made a steer dies, you might start to think we done it wrong."

Page Lambert

Page Lambert, a Colorado native, was recently featured in *Inside/Outside Southwest Magazine* as a notable woman writer of the contemporary West. Her nonfiction book, *In Search of Kinship*, (a Fulcrum Publishing Denver bestseller), won unanimous praise and has been excerpted in numerous anthologies and national magazines, including *Chicken Soup for the Soul* books, New York's *Parabola: Magazine of Myth and Tradition; Bugle; Journal of Elk Country; Range: The Cowboy Spirit of America's Outback; Woman's World* and *The Christian Science Monitor.* Her novel *Shifting Stars* (a Mountains and Plains Book Award finalist) met with equal success, drawing high praise from legendary author Dee Brown. A contributing author to *Ranching West of 100th Meridian*, Lambert was one of fifteen women writers selected from around the nation to contribute to *Writing Down the River: Into the Heart of Grand Canyon*. As a result of this project, she now facilitates annual, five-day River Writing Journeys (for women) on the Colorado River. Her essays also appear in *Woven on the Wind; Leaning Into the Wind, Stories that Shape Us,* and *Tumblewords.* As a speaker and presenter of more than one hundred fiction and nonfiction workshops nationwide, she has lived for the last sixteen years with her family on a small ranch in the Black Hills of Wyoming. She is currently at work on three novels, including *The Water Carrier*, a contemporary story set in Denver, and two nonfiction books, *Stories about Stories* and *Lifeblood: Rivers of Living Water.*

From *The Water Carrier*

Nori and Selu
The Evening of the Storm

Nori eased her truck up to within two hundred yards of the lake, then let the vehicle idle. She rolled down her window and adjusted the fresh air vent so that a slight breeze cooled her forehead. Odd — such warm, humid air in April. Especially after a late winter. She picked up the evening paper from the empty passenger seat next to her and glanced through the headlines, searching for coverage of the President's recent speech on the environment.

Instead of feeling ecstatic when she read the news release, her hand shook. Another thunderstorm was building.

Washington — The American bald eagle has been removed from the endangered species list, the President announced from a platform on the South Lawn of the White House. After three decades of struggle to protect the bald eagle against pesticides and habitat encroachment, the majestic bird, living symbol of the nation since 1782, is back from the brink of extinction.

Nori glanced out her car window at the few remaining bald eagles still roosting in the cottonwoods by the lake. Most of the other eagles, over ninety of them, had already headed north. All but these few, and the Refuge's only nesting pair, were gone.

A biologist at the Wildlife Refuge since 1988, she had never grown accustomed to the fact that the twenty-seven square mile refuge, 17,000 acres, had been a weapons arsenal during World War II. Considered dangerously contaminated, the arsenal, less than ten miles from the heart of Denver, was once known as "the most polluted square mile on earth." Toxic chemicals and pesticides still tainted the land and water.

She took a deep breath, peered at the gray wall of clouds rolling in over the mountains to the west, and readjusted the truck's air vent. A wisp of ginger-colored bang fluttered on her forehead. She glanced out the corner of her eye at the cell phone, then went back to the news release.

> *Challenger, the eleven-year-old bald eagle blown from*
> *a nest in the wild as an eaglet, joined the President on*
> *the lawn. The bird, unable to survive on his own because*
> *of too much human contact, will be the star at the Earth*
> *Day Wildlife Exhibit to be held in Denver, Colorado.*
> *During the President's remarks, Challenger flapped his*
> *seven-foot-long wings and screeched.*

A sudden bolt of lightning burst from the apex of Pikes Peak, where the clouds blanketed the mountain range. Nori dropped her hands to her lap, braced herself for the inevitable thunder, fought her irrational fear with fact. *It is the rapid expansion of the air, heated to 50,000 degrees by the lightning, that causes the thunder.* She had learned as a child to use science like a salve — an ointment to counterbalance eerie flashes of intuition. More like premonitions, really. She'd learned, finally, to trust her instincts. Explore them. But despite the emotional salve of science, storms petrified her. Eagles and storms paralyzed her. Nightmares of the stormy childhood day on the Stikine River, when the eagles rose from the spawning smelt and blackened the sky, still plagued her.

The thunder never came, yet silence charged the air. She thought of her husband Daniel — tracking the pending storm, his helicopter whirling and dipping more than a thousand feet above the city. Lightning posed a serious threat to a chopper pilot. But hail was worse. Hail could render a chopper's blades useless, like clipping a bird's flight feathers, causing a helicopter to plummet twelve hundred feet to the ground. Nori searched the sky for hail-producing clouds, didn't like the dark, vertical giants towering over the plains to the east. Odd. Storms coming in from both the east and west. She glanced again at the cell phone, then swiveled the spotting scope mounted on her truck window toward the thunderheads and shivered. The temperature was dropping rapidly. Wind began churning the clouds, pushing them toward the Refuge.

A drop of rain fell from the shrinking square of cloudless sky hanging over her, landed on the truck's windshield, then ran down the glass, leaving a tiny streak of water. Raindrops from blue sky. Odd. Uneasy, Nori tossed the newspaper into the back seat, tucked the phone into the pocket of her field coat, grabbed her binoculars, and stepped outside.

Easing her way through the grassland, she startled three does. They bounded into a cluster of bare-limbed cottonwoods, white tails aloft. The call of a red-tailed hawk spiraled through the dusk. Nori stopped and lifted her binoculars. A snag, towering 100 feet in the air, stood silhouetted against the horizon. She scanned to the right of the snag until a second tree, with a huge stick nest, came into focus. Even in the failing light, the white head of an adult eagle shone against the starkness of the bare tree limbs. The female, she guessed, based on her larger size. She peered at the nest, held her breath. Finally, next to the adult, two dark fuzzy heads bobbed up. *The eaglets.* Relieved, she watched them a moment, then scanned the other trees for the second parent.

This was the Refuge's first pair of breeding eagles. They had been nesting out here for several years, but never before had stayed to lay their eggs. Perhaps the commotion from Denver International Airport kept frightening them away. Who knew? Then miraculously, late this winter, two eggs appeared. The whole Refuge buzzed with the news. Even the workers cleaning up the arsenal's deadly contamination asked for daily updates as hatching time approached. Then, on the spring equinox, the first egg hatched. A day later, on Denishia's fourteenth birthday, the second egg hatched.

The upper branches of the cottonwoods creaked in the wind. Nori saw no sign of the father. She switched her gaze to the sky. A distant rumble vibrated the air. The lone patch of blue had disappeared. She scanned the horizon and finally found the male circling nearly as high as the clouds. The burrows of a prairie dog colony lay directly below him. The eagle's flight began spiraling, lower and lower, erratic at times as he fought the stormy gusts of wind. Then suddenly he dove toward the hard-packed earth at nearly a hundred miles an hour. As quickly as he dropped, he rose, the limp body of a rodent dangling from his yellow talons.

A bolt of lightning flashed to the east. Nori jumped, skittish as the whitetails had been. She should head back to the truck. Instead, keeping her eyes on the eagle, she slipped on her rain jacket, pulled the hood up over her head, and eased in closer to the trees. She wanted to watch the feeding.

She was within two hundred feet of the cluster of cottonwoods when the scene in front of her suddenly went dim. Every hair on her body tingled. Then a wild, errant bolt of lightning flashed, illuminating the towering snag. As if in slow motion, Nori watched the male eagle fly toward the dead tree, then land on his free foot. A strand of blinding white light zigzagged from sky to snag to eagle and a horrendous crack split the air. Horrified, Nori watched the eagle's body sway as he teetered precariously on the limb. Then the great bird's wings slowly folded and he toppled from the snag, falling to the earth below.

A tingling sensation, like a thousand pricking needles, traveled from the ground up Nori's legs and spine. The thunder broke and violent sound waves came crashing down. An eerie silence followed; a scorched smell hung in the air. The ground beneath her seemed to undulate, like rippling skin. Stunned, Nori walked toward the smoldering snag. Black streaks, still hot to her hand, ran down its trunk. She found the eagle lying dead on the greening spring grass, his feathers burned, his yellow eyes sunk into blackened sockets. Still clutched in the eagle's talons was the prairie dog, charred beyond recognition.

Selu stood on the dark veranda of the old adobe house and pulled the fringed blanket up over her shoulders. Wind whipped through the historic highland neighborhood, rattling the budding limbs of the cottonwoods. A shingle flew from her neighbor's roof, rode the turbulence, then plummeted to the ground, landing among the yucca and cactus in Selu's yard. From somewhere high overhead, she heard the droning whirl of a helicopter.

That the flood was coming did not surprise her. Every time she looked across the valley of the Platte from the bluff, she was reminded of the river's prowess. Like a passionate woman, the river was capable of erratic behavior — sinewy and sultry one moment, full bosomed and headstrong the next.

She and Carlos had stood in this very spot fifty years ago and watched bulldozers rearrange the river's course, pushing tons of ancient sand more than 1,000 feet to the west. To build a highway in a riverbed? What foolishness. To rid Denver of the squatter shanties that grew along the waterway? Such was the engineers' real motive. But time and again the river sought revenge, returning to her old bed like a queen refusing to give up her throne.

She jumped as a bolt of lightning ran jagged across the night sky, illuminating the entire valley below. For a split second she saw the massive, golden steel loops of Elitch's new roller coaster. A second bolt of lightning, followed by a horrendous roar of thunder, stabbed the darkness, illuminating the Ferris wheel. Electricity crept up her spine, flaring the fringes on the blanket and the hairs on the nape of her neck. She stepped deeper into the sheltered darkness of the veranda. Overhead, on the apex of her tiled roof, a clay gargoyle perched — wings spread, mouth agape.

The old valley highway below — I-25 the newcomers called it — ran slick with rain. Headlights cast blurred beacons of light that streamed into the night. Rain poured from the rooftop of the old Forney Museum, down the sides of the new Mile High Stadium, down the swollen banks of the river and into the swirling waters. For a moment she was tempted to walk down to the confluence, to the heart of the raw power.

For a week, heavy rains had been inundating the Front Range. Unusual warmth was melting the mountain snowpack, filling Dillon Reservoir to near overflowing. There was flash flooding in Glenwood Canyon. Trees began toppling in the Turkey Creek area, downing transmission lines. Fierce flooding hit the south — La Junta and Pueblo and Manitou Springs. Tonight, the sky held more wattage than did the city's power lines.

Earlier that day, the clerks at the Sheepskin Emporium where Selu worked could talk of nothing but the storm as they peered out the store's plate glass windows. The wind tunneling through downtown whipped the rain into froth. Traffic signals on 16th blinked sporadically, and manhole covers floated away. Water flooded the huge parking lot at the new $180 million dollar sports arena. *I hear they might cancel tomorrow's Earth Day concert. Imagine that, 20,000 angry people. And to think, I almost got tickets. . . .*

Selu had listened to their talk but kept her thoughts to herself. She, too, peered out the shop windows to the deserted streets. The carriage horses in front of the Tabor Center were gone, the tourists had withdrawn to their fancy hotels, the street kids and their skateboards had disappeared. The Daniels and Fisher Tower stood like a lone sentinel. Even Denver's homeless sought early shelter. Tonight, she had decided, the bus would take her home.

She had kneaded the fleece linings of the sheepskin coats with her arthritic fingers. She fluffed the soft Merino pelts, re-stacking them one upon the other — pressed the wavy whiteness of their wool against her cheeks, running her fingers across their velvety underbellies. To touch them was to feel the earth of home. She ran a wool duster over the emporium's shelves. She refolded her own hand woven serapes, consigned to the store for half their worth.

Her old body had moved slowly, but her mind had raced. Like the river, it raced over ancient ground layered with the memories of countless springs.

To think of spring was to think of Carlos. To think of Carlos was to think of El Chapultepec's. Mariachi music and margaritas and a pulse so rapid that Selu had feared her young heart would flutter from her breast and fly away. Running her hand over the stripes woven into the serapes, her heart still fluttered. The rain beat against the windows, and her old heart fluttered like a girl's.

To think of Carlos was to think of the war. Long factory days helping to build unspeakable weapons. Ammunition. Artillery shells. Bombs. Poison gasses. Long nights spent together in favorite taverns, trying to forget the tedious days. Latin music and dark hair, soft like silken corn tassels. Carlos. Brooding eyes as mysterious as night. Heads bent toward candlelight, bodies touching as they sat, night after night, in their booth at El Chapultepec's — hip to hip, shoulder to shoulder, fingertips making light daring caresses across bare skin.

Spring with Carlos was crab apples blooming on the parkway, lilacs full and fragrant, plum blossoms to keep one's thoughts far from war. Slow evening strolls along Cherry Creek. Carlos had a childhood limp that meant he would never go to the front lines, would never die at Anzio like her father.

Still, she could not turn away her fear — could not call forth the ancient dragons of her ancestors. Her medicine was too weak.

Another bolt of lightning seared the sky above the river, coming down like a rapier over the steel roller coaster. A white-hot light coiled itself around the three loops of the Boomerang and a tremendous crack rent the air. Then another bolt struck, illuminating the amusement park's tall white tower. For a moment, the sky froze in yellowish-blue light. Then a scorching odor permeated the night and darkness engulfed the valley.

Rain dripped from the eaves of the old adobe house, puddling at Selu's feet. She shivered. Every hair on her body seemed to be standing on end. She pulled her long, gray braid over her shoulder and ran her hand down its length. Static electricity sparked out the tips of her fingers. She thought of her mother — imagined her lying limp at Crazy Woman Creek, her own braid a coil of fear. The war, in its own way, had claimed many victims.

Selu had returned to the Wyoming ranch only once since her father had died at Anzio. "Why do you use firecrackers to scare away the coyotes from the ewes?" she had asked her brother Domingo. "The War," he answered, "has taken all the bullets." Then he turned his back to her and walked away.

She looked once again out into the darkness of the storm. Another flood would come. The only question was when. She turned, opened the door of the near-empty house, and entered. She could still smell Carlos' cologne, all these years later.

Earth Day, the Morning After the Storm

Selu lifted a pot from the wood-burning stove and poured strong coffee into a clay mug. From beneath the fringed blanket covering a cage which stood in the corner of the small kitchen came soft cooing noises. She set her mug on the stove and lifted the blanket, draping it over her arm. She had chosen the colors favored by her mother's Cherokee ancestors to weave into this manta, deep reds and bold yellows.

"*Mis palomas,*" she whispered, "the *torrente* is over, no?"

Two brownish-gray mourning doves cooed back. The male spread his long, tapered tail and began pruning iridescent neck feathers. Black eyes, rimmed by tiny, pale blue feathers, sparkled in the early morning light. The female lifted herself from the nest where she had spent the night and stretched her dark wings. A downy breast feather floated to the bottom of the cage.

Selu clipped the door of the cage open with a clothespin, then reached in and removed the food dish. Barefoot, she crossed the earthen floor, then opened the door and stepped outside. Only the drops of rain clinging to the yucca and the pools of water gathered here and there spoke of last night's storm. A clear sky greeted the dawn. She shook out the blanket, blew seed husks from the dish, then returned to the warmth of the small adobe dwelling. *Cooh, cooh, cooh, coo* the male dove called out.

"You are hungry, eh?" she asked the birds, draping the blanket over a butcher-block table which stood in the middle of the kitchen. "Then you shall eat."

Never, when Carlos was alive, would she have placed the blanket from a birdcage on the table at which they ate. But these things no longer mattered. They had not mattered for a very long time.

She pulled a sack of mixed seeds from an open shelf, added some bits of dried fruit, then lifted the lid from a large crock. She peered into its darkness, shaking her head. She reached her arm in, up to the elbow. "Empty," she muttered, pulling her hand out and putting it on her back to rub the ache. She straightened up.

"Well, it is a good morning for a walk," she said, but she did not feel as sprightly as she sounded.

The birds cocked their heads expectantly. She put the food dish back in the cage. The female poked her beak into the dish and rummaged around, then pulled her head out and bobbed it up and down. "I know, I know," Selu said. "Do not nag me." She took two, long drinks of her coffee, sat down in her willow rocking chair, brushed the dust from her feet and pulled on a pair of knee-high moccasins. The female dove strutted back and forth on her perch while the male teetered half-in, half-out of the cage.

"Without your corn, *mis palomas*, you are like sheep herders without their *chahakua*." Selu's words tumbled out like the mixed seed, sometimes the language of Carlos, sometimes her mother's Cherokee. And once in a while, like now, when the day was young and the mind was still lost in dreaming, the Basque language of her father would slip in. Sometimes the dreaming was good. Sometimes it was not so good. Today had the feel of a dream about it — like when she and Carlos had first met. Today felt as if the whole world was holding its breath — waiting. Perhaps she would meet someone new this very day.

She took another long sip of her coffee, then set the mug on the stove, stuffed a small wad of bills into the pocket of her long floral skirt, and pulled the blanket from the table, draping it over her shoulders.

Outside, sunrise — from rose quartz to topaz yellow to orange jasper — streaked the Denver skyline. "The colors are good," she said out loud to the morning. "Very good." Then a memory came to her, as bold as the sunrise. A mere child, she stood with her mother drawing water for the bum lambs from Crazy Woman Creek. The same colors streaked the dawn. Look, her mother had said, pointing to the east. Do you feel the light moving within you? It is the energy of the earth and heavens coming together in your heart. *If your heart is ever stilled by grief, seek out the rose quartz.*

Then another memory came to her — Carlos, holding her young hand, leading her up to the huge gates of the old Elitch Gardens on West 38th. *It will be all right, Selu, don't be frightened. But, Carlos, you are Hispanic, I am Basque — and Cherokee. They will not let us in. What did I tell you, Selu? For tonight, we are Italian, Selu. Italian! They will let Italians in the gates, you will see. Buona sera, signorina. Che bel tempo! What a lovely evening! Grazie, grazie.* And so finally, after all her father's promises, she had made it to Elitch's. And she and Carlos had danced until dawn beneath the soft lights of the Trocadero Ballroom.

That night, they forgot the war, forgot the limp that had kept him safe — remembered only one another. *Marry me, Selu. Marry me.*

She had answered him with a kiss — a passionate, swirling kiss. And then he had shouted to no one, and to everyone, "Yes! To me, she says 'yes'!" Together they watched the sky turn — from rose quartz, to topaz yellow, to orange jasper.

This Thing Called Place

A polar projection map of the world depicts landmasses clustered amid a broad expanse of blue ocean. The land herself, though fragmented, appears to resist the centrifugal force of a spinning planet that casts her off into islands and continents. Man has attempted to draw boundaries on, and color the borders of, these dispersing pieces of earth — to measure her from north to south, from east to west, as if she were stagnant, not alive.

Wyoming, they tell us, is a landmass of 97,914 square miles. She centers herself upon the Great Plains of North America, the northern continent of the Western Hemisphere. According to the mapmakers she is rectangular in shape, and can be found north of the equator between forty-one and forty-five degrees latitude, and west of the prime meridian between 104 and 111 degrees longitude.

This is useful, but uninspiring, information. It tells us nothing of the land herself. We cannot feel her heartbeat — the rivers pulsing in her veins — her Big Horn and Platte and Green and Snake. We cannot hear her breath — the gentle inhale of her warm Chinooks, the wild exhale of her winter winds.

I live in the Bear Lodge Mountains of the Black Hills of Wyoming, mountains formed of granite that rose from the earth two and a half billion years ago. The land seems indifferent to these measures of time and space. She pays attention instead to the creeks and drainages of her watershed, to the flora and fauna that root and rut in her red earth.

Wyoming is a land inhabited by fewer than 500,000 people, less than five people per square mile. New York, with half Wyoming's landmass, is inhabited by more than seventeen million people, about 346 people per square mile. Here my nearest neighbor is two miles west, on a dirt road often times impassable in the winter. I see more signs of fellow travelers (white-tailed deer, sharp-tailed grouse, bushy-tailed fox) when snowshoeing than when shopping. My morning conversations are more often with cows than with co-workers. Animals populate my stories because they characterize my life. And through them I learn of my connection to the land.

The Lakota Sioux call the Black Hills *He Sapa*, "the heart of everything that is." Here, traditional people believe, the whole song of the universe could once be heard. Many fear that barely a whisper of the ancient song remains. Yet I believe that if we share our sacred stories — simple stories of family and landscape — that we will once again be graced with a universal song, an understanding of our kinship with one another, and with the earth that sustains us. Through story we come to know life.

One day, while snowshoeing, I discover a coyote den dug into a snowdrift that covers the boneyard. The entrance is carpeted with deer hair and littered with gnawed ribs. Spring comes and the snows melt. One of our heifers births, then loses, her first calf. We take the calf's body up to the boneyard, but the heifer will not leave the place where he has died. His scent and the memory of him lying there tether her to the ground as surely as if she were staked. Not until days later does she give up her vigil. When I pass by this place I think of her, and am reminded of him.

Our number five ewe has twins and a week later I find the larger lamb drowned in the stock tank. I lift him by his hind legs from the water; his wool is soggy, his stomach swollen. The ewe wanders away, content to let the surviving twin suckle. My daughter takes the dead lamb to the boneyard. When I pass by the boneyard I think of her, and am reminded of all of them.

Intimate stories. With emotional context and earthy sensuality. These form the melody of my own personal song. They are the tools of navigation with which I seek and find my bearings. Through story I am able to tunnel beneath the surface and touch heartland. My vision, by the very act of riveting down to view life at its simplest, is able to broaden and take in the world. I explore and share my truth and am better able to understand yours.

I follow the path our sheep make as they trail out to their

pasture, and find telltale wisps of wool snagged on the barbed wire fence where they have crawled into the forbidden hayfield. I begin to understand their migratory nature and am thus better able to understand the nomadic sheepherders of Tibet's wind-swept Chang Tang Plateau.

Standing beneath the oaks in our sheep pasture, I watch a ewe struggle with the last stages of hard labor. Her water breaks and she licks the salty fluid from the earth. I think of the desert bighorn sheep that live in Colorado's plateau canyon country, and am drawn to my own birthplace. Finally, a lamb is born — front hooves, a tiny nose, the forehead pushing into daylight, hips struggling to free themselves. The ewe, still standing, circles and bends her neck to see behind her, as if to ask, "What is this thing that has dropped to the earth?" She sniffs the lamb, recognizes the smell as her own, licks the sack from the lamb's face.

Before she can clean the yellow birthing fluids from the lamb, she is distracted by more contractions. The first lamb has broken the trail of the birth canal, and within minutes another lamb comes slipping out. The ewe begins the cleaning process anew but is barely able to start before a third lamb slides wet and wooly onto the ground.

Matt, our fifteen-year-old son, my first born, comes home and waves, then joins me beneath the oaks. Together, we watch the oldest lamb take his first faltering steps on long, lanky legs. "Three lambs, Mom," Matt says, awed. "I can't believe she had three." It is a difficult number for a ewe. I nod and reach my hand up — place it on his shoulder.

The ewe turns from one lamb to the other and rumbles in a low, maternal voice. The lambs answer in tiny bleats — imprinting their calls upon the ewe, and upon each other, just as she imprints her voice upon them. Later, when separated out in the pasture, the foursome will call out to each other and be recognized — each voice as distinct to the discerning sheep as map coordinates to a cartographer.

Standing side by side we watch the ewe eat her afterbirth. The silence hollows out a safe place for conversation between mother and son, and soon Matt is asking me questions of birth and maturation. "What happens to people's afterbirth when they're born?" he asks. "What happened to yours?"

The question gives me pause. "The hospital threw it away, I suppose," I answer. "In the trash. But it didn't used to be that way." And then I tell him a story from Marilou Awiakta's *Selu: Seeking the Corn Mother's Wisdom*. Her Appalachian grandfather, upon the birth of each of his five children, lovingly buried his wife's afterbirth in the Tennessee woods in honor of the fact that, "We come from Mother Earth and when we are old, we return to Mother Earth."[1]

When Marilou Awiakta asked her own mother if her daddy had buried her afterbirth, the answer was the same as mine, a gentle no. But our stories don't end there; they are no more finite than is the landscape stagnant. With the telling of this story, our own sanitized birthing stories are somehow healed, and new stories begin.

The ewe and lambs are tied by birthing blood to this piece of earth. The ewe eats her afterbirth for nourishment and to hide the story of her birthing from the coyotes who may visit this same place during the dark of night.

Matt and I, through story, have become linked to each other, to another family, to this place beneath the oaks, and to a new landscape. We no longer simply stand beneath the bur oaks of the Wyoming Black Hills but have set foot also in Marilou's Tennessee mountains.

The mountains and deserts of the American West used to be home to great numbers of wild bighorn sheep. In an attempt to repopulate these areas, outside herds have been introduced, but without success. In Scott Russell Sanders essay *Telling the Holy*, he writes, "The problem. . . is that the sheep do not know how to move between their summer range and their winter range, so they starve. Biologists. . . cannot teach them the migration routes, which bighorns learn only from other bighorns. Once the link between sheep and ground is broken, and the memory of the trails is lost, there seems to be no way of restoring it."[2]

The cattle who summer up in the Bear Lodge have passed on a genetic memory to the herds which tell them when it is time to migrate out of the high country pastures in the pines and head for the lower pastures and home ranges. Come October, or late September, when the first cold blasts of winter assault the mountains, the cattle start leaving — heading out of the forest and onto the logging roads that eventually lead them home. They wander past our place, leaving telltale imprints in the dirt.

I fear that if my children, our children, do not hear the stories of their ancestors, and do not create their own stories of the land, they, like the bighorns of the desert, will become forever lost. At times I feel lost because my ethnicity is diverse and fragmented, and thus I have little heritage to pass on. No one has shown me the migration trails. I have called at least a dozen different places besides Wyoming home, and have crossed the borders of more than twenty-seven countries. "Who are your people?" one indigenous person might ask of another's tribal affiliation. In the past, had this question been asked of me, I would have shrugged my shoulders in an apologetic stupor.

But I am beginning to understand that asking, "Who are your people?" is really just another way of saying, "Tell me your stories."

I am linked to people and landscape by story, far more than by race or nationality. My tribe is a tribe of tales, and sometimes I gently lift another's tale and turn it inside out. Not a sacred story, never a sacred story, but an anthropological story from which I can learn.

Robert Lawlor has immersed himself in the Aboriginal culture of Australia, and has written extensively about it. In an interview with *Parabola*, he talks about their concept of land and story. "Aboriginal people travel constantly and rarely camp in the same spot; however, when a child is about to be born, the grandmother brings the mother to a particular place, she scoops out the earth, and the mother squats above this place and delivers the baby onto the earth. . . [The child] inherits the stories of that place and the sacred responsibilities for the sites of importance in that area. . . . . He alone carries the songs concerning the Dreamtime origins of that place. In other words, his dignity, spiritual knowledge, sense of identity, and social responsibilities and rights are determined by this place. . . spun out from his birthplace into an extensive kinship system that spreads human relationships across vast distances."[3]

What do Wyomingites have in common with Aborigines? Wallace Stegner tells us in *The American West as Living Space* that, "Whatever it might want to be, the West is still primarily a series of brief visitations on a trail to somewhere else; and western literature. . . from *The Log of a Cowboy* to *Lonesome Dove*, from *The Big Rock Candy Mountain* to *The Big Sky*, has been largely a literature not of place but of motion."[4]

When I moved fourteen years ago from Colorado to the Black Hills, I felt disloyal to the land of my birth. No place else, I was sure, could ever *truly* become home. A few summers ago, when I left our beloved ranch to spend two weeks in the depths of the Grand Canyon on a writing assignment, I wondered how a northern Wyoming woman would ever acclimate to the heat and hardness of the Canyon. I returned to the Black Hills shaken and unsure, because I had felt so quickly at home on the river among the cholla and chuckwallas of the desert.

What *is* this thing called place? How can we be so deeply rooted to it, yet so easily transplanted from it? If a sacred place is a place where two worlds intersect, can it also be a place where two stories meet?

Ellen Meloy of southern Utah tells us in her essay *Brides of Place*, that when camped alone in the Colorado Plateau canyon country she awoke to find a band of wild desert bighorn sheep browsing nearby. "The ewes and lambs around me exercise a remarkable and dangerous fidelity to place . . . From the older ewes the young learn where to forage, quench their thirst, bed down, mate, give birth, seek escape, and die, all of it usually within range of an ancestral water supply. The bighorn became a desert bighorn by forming a relationship with its environment . . ."

She goes on to point out that, "The press of modern

culture tends to homogenize biological diversity. Those life forms best suited to a changing world, the most aggressive and adaptable species. . .survive.

"Look into the eyes of a domestic sheep," she writes, "and you will see the back of its head. Look into the eyes of this bighorn. . . and you will see a lost map to place, a depth that we may extinguish before it touches us."[5]

These last sentences made me cry — because of their truth, and their misperception. The sheep that graze in our meadow cannot be blamed for their domestication. I have looked into their eyes and have seen many things, but never the back of their heads. I have seen the fear — a trace of the ancient and wild — which comes from being suddenly transported to a strange, new place — where the ancient genetic map of place has lost all bearings. I have seen the trust that comes with kind stewardship, and the encoding of a new genetic map — marked with creeks and springs and favorite grasses that return each new season. I have seen the pain of birth gone wrong, of legs and heads twisted and bent within a womb that is too old to unfurl itself. I have held the pain, and responsibility, for this dying in the palm of my hand.

I have also seen, in their eyes, a reflection of modern man — tamed, severed from ancestral lands, living in a manicured world where homogenous buildings have sprouted from every terrain — desert, high plain, alpine, wetland, canyon land, and rain forest. What Ellen Meloy warns us about is what Scott Sanders has testified to, that if domesticated, "This band's ancestral fiber of desert woven into living tissue hundreds of years of of wild faith to wild place — would shred, unraveling the seams of time."[6]

How *is* it then that we domesticated human beings, torn from our places of birth again and again, can feel such strong ties? Or, perhaps, no ties at all? Do stories do for us what hundreds of years of wild faith and wild place did for the desert bighorn?

I think so. I think that is why I write stories, and why I read stories, and why I tell stories, and why I listen to stories.

New stories and old stories. They pump heart blood into the dormant fibers that connect us to each other, and to place, be it rural or urban. They encode us with new genetic maps to guide the ancient tissues of our modern souls.

1 *Fulcrum Publishing, 1993, Golden, Colorado, p.156, 157.*

2 *Parabola: Magazine of Myth and Tradition, Summer, 1993, New York, NY, p.8, 9.*

3 *Parabola: Magazine of Myth and Tradition, Summer, 1993, New York, NY, p.16, 17.*

4 *University of Michigan Press, 1987, Ann Arbor, Michigan, p.23.*

5 *Northern Lights, Summer, 1998, Missoula, Montana, p.11, 12.*

6 *Northern Lights, Summer, 1998, Missoula, Montana, p.13.*

Part Two

Farther West

"Oka-san keeps stuffing rags under
the barracks door, around cracks
in the window, to keep out smells
of snow, sage, and cattle,
families pressed around us.
My feet, my mind, become numb
from standing in line all day —
lines to eat, shower, shit
in the dirty outdoor benjos.
Evenings I sweep my anger
off the barracks floor,
but the next morning it's coated
with dust, corners filled again."

Lee Ann Roripaugh

(From *Beyond Heart Mountain*, poems based on voices from the federal internment camp at
Heart Mountain, Wyoming, where Japanese-Americans were imprisoned during World War II.)

Barbara Smith

Barbara Smith is a professor of English and chair of the Humanities Division at Western Wyoming Community College in Rock Springs, Wyoming. Known primarily for her poetry, Smith's work has been published in collections such as *The Last Best Place, an anthology of Montana writers; Ucross: the First Ten Years,* a chapbook of Ucross residents; *Letters From Wyoming,* a collection of Wyoming Arts Council literary fellowship award winners; *Drive, He Said,* an anthology about Americans and their love affairs with cars.

Her work is included in *Leaning Into the Wind,* a collection of western women writers writing about the land, and from the same publisher and editors, *Woven on the Wind,* a collection of western women writers centering on women's friendships in the west.

She earned her B.S. in English Education from Montana State University-Northern, in Havre, Montana, and an M.A. in English from the University of South Dakota. She serves as a board member for the Wyoming Council for the Humanities.

Selected Poems

Interstate 80

This SOB never has been an easy passage
Oh, maybe for twenty minutes
after they finally finished the last stretch
around "This Is The Place" in Parley's Canyon
before it started heaving up from frost freeze
or grooving in the heat, but mostly it's a bitch
requiring your full attention
even if you drive the same forty miles
morning and night to work
and know every pimple on the lady's ass
every curve or incline
you could drive it in your sleep or blind
like you do half the time in January anyway
whiteout white knuckle terror
braced against the blast of triple trailers
whipping like rattlers in the ruts.
This road will give you religion, mister.
The pioneers took the long way around

but still ended up on this road
near a fort over by the Green.
After bucking the river, the heat,
the mountains, the mosquitoes and every other
damn thing, perhaps Brigham Young saw
the look in one of his wives' eyes
like the look a man gets today
when he passes the last rest stop for 125 miles.
Perhaps he saw that look
after crossing the knifelike cut
into the wide flat valley
promising sparkling blue in the west
and declared "This Is The Place"
before she could say anything.
How was he to know that lake was salt not sweet?
Later they got down and prayed
like a lot of folks on I-80
coming through that pass
across a radiator-boiling desert
or around Elk Mountain,
the interstate twenty miles too close
because a highway engineer fell in love
with a pretty drive in the summer
through bowls of wind etched rock
where nothing lands long enough to grow.
The mountain mesmerized him,
made him forget what he shouldn't.
A motorcyclist crossing the Bonneville Salt Flats
with his sandblasted wife in the side car
cranks up the Christian radio network
and prays she doesn't notice highway signs
Dust Hazard near Devils Gate
No Services.

Sisters

The wind blew down the valley from Green River
in the afternoon about 2:30.
She looked at the clock, the usual time.
The dust sifted in through the sliding glass doors,
lingered a bit in the air, settled softly down to rest.
She wiped the top of the dishwasher
and thought of other women.
Back then, when the wind blew, what did they dust?
The shelf on the side that served as a cupboard?
The handmade table? The dirt floor?
What did they dust, those women?
She remembered pictures of pale, wisp-blonde women,
not-yet-grandmothers, homesteading, standing by the sod
with aprons blowing in the wind.
Hair twisted in a knot, arms folded tight under their breasts,
bellies big under full skirts, as usual, they stood tall.
She bent over to pick up a toy,
the baby pushed back hard under her ribs,
a strand of fine hair fell across her face.
She remembered a story told often when she was young.
Two pioneer women would dance together
around and around their kitchen when they visited.
They danced twice in five years,
they saw no one.
What did those women do when the men were gone in the fields
and the wind came every day at 2:30?
She sat down at the table by the sliding glass door
and watched a dust squall whirl its way into the subdivision.
She didn't know her neighbor.
She wondered, did she dance?
She drove off every day in her new car.

Some pioneer women took laudanum for headaches.
Some died in the long afternoon.
Some waited five years to dance together and dream.
Sisters, she thought, we're sisters.

Rock Springs, from the Inside

Immigrants from the hot mines
in Germany, Greece, the Baltics
came here to this sun
desert-wide place
years ago to work the mines.
The American Dream
bringing their trade
forming the narrow winding streets
like back home
where there wasn't much room
even though the high plains
has nothing but space.
Old town is cramped wall-to-wall
narrow vertical steep.

When they could swing it,
the miners walked out
and dug their own coal.
Freelancers jury-rigged
in the side of hills
around the fringes,
secret mines
one man's dream
apart from the company
paying in scrip.

So now, in the new subdivision
up on the hills for the view
something shudders, shifts
as somewhere deep
in that secret spot
the hill remembers.

Transplant

Trailer once battened down
skirted against the blow sand
construction, she laid sod.

Sent for a tree from home
where water fell unplanned
dogwood transplant against sagebrush.

Dug a garden from cracked clay
they watched behind thin curtains
she tilled the rows ready.

What grows here? Tomatoes, zucchini
strawberries if you water good.
Season doesn't hold for melons much.

She staked them high, thinking of
crowders little ladies field peas
muscadine fig preserves mimosa shade.

Around the plot she laid ground cover
gold red surprise across the baked
edge sucking leftovers from the hose.

It grew not near so tall but green
fierce fruit clung in the gusts
ripening against all odds.

Taste this, she gave to her neighbor.
Brushing dust she bit red juice.
It's hard to get but worth more.

Next year I'll help you
if you like. I'm planting potentilla
perennials all along the west.

If that dogwood dies,
I'll get a cottonwood;
it's native to this place and thrives.

Boom Town Grocery Store

She was accustomed to driving the wrong way
on the oneway by the post office.
Everyone knew her '54 Plymouth,
knew she couldn't remember
about that silly business.

But then a boom hit town,
she couldn't drive that fast,
they ran her off the road.

Construction workers rented her house
out back for a fortune, but smoked dope
in the bed where she had her oldest boy,
killed the lilacs she planted in the '40s,
run over them in a 4-wheel drive.

She shopped down at the Merc
where they used to take the scrip
her old man brought home from the mine
before the black lung got him.
Back then, clerks could speak
the languages of all the miners
from Europe, like her dad,
China even. The melting pot they called it.
The aisles were narrow, used to women who shopped early,
after hanging a wash before dawn, taking their time.

She didn't like these transients in her store,
longhairs buying her polenta flour.
They wouldn't go right down the aisles,
grabbing up everything,
flashing big bankrolls at the counter.

She rammed her cart right into one of them
standing over the pork sausage and kielbasa,
looked that trailer trash right in the eye,
"There," old Nona said, "Out of my way for once."
He laughed but moved, "Easy now, old lady.
They told me locals here used to be so friendly."

Peonies

A humped-back trunk sits in the corner,
my grandmother's trunk filled with photographs
a wedding dress, baby blankets, certificates
worth another look, and preserved collectibles.
It is my trunk now.

Grandma loved to watch me dress up
from that trunk under the eaves
in the unused upstairs.

She'd wait below in her leather rocker,
bought fifty years earlier in Chicago
as proof he could support her,
carted out West with the trunk
filled with valuables from her youth,
and some dishes from her weeping mother,

She'd wait for me to clump down those steps
in Aunt Hazel's sling backs, a crepe de Chine dress
wrapped and folded up with a belt,
and her old fox fur, eyes and nose
pointing to the end of things.

Her eyes would shine 'til she'd cry
at my black hat squashed flat
but cocked anyway with that bit of net
pulled down past my nose
and an enormous pink silk flower
smelling of stale sachet.

Off we'd walk, holding hands,
slowed from my wobbly steps in heels
and her arthritis. We'd make our way
around the lettuce patch to Mrs. Knudsen's,
past the Sarbrums, where the youngest girl
would die at seventeen of female troubles,
down the path through the trees to Old Ruth's
for a game of Canasta.

On the way we'd stop where Annie Mae was buried.
Her old doll brought West and dried up,
with a cracked china face and a bald head by my time.
I used to spank her for her own good
until the pins wouldn't hold
and we laid her tired body down
in the peonies one summer day.
We'd say a few words of comfort to Annie Mae
and move on through the heavy scent of peonies
for tea and toast and games.

After Grandma's funeral, when Grandpa had that auction
and Old Ruth took him up as card player and companion,
someone who knew bought that trunk for me.
No one remembers where the fox fur went
much less the silk flowers and net,
but when I open that trunk
the laughter and lace, the slap of the heel,
the feel of fur, and the bright eyes of the fox
drift up through the peony afternoon.

This Place Has Claimed Me

I am the granddaughter of immigrants who came west from a variety of places and countries, the daughter of parents who themselves moved farther west to Montana, and a woman who found my own western experience in the high southwestern boom-and-bust desert town of Rock Springs, Wyoming. These experiences have served to shape and inspire my writing.

My maternal grandfather, Hilmer Johnson, came as a nine-year-old orphan from Norway to be exploited in the coal mines of western North Dakota. As a teenager, he escaped to a wheat farm, and when the opportunity presented itself, set out on his dream of owning his own land by going homesteading in Saskatchewan, Canada. He was going to make a go of it like the sodbusters of a generation before him. My grandmother, Amelia, was born on her father's homestead in North Dakota and, except for her honeymoon year, lived on that land her entire life: it was her place in the world.

Amelia's greatest adventure was marrying my grandfather and going with him to his Canadian homestead to finish proving up the land. I grew up hearing her stories about the wildness of the prairie, where when she spun three hundred and sixty degrees, she was the tallest thing on the earth. I imagined the sod hut, and later the one-room shanty he built for her, which she called her "honeymoon cottage." I could hear the wolves howling in her story of how she outwitted a pack when they caught her between the barn and the house one evening at dusk. She sat up on the haystack all night long, with nothing but a broom to defend herself against the circle of eyes watching her, listening for hours to the harness bells, as her lover, my grandpa, drove the team home from town to rescue her. All those stories. And in them there was more, glimpses of the sheer isolation of living for months without seeing anyone but her husband. There was the fear Amelia had in discovering herself pregnant, knowing that now she would certainly have to go back, Hilmer would have to take her down to the Montana Hi-Line and put her on the train back to civilization. What would Hilmer do when he found out? Would he stay on the homestead or would he follow her? He proved up the land and then turned away from it. Yes, there was the knowing all her life that Hilmer gave up his youthful dream, gave it all up to take up the yoke of that North Dakota farm, to serve as steward of the land, to shepherd five kids through the Depression and two world wars, and he did it for her. God, it was grand! I sat on the footstool in her North Dakota kitchen and Grandma spun her magic.

My mother Bernice, who grew up on that North Dakota farm, didn't see the least bit of romance in any of it. Her experience was that of the Depression kid who had to work hard to survive. She told me different stories. During harvest one year, she was forced to leave her own thirteenth birthday party, wipe the cake off her mouth and go out and drive the hayrack all the rest of the day. The hay was ready and her dad said it had to be done before it ruined. Angry, she refused to change, wore her good dress out there with no hat and was badly sunburned. No one apologized; it had to be done. The land determined what they would do and when they would do it. I see pictures of her at that age, squinting at the camera, fierce and determined to somehow get off that place. She picked my father as the one who would most likely help her escape, and by God, they did it.

My father, Howard Taylor, was dissatisfied and innovative and wanted to do anything but farm with his dad. His parents emigrated from Chicago due to my grandfather's health. Homer had developed extreme asthma and the Chicago doctors told him to leave that climate and move to a drier one or die. So Homer quit an excellent job he loved on the Santa Fe railroad, and he and my grandmother Clara set out on their own adventure, wandering about the West in search of a place where he could breathe. First they went to Oklahoma, then South Dakota, and finally, North Dakota. When Homer woke up in the morning with no asthma, he told Clara, "This is it, this is where we stay."

Once again I was captivated by family stories of the olden days out in the West. Who in the world moves to a place in this way? Think what it must have been like for Clara to pack up her belongings and leave the city, the security of jobs, family and friends, and head she knew not where? Once when camping beside their old Model T somewhere in South Dakota, Homer and Clara woke up the next morning to find a fat old rattlesnake curled up and asleep in the frying pan next to the campfire! It had been still warm when they went to sleep the night before, enticing the snake to bed down there. They crept around it, packed up, and left the precious frying pan there for the snake, still fast asleep. Grandma told me she never slept on the ground again.

As a child I thought of all my grandparents as pioneers, just like those going to Oregon in the covered wagons from my history books. What adventures they had! My favorite book was *Caddie Woodlawn*, about a red-headed pioneer girl who tore about the wilderness, fraternizing with her brothers and the Indians, and defying all her mother's best efforts to keep her civilized. And it seemed to me that the West was all gone, all frontiers were settled. I lived in towns, and most roads were paved. My history books said the frontier was closed.

I spent my early childhood wandering through the North Dakota cemetery where some of my ancestors were buried, strong men and women who pulled themselves up and out of immigration poverty by their own efforts. I used to lay down on the grave of my great-grandmother with my arms crossed and watch the clouds move. If you lay still long enough, you could feel the rotation of the earth. Lying there, I'd listen to my grandmother in the country church, practicing the organ music for Sunday, and dream up stories about the names on the tombstones. Later on, I'd tell her my stories over coffee she served me country style, thick with cream and poured into the saucer to cool. She'd laugh and nod at me to continue. Perhaps it is why I became a writer.

By the time I was thirteen, my family had embarked on our own Western adventure. We said goodbye to our weeping grandparents, to North Dakota, and moved west to Montana. Horace Greeley's exhortation, "Go West, young man," worked for my parents, and they always felt that they had made the right move. Coincidentally, Havre, Montana, where we settled, is not far by western standards from my grandparent's homestead in Saskatchewan. They came for a visit the summer of their 50th wedding anniversary, and we drove up to Canada and found their old homestead. The honeymoon shanty was still standing, now converted into a granary. With surprising strength, my grandmother ripped the door open, and there, still hanging on the wall, was the little shelf Hilmer had build for his bride for her spices. My grandparents had never been back, had long ago sold that property, which had been so hard to prove up. It was now all wheat fields and, as we stood there surveying the land, we were still the tallest things on the earth.

I grew up a protected, nurtured town kid in Havre, Montana, with all the conveniences and advantages my parents didn't have. They made sure I didn't have to worry about going to college the way they did. I made my way through school, then graduate school, and soon found myself with a contract to teach at Western Wyoming Community College in Rock Springs, Wyoming. It was all very civilized, but as I embarked on this move in the fall of 1969, I suddenly felt that this might be my own western adventure. I was striking out on my own. I drove down from Montana, gradually leaving well-kept fields for the Wind River Canyon, which from the Thermopolis side truly looks like a descent into hell, and over the South Pass. Somewhere along the way I started to feel like a pioneer. I had all my earthly belongings in my backseat and had made a commitment to do this, to not turn back, come what may. I stopped at the Oregon Trail marker on the east side of Farson and saw the ruts made by the covered wagons, still there. No other cars passed by and I was truly alone with the wind.

I had been in college during the turbulent sixties, so when I first arrived, Rock Springs seemed like a town straight out of "The Last Picture Show." While its history as a boom and bust coal-mining town was very different from my previous experience, I recognized many of the characteristics of small towns where I grew up. People knew each other, things were done with a handshake, and everyone was very polite and kind to the new school teacher. The local people were very proud of their fifty-seven nationalities and their willingness to welcome newcomers. There was one movie theater and no stores open on Sundays. Situated on a stream called Bitter Creek, the town was surrounded by high plains desert. You had to be a member of the Elks to eat out or buy a drink on Sundays, and women didn't qualify. Once a neighbor lady told me, "Oh, you'll probably always be considered an outsider of sorts 'cause you're not from here." I was to some extent an observer. My mother had to convince me to sign my contract for a second year. "It looks better on your resume if you stay a little longer," she said. That was almost 30 years ago. Like it or not, this is my place. It chose me. Like my ancestors who found their own places before me, I found it here. I belong here.

In the early seventies, things got interesting in Rock Springs and I seemed to get caught up in it. Events came together in my experience and imagination which have shaped my writing. Starting in 1973, a major boom hit Sweetwater County. People flocked here from Texas and other foreign places and no one was prepared for the social costs: the effects on people, sewer systems, police and schools. The community embarked on a boom such as no one still living had seen, and everyone was displaced. The newcomers were displaced, arriving to find that while there were high paying jobs, there was no housing, few amenities, long lines, and increasingly short tempers. People were living in tents out on the desert. Companies who had for some reason kept their little secrets from the local authorities about all this had to start throwing up man camps for their employees. It was a dog-eat-dog world for a while.

The locals were also displaced. Their little town with its self image of fifty-seven nationalities getting along together through western hospitality and tolerance was gone, blown out of the water by pimps hauling their girls in from Denver to walk

K Street. The locals were displaced and outnumbered by people who didn't observe the customs of the place, crowding in ahead of others in lines, demanding things, and complaining about the lack of trees. Signs appeared: "No Construction Trash Allowed." Some took advantage and made a killing, jacking up the rent four hundred percent, selling shower facilities for five bucks a person, throwing up stores here and there.

I was displaced, too. During this period of time, I married and started having babies, shopping for groceries in stores that ran out of bread by ten a.m., and fighting for a dryer at the laundromat with the rest of them. It was an exciting and frustrating life, and I felt as though my husband and I were all alone out there, breaking new ground. We didn't have the support of any extended family network in the community, like those we had both grown up in.

Waiting in lines with all those other women, transplanted and displaced, who nevertheless were trying to make a place for themselves in this alien, hostile environment, a new world not of their own making, I started to see the other people also as pioneers of a New West. I watched the local second and third generation Rock Springs women as they tried to pick up the pieces after forces beyond their control, executives in the towers of the East or West coasts, had cut the deals that blew their lives apart forever. I also suddenly found myself remembering my grandmothers' stories of homesteading, of pulling up roots and taking what comes with the wind.

I started writing with a seriousness I had never experienced. I saw the connections between the contemporary pioneers, trying to survive in the here and now, and those other generations, those other pioneers from my own family, other Rock Springs families and even the Oregon Trail wagon trains. Across time, we had things in common. We were each struggling to come to terms with a hostile desert, with the constant necessity to remake our lives, to change and adapt to circumstances not of our own making, but determined by forces over which we had little control. Even though the times and the challenges were different, the human spirit, ingenuity, and capacity to work as a community to survive and make a place to live was exactly the same. Some, like my Norwegian grandfather, left their dreams and went back home because their families could not live here. Many came and went. Some, like my Chicago grandmother, uprooted from everything they held dear, stayed and made this new place their place. They found something they had not expected. Something – the land, the town, the people – claimed them and became their home.

It's hard to explain it. There's a fierce pride and maybe a bit of lifeboat mentality in the community for having survived the boom-and-bust life which Rock Springs seems to have endured throughout its history. I've only survived one of these things; there are many families who have been here for generations, who came here back when the big bad boys back East pulling all the strings were not coal or oil but the railroad. It does something to the nature and spirit of the people who survive and thrive despite all the abuses of nature, politicians and big business. The western landscape exists in these people. They survive now, as the ancestors of this place survived then, and their stories and self-concept as a community sustain them.

Because I often give memoir writing workshops for senior citizens and the community, I am familiar with many of the stories of survival. The Rock Springs reputation around the state is that the natives are tough and can take a punch. I heard one story about early football that exemplifies this. The football field back in the old days was situated behind the old high school where there had been a coal slag pit. That leftover coal slag was sharp and would cut the boys from the visiting team to pieces if they slid on it. The Rock Springs team practiced on that field and their skin had toughened up, so they had a decided advantage. It was hard to beat Rock Springs at home in the old days. There are many stories like this told and retold in the community, which show a certain pride in turning adversity into an advantage.

There are other stories of hard times, stories of women waiting for the whistle, always keeping an ear cocked to hear which mine would work, when the man of the house would come home or, God forbid, when there had been an accident and he might not come home at all. Then, if he was dead, the choice she faced: she could send her son down into the mine to take his father's place or move out of the company house after the funeral. There are stories of neighbor helping neighbor at times like these as well, and stories where people came together to put a stop to such abuses of the human spirit. These stories are handed down in families to remind descendants of what it took to get them this far. They also serve to remind us in the community of the connections we have to the people in the past, in this place. They too were often subject to forces beyond their control. They too often had to mount up David and Goliath battles to improve their lives and their children's lives. The wind we face blew then, too.

When I write, I often find my voice is co-mingled with these other voices grounded and shaped by this place. It has claimed me.

Geoffrey O'Gara

Geoffrey O'Gara of Lander is the author of numerous literary nonfiction books and travel guidebooks. They include *What You See in Clear Water,* an exploration of the battle over water in the West, which won the Western Writers of America best non-fiction award in 2001, and the *National Geographic Outdoor Guide to the Far West,* published in 2001. His articles have been published in the *New York Times, Los Angeles Times, High Country News, National Geographic Traveler, Sierra, Northern Lights,* and many others. O'Gara has been a recipient of the Arts Council's Neltje Blanchan Award for Nature Writing and a literary fellowship. He writes and produces "Main Street Wyoming" and other productions on Wyoming Public Television. He is working on a book of fiction called *Prosper, Wyoming.*

From *What You See in Clear Water:*
Life on the Wind River Reservation

Chapter XII

North Fork

Out the courtroom door, away from the old men in robes, away from the cologne-scented, hair-in-place former-debate-team-captain players in the game of words, and back to the paths of water, the cobble streams beneath leaning cottonwoods.

In the fall of 1989, when farmers in the Wind River Valley sat burnt-neck exhausted at the kitchen table wondering at the end of the day if they had any future left here, when the phones at the Tribal Water Engineer's office and the U.S. Fish & Wildlife Service rang and rang with edgy-voiced questions from bosses pissed off about leaks to the newspapers, when the Shoshone were fighting each other over who qualified for tribal membership and the Arapaho were fighting each other over where the tribe's money went, Richard Baldes took his son Jason fishing.

In late August the rabbit-brush blooms yellow on the banks of the streams in the Wind River Basin; the nose-clotting clouds of insects are quelled by the cooling nights, the cloven prints of white tailed deer zig to the water and zag around the bramble of wild rose and under the willows to the beds of cool damp earth, and you can see in the clear water the yellow belly and red maculae of the brown trout turning and the soft pink brush stroke of the rainbow trout. Baldes steered his truck up a two-track that climbed the ridge between the South and North Forks of the Little Wind River. They drove up the backslope of a sea rolling west, a wave of tawny dried-out ocean bottom combing toward the steep granite cliffs of the Rockies. Here and there this westward surge of foothill is broken dramatically by a stream, which cuts through it like a surfer breaking through the back of a curl. Baldes stopped on the lip of one of these canyons, the North Fork of the Little Wind River, and they descended on foot, he with his fly rod, and Jason with his spin cast rig.

The North Fork of the Little Wind River is not a particularly big stream, but it's a healthy one; its path is skewed usefully by unyielding outcrops and big boulders. It's hard for anglers to get to, if they even know about it, so the fish do wonderfully well.

Father and son worked their way up the stream, hooking a small trout now and then and throwing it back, as they customarily did. One of the pools had a crinkly riffle where the current skirted a bison-size boulder, and then a deep spot where the water smoothed. A small place with good possibilities. It was late afternoon, and you could see the little gulping rises of unfrenzied fish, methodically dining on a meal of mayflies. A spin-cast lure would not be much good when the fish were watching the hatches on the surface, so Baldes offered Jason the fly rod. The boy had been asking for it all year, rolling his eyes when his father told him he was too young.

Small shrubby streams make mock of the graceful, spacious art of classic fly casting — they respond to a more cramped style of attack, which can look pretty artless but in fact requires precision, patience and stealth. Of these qualities, eight-year-olds often possess stealth, and not much else. But there seemed only enough room for one fisherman at a time on this pool, so Baldes offered Jason the old fiberglass pole he'd been using for twenty years.

First the son had to endure his father's demonstration of good casting technique, which he watched sideways with his raven head propped on skinny arms across his knees. He'd been quietly studying his father's moves for years, and knew, like most sons, the large difference between doing and saying.

When he was handed the rod at last, Jason positioned himself on a rock at the bottom of the pool — out from the shore, safer from snags — and began casting. The movement was stiff-armed at first, but his father held back, watching. Attached to the tippet was an elk-hair caddis. It must have been his tenth cast when the fly looped up to the riffle and came bobbing over the small standing waves and into the deeper, smoother water.

In the clear water, they both saw the trout rise to the fly, which it took with a sudden, sideways jerk of the head. Jason looked wide-eyed at his father, who kept his distance. The rainbow dove with the fly, but when the pull on his jaw didn't give, he charged angrily to the surface, where he jumped and danced, trying to throw the hook. The fish was bigger than anything Jason had caught before, a good twenty inches.

"Just let it run," said Baldes, watching Jason's left hand pulling on the loose line and dropping it at his feet. The fish darted up and down the pool, erupting now and then for another head-flopping Charleston. Jason's eyes were narrow, watching. For more than five minutes the boy and the fish pulled and gave. Finally, the tired trout surrendered, and let itself be dragged into the shallows, where it lay defenseless on its side with an unblinking eye taking in the sky.

"Nice fish, Jase," said Baldes. "He put up a good fight. Let it go?"

To his surprise, Jason shook his head no. Almost always, they released the fish they caught. But this was the boy's first catch with a fly — a hefty, husky fish with a bright red slash down its side.

They ran a stringer through the trout's gills and placed it in shaded water. Jason ignored the pole leaning against the rock — no interest in more fishing, after this glory. He crouched over the fish and said nothing. Let him think about it, Baldes decided.

He took the fly pole and started up the river. He went from pool to pool, hooking a few small browns and letting them go. Every now and then he would look back. Jason was squatted by the river, looking at the fish.

A while later, he came back down.

For a moment, he watched his son, who seemed transfixed by the very slight movement of the rainbow. Then he said, "Okay, you want to keep this fish or turn him loose?" Baldes believed in letting the big fighters go, but he held no principled opposition to killing: his freezer was full of game. Anyway, it was Jason's fish.

Jason looked up. "I think you're right," he said. "I think we better turn him loose."

Baldes felt a surprising rush of relief.

As they walked back up from the river, he tried to see in his mind's eye Jason's face, and what was on it, when the boy was crouched over the helpless fish in the shallows. Something might have been going between them, something that took awhile.

From atop the ridge where Baldes and his son drove, you can see the green path of the South and North Forks as they journey east to Fort Washakie, where they join. The steep sides of the canyons flare out and flatten like a collar opening at the neck, and the bald, steep rocks smooth into green fields. Fences appear, then livestock corrals, shacks. The twisting path of the river is marked by tottery cottonwoods and thick borders of willows. Only barely visible in these bushes is a hump of brown canvas set back from the riverbank, with a trail of smoke rising from a smoldering fire.

Sumner Marlowe pulled his shirt over his head, freeing his long tail of shining hair, and stripped to his shorts. The first of four red-hot rocks had been carried by shovel to the door of the sweat lodge and placed in a pit just inside. The river was low, its bumpy surface dimpled with light from the setting sun. The lodge faced east, toward a clearing where burning cottonwood log sandwiched river rocks, heating them for the sweat. At least a dozen people stood around, including shy teenage girls, an older white man with a cigarette dangling from his mouth, Shoshone elder Ben Shoyo, and leaders from both tribes, including Virginia Sutter and John Washakie — a motley, convivial group, moving about, shaking hands, talking and laughing. It might have been a weekend barbecue, except that there were only rocks on the fire, and the guests were in various stages of disrobing.

Every year, Zedora Enos' family erected a sweat lodge on their property along the North Fork, and several times a week people squeezed into the sweat lodge to pray and purify themselves in a wash of hot steam and darkness and sweet cedar fumes. There was no set schedule — someone who might be ill or stressed or wanting to reconnect with the Creator would call the family and ask for a sweat. Other people would hear about it, and would come to help and support, or perhaps to deal with some problems of their own. There was a core congregation that showed up regularly, but others like Sumner Marlowe were welcome to drop in occasionally.

The lodge was built by anchoring green willow branches in the ground and bending them over to form a shelter. Several layers of dark-hued tarps were then lain across the willows, until it looked like a brown beanie cap, or an enormous drooping mushroom. Facing the east, and the fire, was an opening where people entered, with the flap thrown back. Within was a shallow pit at the center where the red-hot stones would be placed, a bucket of water and a dipper, and, sitting at the rear of the pit, James Trosper, Zedora's son, who would lead the prayers.

The number and variety of guests at these sweats increased the likelihood that old feuds and enmities might be circling the altar, but some of these folks were Marlowe's relatives, and he felt welcome. A sweat diffused tension. Anyone who was there had a spiritual need, or at least a wholesome desire to cleanse themselves, and when the ceremony began they would be asked to pray for others — knowing that, you might look on an enemy with new generosity.

During the four rounds of sweating, prayers would be offered up in silence and out loud. Marlowe always had reasons to pray: In the past, he had prayed for a job, for his family, for a plan to catch some wily horses. "It's not hard to think of people who need help, in the hospital or somewhere else," he said. During the long years when he drank and smoked dope, he prayed for help controlling himself, and sometimes it worked for awhile.

The sweat lodge has been called the "little brother of the big lodge," meaning the Sun Dance, which is the most vibrant spiritual event in the lives of many Indians today. Strength and insight, even visions, can be infused in a sweat, but *nothing* can happen as well. There are men who have gone repeatedly into the Sun Dance and never had the sort of seizing vision that throws a man to the ground, unconscious or in a dream, and teaches him secrets — but their regrets are mild, because the days of thirst and prayer at least cleanse their bodies and minds. "Sometimes you want the power strong, you want it to manifest," said Trosper, who is a Sun Dance chief, "and it just doesn't happen. It's not up to you."

In 1985, Marlowe was asked during a sweat with Arapaho elders to pour water. It's an important role and an honor: the one who pours decides how hot the sweat will be, by the amount of water turned to burning steam on the rocks. The sweat begins when the red-hot rocks are brought into the lodge — usually four rocks to begin — and people enter, silently, hunched over as they circle the lodge clockwise and seat themselves. There are four "rounds" to the sweat, between which you can leave the darkness of the sweat lodge and stand in the open air. During Trosper's sweats, there is "doctoring" in the third round for people with ills, and a chance for everyone who wants to talk of their travails, their gratitude, their hard road. After three rounds of prayer and proximity, shy people spill their guts, and in the darkness tears are shed. When Marlowe poured the water for the Arapaho elders, he was asked to pray in the third round. He asked for help to go straight and quit his drinking and doping.

He had asked the same thing as a dancer in the Arapaho Sun Dance, when he had a wife and two small children and no steady paycheck, and it wasn't as fun as it used to be. He didn't drink every day, but when he had a birthday coming up, or some other excuse, he'd start a party that would last for days. His marriage was shaky — his wife drank, too, and Marlowe had trouble with her family. Only a month earlier, Marlowe had taken a vow in the Catholic Church to quit his binges, and the priest at St. Stephen's had him sign a pledge. He noticed that the written pledge included abstinence from smoking marijuana, and he told the priest he simply wanted to quit alcohol, but he planned to continue smoking. The priest crossed marijuana off the list, and Marlowe almost laughed with glee as he signed it.

So there was reason for skepticism when Marlowe lay on the ground resting after the sweat with the Arapaho elders. One of the old men came up to him and started talking about his own troubled times with the bottle. "A pledge is just a piece of paper," he said to Marlowe. "It's got to come from the heart." He tapped his chest. "The only way to quit is, you've got to have the *want* to quit."

Weeks later, in his dreams Marlowe was still gulping liquor, but he would wake himself up — he could do that — and start another dream, with a different subject. At his father's urging, he was heading back to school. His attempts to restitch his family failed, and so he took his journey through higher education largely alone. Then his son's troubles swept over his life like a black wave. But ten years after he quit drinking, when he ducked into Trosper's sweat lodge, he was still sober.

He was glad to be seated inside when the flap came down across the entrance and swaddled them in darkness. He felt the wet touch of the shoulder next to him, and heard the labored breathing of an old person on the other side. Trosper's voice came out of the dark sounding small and tinny, far away, giving thanks to the Creator. There was the fizzy sound of water pouring on the rocks, the sensation of his own liquid core springing up to the heat, and the music of the river just outside.

Marlowe always had reasons to pray.

Out of Place

Though the usual backdrop of my journalism, my nonfiction books, the novel in the bottom drawer, and my own life from birth is the American West, the designation "Western writer" leaves me cold. . .or rather hot: It puts me in a sun-sapped, sorefooted mood that's not much good for writing.

Nor, in this occidental torpor, am I much good for reading, if the bibliography is Important Books of the American West. Now and then I try, but the crowded shelf of a slow reader sags at the thought of another Owen Wister or Gretel Ehrlich. When you have spent your whole life futilely trying to "catch up" on remarkable books, and the end (of the life, not the library) is likely closer than the beginning, impatience sets in. At some point, I began dodging landmarks of the Western canon that had once seemed essential blazes. I haven't read everything Edward Abbey wrote, or even all of the estimable Wallace Stegner. I offer this more as a personal confession than a cultural critique: While the West is my literal home, it is not my literary home.

It is, I should add, a very good place to write. I'm trying to make a distinction here, trying to parse this business of "place" and its importance to the writer. There is a widely held belief that the West — a pretty big place, from Jack London's frozen tundra to Mary Austin's baked desert — has its own literary gene, a regional pigment that enriches the work of its writers. We're talking about something more than just a landscape set behind a story, or a writing table with an inspiring view. The finest "western" writers are simply born with the pedigree — Stegner, of course, and Ivan Doig and Norman MacLean — but in this age of mobility and gene-splicing, others have been able to overcome a lesser birthplace and *become* western writers.

It gets more complicated in my generation, when it is

possible to grow up in the West and still have to move to the West. A writer who attends grade school in Las Vegas, or Portland, or Salt Lake City, is a city kid like any other, and will have to find a rural post office box to evolve into the real thing. Many of us "natives" are a generation or two removed from the wheat farm homesteads or the gold camps of our ancestors, and to qualify as a regional voice we may have to seek out the space and wilderness and aridity that feature so prominently in the literature.

But here we are. Writers of the West. The connotation is not provincial or negative, it's valuable cultural coin. Writers are *moving* here to be part of it. If it starts to feel a little close — we need space, remember — then try Writers of Wyoming, even more rarified.

Some of my best friends are "western" writers– I mean it — and if we root for and steal from each other; why can't we be a regional movement, a literary cell with its own manifestos? And, practically speaking, why not grab some shelf space in the Literature of Place, particularly when the place is west of the 100th meridian, where a blurb from William Kittredge will sell a few more copies?

Because there is something fundamental missing. Scratch away at the straining adjectives and prayerful soul-searching in our meditations on the West and you often find an alpine lake: a beautiful, ball-tightening, mint and ineffable pool, frozen-out sterile.

It might help to glance at the region of the United States that made literary regionalism a label of proud exception rather than provincial limitation: the American South. If William Faulkner or Tennessee Williams had set their sweaty stories in Colorado, say, or Connecticut, they would have been dismissed and ridiculed — well, they are sometimes ridiculed, but they're also deified. There's no trouble telling them apart from the uptight Yankee writers, and we link their talent and license to the distinctive Southern environment that grew them.

But the Great Plains are a distinctive environment, too. Yet outside of Willa Cather and a few others, plains literature hasn't come close to matching the South's oeuvre.

What distinguishes the South are its tragic social and economic histories, the great wreck of it: the plantation system, the Confederacy's pride and sacrifice in the Civil War, and the despair of defeat and disesteem. Where the Confederate military failed, literature would triumph: the idioms of the South, enriched by loss, would rout the flat Yankee dialect.

For Southern writers, regionalism was a way to turn their insecurities to advantage. Their degrees were not from Harvard, but from Vanderbilt. They spoke not with the New England twang of the publishing houses, but in a Southern drawl. Long after the conflict, Southerners still needed to pose as rebels to get their juices flowing. Robert Penn Warren and his group called themselves the Fugitives, a hyper-version of a writers' support group, hanging out and yelling their dreams at each other. Where in all the dull dead writing from New York, they asked, would you find such language, such subjects? They liberated an army of truly original voices, and the notion of regionalism as a wellspring of great American literature took hold.

Can we get the same vigor by declaring a literary region of the American West? The idea persists. The West as a literary fashion comes whooshing back into New York publishing every few years like a shift of the Gulf Stream. There is a squad of academic supporters that line the contours of Western regionalism in essays and courses, there are editors who hear a special music when they visit western writing workshops, and there is a loyal readership ready to plunk down its dollars for books about western places and western experiences.

It's something different from the literary culture of the South, with its hot-house language and theatrical dialogue. Instead of idioms, we have landscapes. These are landscapes distinguished by the aforementioned space and wilderness and aridity, very different indeed from the fragrant and overgrown English garden that inspired Romantic poets and some nineteenth century American writers. Only here, slabs of tall cold granite, sheets of sand, wind-rippled grasses that go on forever: an elemental tableau baked by sun and scoured by blizzards. The monumental distances are uncluttered with human detritus. Stand on a butte above a scalloped valley up the DuNoir Valley and watch a pin-dot grizzly make its way across a deep meadow of fescue and silvery lupine and balsamroot, and you've arrived at a new, wild place, even if it's not the first time. If you write or draw, you're scribbling your discovery with trembling fingers.

But what is the *story* to be told in this setting?

"How will human beings be able to endure this place?" asks the Dakota emigrant farm wife in *Giants of the Earth*, beginning her slide into madness. She should have been a literary critic. From O.E. Rolvaag to Wallace Stegner's *Angle of Repose* to Ivan Doig's *This House of Sky*, so much of the best writing from the West poses that question and tells the story of someone who tried. (I dare not say all the great literature of the West — I've already confessed my failure to stay awake through it. There is, for instance, that category of Louis L'Amour literature that celebrates the cowboy and the Indian during their brief guns-and-ponies glory; and then the corrective debunking of the same era, by writers like the extraordinary Cormac McCarthy.)

My question: Is a rich regional literary culture likely ever to evolve in a place that defines itself by its resistance to humankind? You can write a few great books about it, we already know. But this hostile soil hasn't yet given root to a full-blown literature of its own.

The ability of the West to confound and often defeat those who would settle and civilize it is part of what today's writers love about it — especially when they themselves are not defeated, but in fact find they have that rare gene that fits this place. This discovery is often prefaced by alienation in a previous setting. The story goes like this: Reeling from a soul-killing setback in the Other Place (the city, the marriage, the job), our Protagonist retreats to the Empty Quarter to lick wounds, and finds him or herself tested anew (the weather, the loneliness, the peaks, the quirky locals) before finding in the subtle and secret places (well, less secret now) a hard-won renewal — and a commitment to place that will never, ever falter again.

I realize I have a few less friends now than when I began this essay.

Today the "native home of hope" attracts a horde of hopeful new settlers, including an inordinate number of personal essayists. They appear on the landscape newborn, admitting in only a few paragraphs the Other Place that spawned them, often back on the other side of the hundredth meridian. Is it unfair to wonder, as they bless the West with their homilies, what they found so lacking, so not worth defending or describing, in the lands they left behind?

Next I will offhandedly, feigning humility, confess that yes, indeed, I, unlike them, was born in the West. . .

Does it make you a little nauseous?

Well, I can't really pull it off. The West where I was born is California, which in many minds is Beyond West, the lotus land of surfers and psychedelics. My mother's family was mining gold in the Sierras in the 1880s, and my Irish half landed in San Francisco a little later. Knowing what counts in the western literature of place, I can mention the family orchards in Santa Clara, Big Sur wild boar hunting in my youth, and black bears raiding our place at the old mine property in Sierra City, but that kind of selective memory greatly distorts the reality of my childhood. I grew up primarily in the California of Disney and Didion, insulated much of the time from the "western" qualities of open space and harsh weather and wilderness.

I'm not complaining. It was a crazy and invigorating place to grow up. Worth writing about, too: Modern California, where the last great crash of migratory surf reached the end of the continent. My family history has a value, to me at least, in a state where history is vague and rarely personal: diaries, the still-standing homes of ancestors, and photographs of the state's early just-becoming days. From them I might pull the idiosyncratic detail that would add texture to a story of the present.

In my forties now, I think of how lucky I am to have material like that. That's the way a journalist thinks, and I've made my living as a journalist, competing for the unreported story or the new angle. That's what brought me to Wyoming, but it's not the reason I stay. Really, it's not quite the way I think anymore. Did I have to get to the Last Best Place to find a voice, or the scenery for a book? Certainly it would never have occurred to me in my youth, when I first began to write, rampantly, without a target. A writer has to write. "Place" may be the clay, but you can make an interesting shape out of any sort of clay, and you don't want to waste too much of your life searching for the last, best clay.

Yet I said: Wyoming is a very good place to write. I can't think of a better place.

It would be a good place to live as a carpenter, too, or an insurance salesman, for all the earthbound, self-centered, cornflake reasons: small towns, safe schools, trout, peaks and G&T's in the backyard under an uncommonly beautiful sky.

There are a few special reasons why it's good for a writer. You can make some easy money at journalism, because there are more stories than there are writers here, and they're interesting stories. You can work in your house, and, when you're not writing, you can work on your house, because your neighbors will help and know more about houses than you do. You can live here a life uncluttered, as free of noise and bustle and cant (at least about writing) as any place left in the country.

When assignments run thin, I sit at my desk and often find myself writing about my childhood, and what I know of my family before me. Good material, thinks the story-pitching journalist in me, and then, because I'm not writing as a journalist, I use the material any way I please, without much respect for how Uncle Jay Orlo *really* felt when he went back down the mine shaft to grab one more futile shovel of ore. A diary is just a suggestion, just a tip, and so is place. Any place will do, or so I believe, if you use it to describe your own heart.

My desk is in Wyoming, where I write about California.

Now and then one of those childhood stories transplants on the page to a hot spring in the foothills above Dubois, or a basketball court in Jeffrey City. I seem to be slowly moving this way.

Charles Levendosky

Charles Levendosky had been teaching at New York University and had completed two books of poetry by the time he was invited to be Wyoming's full-time Poet in Residence in 1972. Two years later he won a National Endowment for the Arts fellowship and taught poets how to work in the Poetry in the Schools Programs throughout New Jersey, New York, Georgia and Colorado. While in Wyoming, Levendosky ran the Poetry Programs of Wyoming which set up and coordinated poetry residencies and readings in schools and colleges around the state from 1973 to 1982. In 1983 and then again in 1987 he received the Governor's Arts Award in recognition for his contributions to the arts across the state. In 1988, Levendosky was appointed Poet Laureate of Wyoming and served in that post until 1996. In addition to his work as a poet, Levendosky works as the editorial page editor, columnist, creator, and editor of the *Casper Star-Tribune*'s First Amendment Web site (FACT). He has won numerous awards including the Hugh M. Hefner First Amendment Award for Print Journalism and the John Phillip Immroth Memorial Award for Intellectual Freedom, both in 1987; American Library Association, 1987; the Baltimore Sun's H.L. Mencken Award, 1994; American Bar Association's Silver Gavel Award, 1994; Roll of Honor for First Amendment Advocacy — Freedom to Read Foundation of the American Library Association, 1999; Society of Professional Journalists First Amendment Award, 2000; Wyoming Wildlife Federation's Conservation Communicator of the Year Award, 2001. He has also received a Wyoming Arts Council Literature Fellowship and *Prairie Schooner*'s Edward Stanley Award for Poetry.

Selected Poems

Peeping Tom hears

the tiny "no" you say to yourself
yet have never told anyone else.
Those doors you closed and turned
your back upon — even the portals
you didn't know you had abandoned.
Tom hears the promises you make
but intended to break. Hears, too,

when a dream drops like a pebble
down a deep well and finally plips
through a dark mirror sending out
ripples which gradually flatten
as the dream wafts and tumbles
into increasing dusk. Into silence.
Such a deep "no." So many deep "nos"

accumulate like layers of silt at
the lower fathoms of a life.
Weigh it down. Hears even those goodbyes
that lips never speak: the quiet defections
of love, of trust, of spirit.
Unacknowledged finalities
that settle like too many moonless

nights on those who search
for a child lost anywhere —
perhaps no further than within.

Peeping Tom: "never enough"

"Bodies are never enough," he whispers
to himself as he slips into their homes
while they are gone. He reads letters
left open on tables and diaries, and
thumbs through books memorizing any

underlined passages. He fluffs pillows,
sits where they sat, listens to whatever
music is in the tape decks, sets clocks
according to his watch, sniffs perfumes.
He wanders all the rooms touching walls,

noting stains where their hands touched.
Always a must of loneliness in the rooms,
dusty scent laid over a faint ammonia,
like the panties flung into their dirty
clothes hampers. He kneels on the floors

of these women's bathrooms and cries over
the vacancies that invaded their lives —
as if a cruel surgeon had cut them open,
removed half their insides, sewn them up.
He knows nothing of scalpels nor the art

of stitchery, but has an ear for the timbre
from what is hollow: drums, caves, old hotel
rooms, and great loves that have been lost.

In the dark

In the dark, Tom closes his eyes
as he lurks from room to room,
brushing furniture with the backs
of his hands or a tentative toe.
These are not his rooms he wanders
through blindly, they are yours.

He explores the night surface
of things for edges the day dare not
reveal. In his mind, he conjures up
the dimensions of your home, where
you place value, in what possessions.
Is a room a fortress, is it a hollow?

What desires have you stuck in back
of drawers? Where do you lay the warmth
of your life when you aren't cupping it
in your palms? Tom runs fingertips over
dresser and vanity, over desk and chair.
He skims the oil of handprints, scratches

nails have made, nicks of frustration, and
where you have lost balance in life.
He senses the edges you fall over.
Stumbles there, too. Sometimes he thinks
he is you. In those moments, he forgives
himself and your lack of foresight.

Burden of War

Artillery observer on the front lines,
Dad didn't talk much about what he saw
after he returned from Korea decorated
and disjointed — his eyes still focused
on what they had witnessed there.
He could not comprehend, nor could we.

Had been far enough North to see Chinese
"hordes," he called them, "cross the border,
to hear their war cries and battle horns
as they charged." He confessed to us once:
"The clamor could turn a brave man's blood
to jelly. Worse than anyone can imagine."

Lost his young Jeep driver to a land mine.
When drinking heavily, Dad would sometimes
mimic the sound of the explosion, "whump"
and shake his head, his eyes in that place.
Bottle after bottle contained tiny explosions
that dulled those memories — year upon year.

II.

This story then, from a fellow officer:
"An old woman with a child behind her
was walking toward your old man. She held out
a hand, begging for food. Your father dug
in his jacket to find something to offer.
She bent at the waist. I just came around

the corner in time. Granny had an automatic
rifle strapped on her back. It was pointed
at your father. The boy — half your age —
reached for the trigger. I shot them both.
First, the boy, then his old mamasan.
Strange war, women and kids trying to kill us."

III.

I can only guess now that my father
carried them for the rest of his days. Digging down
into himself, into whiskey stupor. Each drink
proved he was still willing to offer food or aid,
unwitting beneficiary of that terrible trade —
two lives for his, a child and a grandmother.

Seldom Heard

To make us listen more deeply,
the sky unfurls heavy snow,
or sometimes thick fog and
lays a hush upon the world.

All things, every event, are
suddenly coated in lush fur.
Fleece clings to rolling tires
and streets, and shattering
glass is muffled by soft pelts,
even the sun peers through shag.

Mornings when it settles so densely,
we feel the pressure of its weight
pushing us down into ourselves, we
listen finally past the pulse of blood
to some distant, much older voices.

The Short Adult Life of the Cicada

"meet my wife" he said
"she tends my home and drinks good bourbon"
then laughed this rancher

i heard a hum
the oak paneled basement of their townhouse
decorated with mounted arrowheads
and antique bottles
i heard a hum in the blue glass
he didn't hear it

her eyes were already leaping
madly flitting from wall to wall
he had sight keen for things forgotten in the earth
but didn't see it

he returned to town one hot august day
found the door wide open
the house empty

dry transparent husk of a cicada nymph
split up the back
and occupant flown

Snowshoeing in the Mountains

Snow groans as it packs
beneath our long, latticed tracks
the only sound we make. Our passage
and the wind through pines hush us.

We leave our too brief history
behind us — silent testimony
to those who follow: a father
and his daughter pass this way.

I taught you to lace the bindings,
how to walk up slopes by digging in
your toes. Now you will break your own trails
where the air is thin and shadows crisp.

We squint against the bright light,
walk together a little way longer.
Our passage hushes us: the sky, a stream
burbling below the snow. We stop for a moment

and look back at our tracks sinking
silently into blue shadows. Our passage
hushes us. The sun crosses the sky too swiftly;
we feel the chill. Our passage hushes us.

Astronomical Lesson for Acme, Wyoming

(Small town bought and vacated by a coal company)

Clapboard houses are ripped
at the sawtooth rim of this open pit:

Black holes, astronomers say
pull into themselves whatever is near.

Their gravity, insistent
and voracious, feeds
upon gas, dust, asteroids, even planets.

What spirals down into the vast darkness, remains.

We know them by their absence of light.

Against the Light, Driving to an Execution

Seconds click by as fence posts
as I drive west, against the light
  — to witness an execution,
  — by lethal injection.

The car's shadow gradually lengthens
behind me — stretching away
from the sun. Toward the onrushing night.

Ravens lift heavily from the body
of a roadkill rabbit. They scold
the passing car. In the yellow light
of evening and glow of golden grasses,
they are black slashes in the fabric
of the sky. Two fight over a small
piece of torn flesh. Against the light.

A hawk reconnoiters overhead; I see
his shadow first, as it slips over snow
following the tracks of his prey.
The setting sun spreads a red gash
across the horizon. Snow turns ashen.
A cold wind begins to blow. By tomorrow
it will have erased all our tracks.

Darkness has outpaced us — only the sun's
small red glow remains. Point of entry
a needle makes. I drive toward that point.

Against the light.

Cityscape and Landscape

When I came to Wyoming twenty-nine years ago to be a full-time poet-in-residence, I was a brash young poet from New York City with two books of poetry and a chip on my shoulder. I knew it all. Peggy Simson Curry, who was the other state poet-in-residence, saw through all that and was kind enough to shepherd me around the state, so I wouldn't stumble over my own ego. Gradually, under Peg's tutoring I began to see below the surface of things in Wyoming. And being a friend of Peg's meant that many people in the state gave me a chance to learn about the Rocky Mountain West, without judging me.

I was first attracted to the boomtowns like Gillette and Rock Springs because they had the kind of frenetic energy that I had lived in and written about in New York City. Those two towns were my entry into a larger understanding of the landscape in Wyoming and some of the landscapes of the psyches of the people who live here. I planned a book which was never completed, tentatively titled, *Boomtown, Wyoming*. It would have fit the general tenor of my two earlier books: *Perimeters* and *Aspects of the Vertical*. *Perimeters* is a log of a bus trip around America, expressing what the travelers saw and their concerns. *Aspects of the Vertical* is another extended poem about life in New York City, a city of skyscrapers and monumental bridges. The *Boomtown* book would have fit well in the series, but the boom faded before the book came to completion, and anyway my poetry had begun to shift ground under me.

In New York City, I had to put blinders on, like those used for skittish horses in races, to keep so much stimulation out — in order to focus on my own vision, my own voice. In Wyoming, there isn't the constant self-absorption by cultural tastemakers who tell everyone what is good or bad in art, painting, poetry, fiction. In Wyoming we make our own way. Almost immediately, I began to open up and my poetry suddenly became more personal, more about my psyche or about those I knew here. I dove past the surface, objective world and began to see if I could catch lives at some turning point or some dramatic moment. My own life became material as well. I had opened up to the subtle nuances in a life.

Writing about New York City, I had been keenly aware of the architecture of the city. That is a city dweller's landscape. Concrete and glass. Hard surfaces, brittle surfaces. And the voice of my poetry reflected that hardness.

One of the poems in *Aspect* has these lines in it:

> *". . . and when you die*
> *there will be one pair*
> *of eyes less*
> *scanning the street*
> *that's all*
> *the street doesn't care"*

Contrast these lines from a memorial column I wrote about Peggy Curry two years after her death:

"Now, when I drive from one town to another, as I still do, to give poetry readings or speeches, I feel Peggy Curry in the land and hear her poetry. . . And I know that this is home for me, too; that we go into the land here; that our spirit infuses the land, gives it a uniqueness, adds to the land's own soul. Gives it mystery — the way details of history are lost and mysterious, the way people fade in our minds but not our hearts."

Landscape as opposed to cityscape is more forgiving. That may be why people try to escape to national parks or forests or refuges to feel a forgiving place, places of awe and beauty that — if we respect them, give us blessings and the silence in which to find our spiritual selves.

I think too that the kind of landscape influences its artists and writers. The lush forests of Georgia and Tennessee and the South in general yield the kind of convoluted prose that is best illustrated by William Faulkner. No horizons are visible, only trees and underbrush and the shadows of forests. Hence the prose must weave in and out to reach a goal. In the West, generally the horizon is a line of sight. Direct. Eye to eye. We admire people who can talk straight and look you in the eye. The prose is spare and direct. And that becomes an influence. The subtle influence on style or vision or voice. Not merely the cliché paintings of the Tetons, but the line of sight statement. In Faulkner, the conniving trickster Snopes can be a hero. In Hemingway, the simple, honest man who respects his world is the hero — as in *The Old Man and the Sea*.

And Western poets like Richard Hugo and Peggy Curry understood their landscapes well enough to use them to explore the inner states of human reality. The outer landscape becomes metaphor for the inner landscape.

The sky, mountains, rivers, weather, high plains, sage, clouds, silence, trees — all these begin to inform my poetry, become more than sight, to include sound and smell and their touch.

"From here I can see the blue of the sky settle into the tracks of a snowshoe hare, how the delicate entry, which the sky makes, dust the edges of the tracks, tumbling flakes and crystals into shallow blue pools." This comes from a column I wrote in February 1987.

I have never ceased to marvel at blue pools of light in snow banks even though I know the physics that makes it possible — having earned my first degree in physics. Snow in urban centers is gray and then black as soot.

But blue snow is only a detail in the fabric of awe that landscape inspires. There are gods of nature. And whether we give language to them or not, we know their presence. . . sacred places that tribal people know.

And so my poetry became inner and sometimes even reflects the awe that I have felt in the presence of something sacred. One must know one's locale, one's geography and the flora and fauna that live upon it, just as we know the people who are our neighbors or our friends.

Poets, more than other writers, I would suppose, know with a familiarity of deep friendship that landscape creates language and the best, truest language creates landscape. We give the reader and the listener new eyes to see the land. It's a gift we offer, if we are lucky.

In such a vast landscape — as far as the eye can see — we, humans, are made small. Our concerns, our sorrows, our fears are put into a larger perspective. A healthy perspective that loses its selfcenteredness.

Coming to Wyoming allowed my poetry to grow in ways that I don't think it could have grown in New York City. In a manner of speaking, the landscape called my name. And I find myself trying to answer as truly as I can in my poetry and my prose.

Warren Adler

Warren Adler has published twenty-six volumes of fiction, which have been translated into more than twenty-five languages. His next novel, *The War of the Roses – The Children*, will be published in spring 2004. Adler's *The War of the Roses* was made into a hit movie starring Michael Douglas and Kathleen Turner. Another book, *Random Hearts*, was adapted into a movie starring Harrison Ford. An earlier collection of short stories, *The Sunset Gang*, was adapted and made into an acclaimed trilogy on PBS. A musical version, with words and music by Adler, is currently in development. His books are available on his web site (WarrenAdler.com) in every format, from e-books to print-on-demand. He is the founder of the Jackson Hole Writers Conference and a former chairman of the board of the Teton County Public Library. His collection of short stories, *Jackson Hole: Uneasy Eden*, offers his insights into contemporary western culture.

Adler was born in Brooklyn, N.Y., graduated from New York University with a degree in English literature, and attended creative writing classes at the New School. After graduation, he worked for the *New York Daily News* and was an editor for *The Queens' Post* in New York. During his Army service during the Korean War, he was Washington correspondent for the Armed Forces Press Service. His byline appeared in every service publication throughout the world. The Adlers maintain their permanent residence in Jackson Hole, Wyoming. They have three sons and four grandchildren.

The Promise

Steadman could hear the tires crackling over the gravel as it cut in from Spring Gulch Road and moved west toward the Circle Bar S ranch house. Thirty years ago, he had sited the house on high ground overlooking the Snake River so that, through the west-facing windows, they could see the jagged peaks of the Tetons, glimmering silvery in the morning light. From the east windows they could see the forest of lodgepoles that gave them the feel of complete privacy. Farther east, beyond the lodgepoles, had been the pastures for cattle.

Now what was that boy's name again? he asked himself as he waited, wondering why he had even consented to see him. Steadman had received offers to buy the ranch before, but he had turned them all down. Actually, it wasn't a working ranch any longer, not since Amy had died and he had sold off his herd.

Without Amy, gone two years now, ranching made no sense anymore. They had been partners in the working aspect of the ranch, a cow and calf operation that made just enough to keep them going from year to year. All in all, it was a hard but happy life, and they both loved it.

They had been married for fifty years and had no children; their family was the ranch hands, and their children were the calves that they helped birth and baby each year, worrying about their health just like any loving parents would. Life was rhythmical and predictable, almost, depending on the weather. The ranching way of life suited them, and if there were hardships, they got through them with cheerful resolve.

Steadman had grown up on the ranch. His father had bought it from the original homesteaders, and when he brought Amy here from Casper, where he had met her at a rodeo, she fell in love with it, every rock and tree, every piece of dirt and sage, every cow and calf and horse. Most of all, she loved the ever-hovering mountains, never tiring of the play of light that made them look different from moment to moment, day or night.

They had designed their bedroom and placed their bed so that the first thing they saw in the morning, when the weather was clear, of course, was the jagged peaks of the range. It was like a morning light show and never failed to thrill them.

"There they are," Amy would say, her first words when she opened her eyes from sleep. "Means we're still alive, Aubrey."

Not having children was a bitter disappointment for both of them. But the power of their love for each other weathered that storm, just as it weathered whatever blows destiny dealt them. But they did believe that life balanced out and that they were lucky to have the gift of this piece of earth in Jackson Hole. They felt certain that they lived in the most beautiful and magical valley on the planet.

The problem was, as Steadman saw it now, that this beautiful fifty-mile-long and twelve-mile-wide valley that stretched from Yellowstone to the Hoback had been discovered by the world. In his mind, the world meant "trespassers," aliens who had no appreciation for the glory and sanctity of this place and whose only motive was material gain.

The evidence was all around him. Land that once had sold for fifty to a hundred dollars an acre now was running into the thousands. Commerce had arrived in the form of stockbrokers, chain stores, fast-food operators, fancy restaurants. Big houses were mushrooming everywhere. Whereas he and Amy once knew everybody in Jackson Hole, he was seeing more and more strange faces. Change appeared to be accelerating quite rapidly.

Not that life in the valley had ever been totally static. There had always been dude ranches attracting folks who craved a Western experience, and the old moneyed families had bought up large tracts for their own recreation, but there remained a sense that the land was sacred, not to be sacrificed on the altar of commercialism. It was different now. The tourists and the developers had invaded the land, and the operative word was "profit." Steadman and the other old locals used another word to describe what was happening. Greed!

"Don't let them do it to the Circle Bar S, Aubrey," Amy whispered with her dying breath. If the situation were reversed, he would have asked her to pledge to the same wish.

"No way, my love," Steadman vowed. "No way."

Many of his ranching friends were selling out to the developers. Selling out was the only sensible way that they could liquidate and provide for their heirs. It was a sorry situation.

Inevitably, he knew, he would have to sell the ranch before he died. Dying without heirs would put the land at risk; it might be auctioned off to the highest bidder to do with as they wished, without restraint. Steadman was determined to pass it on to someone who would respect it, create a home here and not develop it as a subdivision. In Steadman's mind, subdividing would be destroying its integrity. To him, money was very low on his list of priorities. Besides, he had promised Amy.

Since Amy died, even during her funeral, he had been turning down offers for the ranch on what was almost a weekly basis. Most of them came from real-estate people. He could almost smell the stench of greed before they turned onto the ranch road. They would bring their big smiles and sincere looks, promising the moon, not realizing that he was sizing them up at first glance and rejecting whatever baloney they were selling outright. He hardly listened to their blatant pitches and promises of riches, although he showed them the same hospitality that Amy would have provided to anyone who crossed their threshold.

What annoyed him most was his own loss of trust. Once, he had trusted people. Locals had always lived by the ethic of honesty and straight-talk. People said what they believed to be the truth. A man's word was sacrosanct, and a handshake was more binding than words on paper. Steadman believed that knowing how it once had been gave him a special insight into people and their real motives.

Yet he had never given up hope that one day someone would arrive to whom he could safely turn over the stewardship of his land, someone who would revere and respect its character, someone who would make it his home and not a profit center.

But when someone came with an offer and a basketful of promises, he was always wary and on his guard. He imagined he could sense who would be likely to put another nail in the valley's coffin. So far, a steady stream of that kind had beat a path to his door. He considered them the enemy, the people who were hell-bent on ruining his beloved valley by chopping it into pieces, devouring it like vultures over carrion.

"Thanks for seeing me," the man said. Steadman took him for early fifties, lean, athletic, strong chin, blue-eyes, steel gray hair, serious. No big smile, which was a plus.

"Care for a drink?" Steadman asked. He had set out a pitcher of iced tea, lemon and mugs.

"That iced tea would be fine," the man said. His name, Steadman remembered, was Everett Carter. He was from New York, he had told him on the telephone. Saw his ranch from the air. Liked the setting. Any chance of talking business?

Steadman had liked his voice and his straightforward approach. Why not? He had already said "no" in his mind. Besides, without Amy, life was lonely and people to talk to were rare. Sometimes he was so lonely he would not have turned down a dialogue with the devil.

Steadman poured the man a mug of iced tea and pointed to a chair across from his own. Carter took the mug, sipped, then looked around him, his glance settling on the view of the Tetons.

"Great view," he said, putting Steadman on his guard. He was particularly wary of compliments. This one, however, came without a smile. Steadman merely nodded acknowledgment.

"What do you do in New York?" Steadman asked.

"Investment banker," Carter replied.

"Made a lot of money in the last few years?"

"That I did," Carter said. "Not ashamed of it, either. My father drove a delivery truck for a bakery. Never made much. I guess I figured I evened things out for him."

"You say you're lookin' for land?"

"Not just land. I'm looking for home. I'm planning on leaving New York."

"For good?"

"Why not?" Carter said, drinking another deep draught of his iced tea. "Been through here as a kid. I've always dreamed of a home here."

"Want to run cows, be a cowboy?"

"Sorry. No interest. I'm not coming here to do business, Mr. Steadman. Besides, I don't want the hassle."

"It's a hassle. More so these days. Hard going."

"What I'm looking for is a spread near the river with lots of land, a great view, a place for the kids to come. Maybe keep some horses."

"Got kids, have you?"

"Two. They're grown. One in college. One getting married. I want a place for my grandkids to appreciate and enjoy. Teach them the values of the West. Maybe I'm jumping the gun but that's what I'd like to happen."

"We never had kids," Steadman said, sipping his iced tea. He was sizing up the man, his opinion wavering, but he was not rejecting the man outright.

"Where'd you get the idea I want to sell out?" Steadman asked.

"I told you. I just took a shot," Carter said. "I believe in going after things face to face. If you're not interested, then I'll just be getting on. There's no harm in asking."

"You learned that in the investment banking business?"

"I learned that in life, Mr. Steadman. You want something. You go for it."

"No real-estate people in the bushes?"

"I like to deal direct."

Steadman continued to size up the man. He admitted to liking the man's look. His attitude, too.

"What would you do with this land?"

"Do?" Carter frowned and cocked his head. He seemed confused. Steadman refused to explain himself, watching Carter as he framed an answer. "I told you, Mr. Steadman. I'm looking for a home. That's it."

"You retiring?"

"Hell no. But I have left the firm. I've got lots of interests. And today we hook up with computers and faxes. You can be anywhere."

"Still want to make more money?"

"I'm in the keeper stage. I just want to keep what I got. Live here and keep what I made."

"Got plenty, do you?"

"A lot more than I need. As we say in the trade, I've hit my number."

"What number was it?" Aubrey asked.

"More than enough," Carter said, smiling for the first time.

Steadman shrugged, but didn't pry any further. A man who knew when he had enough was a smart man, he thought, warming to Carter.

"This valley is a way of life for most of us been here a long spell. Was a time we couldn't get green vegetables but once a week. Had one movie screen. Knew everybody in town." Now I'm talking like one of those old damned fools, Steadman thought, stopping himself. Amy would have shut him up fast.

"Must have been wonderful living here in the old days," Carter said.

"It sure was," Steadman agreed, forcing himself to crowd out the memories. The fact was that all his waking thoughts lately were about the past. He grew silent for a long moment, his eyes wandering to the mountains. Still here after a hundred million years, he thought. Saw a lot of us come and go. One day he'd go, too. Problem was he didn't know when. Nobody could predict when their time was over.

Suddenly he thought of the future as an affliction. What would he do without this land? Probably rent a small place in town and head for the desert in Arizona or Utah. Winters in Jackson were rough on old bones.

He might do some traveling. See the world he had missed during those years of ranching. After all, by any standard, the sale of the ranch would bring more than enough to live on for the rest of his life. He and Amy hardly ever traveled. Once they had taken a package tour of France and Germany. Another time they went to Mexico. They had derived some mild enjoyment on the tours but couldn't wait to get home.

"So you just took a shot?" Steadman asked.

"It's the way I operate," Carter replied.

Steadman rubbed his chin, still sizing up the man, but fast reaching a conclusion as to the man's motives and character.

"The point is, Mr. Steadman, are you in a selling mood or not?"

"Could be," Steadman said. "With Amy gone . . . my wife. She died two years ago. Without her . . . well, I just sold off the herd. Too hard for a man of seventy-five." Steadman became pensive, then looked into Carter's eyes. "To the right man, I might be willing to sell out."

"So my shot found its mark," Carter said, chuckling amiably. "Goes to show. You don't ask. You don't get the order. Apparently then, you'll entertain an offer."

"Depends."

"On what?"

"I need a rock solid unbreakable promise that this land stays intact. No development. No chopping it. It stays the Circle Bar S, just like it sits now. Get my drift?"

"Why would I want to chop it up?" Carter asked.

"Money."

"I told you about that. I hit my number. I don't need any more money. As for the name, its got history and character. Why change it?" He leveled his eyes directly into Steadman's. "I'm prepared to make you an offer you can't refuse."

"Yes I can, Carter. It's your promise I need more than the money."

"I get the picture. No development. I'll put it in writing if you want."

Aubrey had given that matter lots of thought. Could he trust a piece of paper? Contracts were made to be broken. Deed restrictions could be ignored. Legal challenges launched. The valley was getting too damned litigious, another sign of a society going to pot. Smart lawyers could do anything nowadays.

Integrity was what he was looking for. There was another dimension to this, Aubrey knew. He had been brought up to believe in the sanctity of property rights. It was a valley tradition that a man had a right to do what he wished with his property as long as he was sensitive to his neighbor's rights and needs. The standard was fairness and common sense, which was embedded more in a man's character than in the rule of law.

"If it was just the money, it would be easy," Steadman said.

"I know what you're thinking, Mr. Steadman," Carter said. He took a deep sip of his iced tea, and Steadman refilled his mug from the pitcher. "You think I'm one of those sharp guys from New York on the prowl for a deal that stacks the deck for himself. And you don't know me from Adam. You don't know my history or my reputation. Hell, to you, I'm just a fellow that dropped from the sky."

"You got that right, Carter," Steadman said. The man had indeed read his thoughts.

"There's no way I can reassure you. As I said, I'd be glad to put it in writing, but I'll bet you don't trust that either. You're going to have to lead with your gut here, Mr. Steadman. You're going to have to judge me by instinct. Oh, I'll give you more than a fair price. You know that. I'll pay a premium for this spot and you know that, too. And the reason I'll pay a premium is because this a fabulous place for me and my family to put down stakes, call home. Just me and my family. Hell, I'll probably be joining up with the folks, like yourself, who want to keep unchecked development out of the valley."

"A good speech, Carter," Steadman said. "But it'll still be a gamble on my part."

"Yes it will," Carter agreed.

"You're probably thinking I'm a damned fool. Take the money and run, you're probably thinking."

"Not at all. I can plainly see that money is not the issue here. What I'm thinking is how I can assure you that I intend no development, that I'd be buying this place for me and my family. I'll be glad to provide you with any references you might want, anything that might help mold your judgment of me. It's your call."

Steadman contemplated the man's face and bearing, looking for the answer to that question. He poured more iced tea and took a light sip.

"Afraid so, Carter."

"But I won't make my offer until you give me a firm commitment as to your intent. Fair enough?"

"Fair enough," Steadman agreed.

Carter slapped his thigh, rose and put his iced-tea mug on the table beside Steadman.

"I'm staying at the Spring Creek Resort for a few days. You think it over and you decide. All I can say is that I give you my solemn promise that I'll meet your conditions whether you want it in writing or you'll take my word for it. Believe me, I understand how important such a commitment is to you, and I'm prepared to honor it."

Steadman stood up, and the men shook hands. He imagined he could sense the man's integrity through the touch of his flesh. Then the man turned, went back to his car, and drove through the trees. Steadman could hear the fading sound of the tires crackling away on the gravel.

He stepped off the porch and walked along the river dike

for awhile, then headed back through the lodgepoles into the pastureland. Lack of irrigation had killed the grass. Now the sage was taking over, getting back its rights to the land. The sage, after all, was there first and was returning to its rightful habitat.

Steadman walked along the gravel road, then headed north beside the now-empty irrigation ditches that fed the grass and the cows along which he and Amy and the hands had pushed the cattle to new growth, then up to the mountains for grazing. It was a good life, and it was over.

As he walked along the barbed-wire fences that still marked the bounds of the ranch, he thought about the man. Was this the person who would fulfill the promise he had made to Amy? He had liked the way the man put it: "I hit my number." It suggested to him that man's greed was finite, that the thirst for more finally could be tamed and harnessed.

"Is this the right man to turn the land over to?" he asked aloud as he headed back to the barren loneliness of the ranch house, hoping that, somehow, his plea would reach Amy and she would respond with some sign.

The walk, which he once could do in minutes, took far longer than it ever had before, and when he reached the porch again he was winded and tired and had shooting pains in his thighs and back. Old age was arriving, and there was no mistaking its onset. It was time, he decided. The old way of life was dead.

That night, he continued to wrestle with the problem. He always had prided himself on his judgment of other men's motives. Wyoming people, he believed, had a sixth sense about people. Was this the man? He wished Amy were here to help him make this decision. She always was better at judging people. She could tell the good from the bad, the innocent from the guilty, the selfless from the greedy.

He hardly slept, and when he awoke he was more tired than he was before he went to bed. After a light breakfast, which he ate without appetite, he called Spring Creek Resort and the clerk put him through to Carter's room. In a voice still hoarse with sleep, Carter answered and the two set up an appointment for another meeting in mid-morning.

Carter hadn't asked whether Steadman had made his decision. The fact of his call, Steadman thought, was enough of a clue as to where he was heading.

"I didn't think I'd pass muster," Carter said, arriving on Steadman's porch a couple of hours after his call.

"Why would you think that?" Steadman asked.

"Investment banker from New York who had made a pile of dough." Carter said. "It sends off a message of acquisitive greed."

"Yes it does," Steadman agreed.

"Well, here we are again. Eyeball to eyeball. What's it going to be?"

"Do I have your word on what we discussed?" Steadman asked.

"You have that, Mr. Steadman. Upon my honor. You can take it to the bank."

"No subdividing. The land stays intact. The name stays."

"Agreed. On all three."

Carter held out his hand and Steadman took it. Both grips were strong as if the strength somehow was the measure of the promise. Steadman was relieved. The ritual of the handshake made him feel secure. He sensed he had struck a good and honest bargain in both Amy's name and his own.

"No second thoughts, Mr. Steadman?"

"None. Except that it will take me a month or two to clear out."

"No need to rush." Carter said, pausing for a moment, then chuckling. "We haven't discussed price."

"Just make it fair," Steadman said, certain that Carter had researched the comparables and knew the land's true value. He was far less interested in the money than in the fulfillment of Amy's wish.

"Will three million dollars hack it?" Carter asked.

Steadman was stunned. The best offer he had gotten was

$1.5 million. What in the world was he going to do with all that money? He considered it a cruel irony that all those years of hardscrabble suffering to make ends meet should end in an embarrassment of riches for which he had no need.

If Amy were alive, he wondered, what would she have said? She was the one who ran the books for the ranch, and the very most they had ever had in the bank was $50,000 and that was only for a month or two after a cattle sale. It was far too late for money. He supposed that he would wind up giving most of it away to charity.

"That'll do fine," Steadman replied, feeling the constriction in his throat.

Carter nodded, and they shook hands again.

"And remember your promise," Steadman said.

"Done," Carter said.

Lawyers wrapped up the financial details, and Steadman arranged for an auction of various possessions that he would not need, keeping only those items that had sentimental value or were essential to the new life he planned for himself. He could not bear to attend the auction. Carter had told him to sell whatever he wanted.

The day he left the ranch for good was a day for tears. He felt hollow and deeply unhappy. With him went all the memories of the old life, Amy, his parents, the cows, the branding, the ranch hands and cowboys, his pets, all his history, days upon days of a good life lived. He could barely see the road through his tears.

By the time he had arranged to leave, it was November and he headed for the desert and bought himself a condominium in Phoenix, where he spent the winter. He hated it, made few friends and missed his beloved valley. In the spring, he went to Australia and New Zealand, then toured China. It was only mildly interesting to him.

Then he booked a world cruise on the QE II, which he hated, feeling out of place and unable to connect with people. He did not like the confinement of the boat, and even though he had booked a large stateroom, by his standards it was small and he felt claustrophobic. The fact was that he missed Jackson Hole.

Above all, he concluded that he was not a social person and had no skill in small talk. He essentially was a rancher and a cowboy, used to long silences and wide open spaces under the big sky. He felt as if he was marking time waiting for the grim reaper to reach his patch.

After two years of what he considered aimless wandering, he came back to the valley. Up to then, it would have been too painful to visit the Circle Bar S and see how Carter was faring. Memories were too fresh. But time somehow had reduced the prospect of pain, and his first act on flying into the Jackson airport was to rent a car.

Low clouds hung over the valley, and he couldn't see the old ranch from the air. The only familiar sight was the peak of the Grand, pushing out of the mist below as the plane punched though the clouds.

He planned to visit the ranch, ride around, see some of the old-timers and contemplate the idea of coming back to the valley, renting a place in town and spending his days in his old haunts telling stories of the past to those who were still alive.

The Circle Bar S, being north of town, was only a ten-minute drive from the airport, and with great anticipation and excitement, he drove south, then turned in toward the river, heading up beside the western edge of the airport.

He could not believe what met his gaze. Stone structures with metal lettering proclaiming "Circle Bar S Estates" were on both sides of the old ranch entrance that had been landscaped with spruce and aspen trees. The old road had been widened and paved with asphalt, and new roads crisscrossed the old pastures. A few bulldozers and backhoes were at work cutting into what had become full-blown sage meadows.

He felt a hollowness begin in the pit of his stomach and a cold sweat break out on his back, chilling him. How could this be, he asked himself. Stunned and confused, he drove the rented car to a spot near a man working a backhoe.

He got out of the car. His knees shook and his legs felt like jelly.

"What's happening here?" he asked the man operating the backhoe.

"Digging a foundation," the man said.

"Carter's house?" he managed to ask, foolishly clinging to that possibility.

"Hell no. Carter lives by the river," the man said, pointing to the stand of lodgepoles in the general direction of where his and Amy's house had stood.

"This a house for one of his kids?" Steadman asked.

"Where you been? He's got eighty going up. Lots sold out like hot cakes. Some are even turning over. Carter's made himself one big pile."

Steadman felt a thump in his chest and his breath came hard and shallow. He turned away from the man on the machine and, with effort, headed toward his car. He couldn't believe it. The man had promised and Steadman had believed in the promise.

He sat in the car for a long time. Somehow the knowledge had sapped his strength, and he needed to rest. He closed his eyes and felt tears stream down his cheeks.

"I'm so sorry, Amy. I'm so sorry," he repeated to himself over and over again.

After awhile, he felt strong enough to drive and he followed the old road to where his house once stood. He felt an incipient rage stirring inside him. He had been so confident that he knew men and their motives. How could he have made such a mistake?

Riding along the path of the old road, he passed through the familiar forest of lodgepoles, then into a long circling driveway to a log house of immense proportions. His old house was gone.   Around the new house was lawn and, close by, a putting green complete with sand trap. In the distance, he could see another golf-hole flag fluttering in the breeze.

With what inner strength he could muster, he tamped down his rage, although he could not control his shaking legs as he walked up to the front door of the house and rang the buzzer. He knew that there was no way to reverse the process, but, for his own self-respect, he decided, he needed to confront Carter.

A young woman answered the door.

"Can I help you?"

"I would like to see Mr. Carter," Steadman said.

"He's in his study. He doesn't like to be disturbed. Is there anything I can do? I'm the housekeeper. Mrs. Carter is off on a shopping trip to New York."

"I'm afraid my business is with Mr. Carter," Steadman said, hearing the readiness in his voice.

"I really don't think. . . ."

"He'll see me."

The woman eyed him up and down with what he imagined was contempt. What business did this old fart have with Mr. Carter, she was probably thinking. She had closed the front door and he stood awkwardly waiting for it to open again.

When it did, Carter, dressed in plaid cowboy shirt, tight jeans, a belt with a large silver buckle, snakeskin cowboy boots and a fringed vest, stood in the doorway. He was smiling, and his hand was outstretched. Despite his rage, Steadman had no time to think and took the man's hand, remembering the last time he had taken it. Now it felt cold and clammy to his touch.

"Mr. Steadman. So good to see you. Come on in."

Steadman was not prepared for the hospitable welcome. He followed Carter into the house, a massive log structure filled with Western antiques, Western paintings mostly of cowboys pushing cattle, braving storms, slogging through mud, sitting around campfires. Others were images of painted Indian faces.

There were many pieces of log furniture and on the walls hung Indian artifacts. Sculptures large and small of wildlife and cowboys on horses adorned various spaces throughout the areas that he passed.

Steadman followed Carter into his large study, dominated by a massive carved desk and heavy leather chairs. Behind the desk was a huge painted landscape of a mountain setting.

"Drink?"

"No, thanks," Steadman said.

"Take a chair, Mr. Steadman. Make yourself at home."

Home? Steadman thought. He was appalled by the idea. Carter went behind his desk, lifted his fancy cowboy boots to its surface and clasped his hands behind his head.

"So what do you think?" Carter asked, still smiling, after a long silence.

"About what?" Steadman asked.

"The house, Mr. Steadman. Built in record time. Catch all that Western art work? Would you like a tour?"

"No, thanks, Carter."

"You back for a visit? Heard you had a place in the desert."

"I think you owe me an explanation."

"I do? For what?"

"You promised. We shook hands on it."

Carter scratched his chin and looked at Steadman.

"Conditions changed, Steadman. Opportunities arose. The county was changing the rules. I had no choice but to act before the door closed on the possibility. Just business, Steadman. Hell, you came out smelling like a rose."

"But you promised. We shook on it. I made it clear. I never would have sold you the place — you said you would never subdivide. . . ."

"I told you. An opportunity came up. I've got eighty lots in my master plan. People are gobbling them up. Really, Steadman, what kind of a dumb businessman would I be if I didn't seize the opportunity?"

"You said you hit your number," Steadman said. "You'd made enough money."

"Hell, can't be too thin or too rich," Carter chuckled.

Steadman felt the bile rise in his chest. His tongue felt dry and his anger made it impossible for him to respond. Instead, he just sat there, staring at Carter, his fancy boots on the carved desk.

"It was a condition of the sale," Steadman said finally, but his voice had weakened and he felt faint.

"You OK, Steadman?" Carter asked. "You look pale."

"And you, Carter? Are you OK? Don't you feel

anything?"

"Me? What should I feel? We did business. And business is business. The trick in business is to recognize opportunity. I saw it from the beginning. I gave you double what the other bastards offered. You came out pretty good. Three mil on the barrelhead. Not bad for an old duffer with a few years left. You could have a ball. No heirs. You could spend it all. You should have no gripes, Steadman."

"You cheated me, Carter." Steadman said, his voice still reedy. He felt weak, defeated, defeated by age, defeated by greed.

Carter scowled, lifted his feet off the desk and stood up.

"I think this little meeting is over, Steadman. Your problem is you let emotion and sentimentality get in the way of your business sense. Hell, Steadman, this place is hot. It's discovered. The big money is rolling in. Money talks and bullshit walks. There's a feeding frenzy for land going on in this valley. Fortunes will be made. You old-timers were here all along. How come you didn't see it?"

With effort, Steadman stood up. Carter was probably right. Greed was too powerful to be opposed. The bad guys had won. The valley that he and Amy had lived in was over. Aubrey Steadman was over. He followed Carter out to the door, which Carter opened. Steadman started to walk outside. He was tired and wasn't sure he would make it to the car. Then he turned and faced Steadman, standing there in his fancy Western duds.

"You'll never be a true Westerner, Carter. All the cowboy clothes and pictures and Indian stuff and wildlife paintings and your big fancy log cabin won't make you a Westerner. Not a real one. You don't have what it takes inside."

Carter slammed the door, and Steadman walked unsteadily to his car. He wondered where he had found the strength to say the things he had just said.

Sitting behind the wheel waiting for his equilibrium to return, he looked up toward the mountain peaks of the Tetons.

You're still beautiful, he thought. I'm ashamed of what

you have to put up with, watching us poor dumb mortals down here.

He turned on the ignition and headed back down the old ranch road, knowing he would never return.

The State of the Cowboy State in the New Millennium

Through the window of our chartered plane, I could see the snow-covered peak of Mount Kilimanjaro and the lush green carpet of the valley below studded here and there with the wandering herds of the Masa Mara game preserve in Kenya. I turned to my companion who shared the seat beside me. Her safari campsite had been rained out the night before and we had agreed to take her on board as a hitchhiker.

"Where in America can we find such a place?" I mused aloud as I surveyed the passing landscape below.

"Have you ever been to Jackson Hole?" she asked. I turned and looked into her clear blue eyes, which sparkled with enthusiasm and personality. I shrugged and shook my head in the negative.

"Do you know it?" I asked struck by the notion of questions being answered with questions.

"I am Jackson Hole," she said with self-effacing glee.

Without dwelling on the philosophical cliché of happenstance and fate, this exchange eventually brought me to settle in what is arguably one of the most spectacular settings in the world, Jackson Hole. My hitchhiking friend turned out to be the late Mary Mead, granddaughter of homesteaders, daughter of the former Governor and Senator Cliff Hansen.

More than a dozen years have passed since that quintessential moment on the airplane. My wife and I live in a house at the foot of the Tetons with a clear view of the Grand whose jagged peak is the first thing we see when we open our eyes in the morning when the weather is clear.

My impressions of the landscape of Jackson Hole remain as fresh, exciting and emotional as it was on that lovely day in May when we savored it for the first time under Mary's guidance. Unfortunately, we have discovered that there is more to a community than its natural endowments.

We hadn't realized it at the time, but we had arrived in the midst of what can only be characterized as an oncoming wave of revolutionary change. The bucolic valley in which we hoped to sink our roots permanently has undergone a transformation so rapid and mind boggling that we can, except for the eternal wonders of the mountain range, barely recognize it as that place of timeless beauty and joyful tranquility we once thought it was.

Now a dozen years is not a long time. The original homesteaders and the four odd generations that came after them have, quite obviously, seen changes that, to them, must seem both strange and probably appalling. Indeed, these worthy descendants have a menu of far more regrets than a newcomer such as myself might profess. To their eyes, I, too, must seem an interloper, indistinguishable from the pack of greedy predators who have ravaged their land with their arrogance and disrespect.

Meeting the various residents of the valley when we first arrived enhanced our initial favorable impressions. We sensed a generosity of spirit and a tradition of tolerance that had more to do with character than material wealth. There was, even then, a democracy of social intercourse. Class lines hardly existed. Working people mingled freely with retired multi-millionaires. Houses were built with a view to restraint and grace rather than as a gaudy expression of one's material wealth.

Showing one's economic largess through one's obvious possessions was considered anathema, even *verboten*. There was an atmosphere of funkiness, which could be seen in the architecture of the buildings and the dress of the residents. Faux western in garb and attitude didn't seem quite so faux.

As a writer, I thrive on diversity. Differences are the ingredients that go into the stew that gives piquancy to the imagination. The clash of ideas and personality is the mother's milk of the novelist's elixir. We bought into the trait of local cussedness as being the warp and woof of the western tradition. Mean-mindedness and smallness of spirit, like the expansiveness of the landscape itself, seemed to have no place in the intellectual firmament and social mores of our newly discovered valley.

Like a snowball barreling downhill, slowly at first, then accelerating mightily, profound changes began to occur. A combined gated country club and residential subdivision appeared, innocent at first, but pregnant with divisive possibilities. Stores around the square, once mostly locally owned, began to disappear to be replaced by national chains.

Greed, once merely a deadly sin, burst the bonds of propriety and fairness to become an obsessively ruthless ingredient of the business environment. Land prices began to skyrocket, pumped up and promoted by aggressive real estate interests. Indeed, it hadn't quite occurred to us at first blush that the most valuable currency in the valley was land, and that its exploitation was whetting the hungry chops of the real estate and banking establishments.

Lured by the absence of a state income tax, the big money corporate types grown fat with stock market profits began to migrate into the valley bringing with them the baggage of their success at manipulation and acquisition. In their wake came the hordes of well-heeled second-home owners who use the valley for brief periods of skiing and summer vacations. Most of them are uninvolved in ordinary community life overburdening the infrastructure and contributing only modestly to the communal social contract.

Unlike Aspen, which attracts glitzy celebrities, Jackson Hole magnetizes the financial bulldogs, many of them active or retired partners in major brokerage firms or executives of Fortune 500 companies. To add to the macho mix have come bootstrap entrepreneurs who, as they say, did it their way and, therefore, are metastasized by their sense of infallibility.

This is not to say they are evil people. Most of them are on the dark side of middle age and have come to Wyoming, aside from a tax haven, for a physically active semi-retirement. Unfortunately, after a brief honeymoon, they discover that they are simply unable to discontinue the aggressive strategies and tactics that won their past battles to achieve economic success. Many of them revert to type and begin local deal making and land speculation, which inevitably accelerates real estate prices to levels beyond the reach of the working locals.

Most have built houses that are truly faux western palaces, too many of which appear on the butte ridges like resting sparrows on a high wire.

As people who cherish their entitlement, they, like the proverbial birds of a feather, naturally cluster together, socializing with only those who are like-minded politically and on the same heady economic plateau. Much of their financial support will go for those institutions like the Music Festival that have the cachet of "culture" where big buck contributions is the admission price of their social acceptance. Such a narrow mindset has become the principal measure of their status and, by its very nature, the instrument of their exclusionary practices. Diversity is not their strong suit.

The result is an ever-widening gap between the haves and the have-nots in every realm of Jackson Hole social life. There are exceptions, of course, but now such acts of inclusion are viewed more as "outreach" than social intercourse, thus adding insult to injury. By its very nature "outreach" implies separation. Reaching out to whom? The perceived underprivileged, of course, and the socially and economically unequal. In a valley our size, the notion that the citizens who serve their infrastructure are somehow "lesser" and need to be "reached" as if they were deprived beings is absurd.

Notwithstanding such separation, we cannot begrudge the economically privileged to their share of the area's wonders, the fly-fishing, hiking, rafting, camping, hunting and skiing, the clear air, the views, the starlit nights. There is an irony here since the majority of the privileged are Conservatives, not of the moderate variety like myself, who rail against the beady-eyed government intruding on their lives. It must be galling for them to accept the bedrock truth that it was the government's foresight, with the acknowledged help of the Rockefellers, by taking much of Teton County land out of development, that has made this area a recreational paradise.

Unfortunately, this paradise will soon be available as a

permanent residence or a second-home site for only the chosen few. Not to be overlooked are the millions of tourists who will invade the landscape for their seasonal fix of outdoor liberation and a western faux experience. Tourism is Jackson Hole's only profitable industry, which accounts for yet another form of separation.

There is a double irony here. The tourists arrive to enjoy their national parks, which is their entitlement and those who once opposed their expansion, the descendants of the homesteaders who had barely eked out a living from the ranching life, now vastly profit in land prices from that which they so zealously opposed.

Of course it can be argued that one need not immerse one's self in these heady philosophical questions and can simply enjoy the scenery, the ambience and the recreational opportunities and turn a deaf ear to the cacophony of change. There are those who are quite content with such indifference and solitude. But if you are, like myself, someone with a nose for curiosity, an eye for observation, and a novelist's burdensome sensibility you can only look about you with a heavy heart.

Land-poor working locals, for example, are beginning to disappear at an alarming rate. The human infrastructure of the area, the schoolteachers, policemen, librarians, nurses, and the like find it harder and harder to make ends meet. And when they leave in frustration it becomes a near impossible task to bring people in to fill their shoes.

On the other hand, there are those who, for a variety of reasons, have made a conscious choice to live here regardless of the economic hardship. They practice their own brand of separation. Many of them hold degrees from some of our most prestigious universities. They have considered their options and chosen to live here despite the necessary sacrifices. It is not uncommon to be waited on at table by a Ph.D. in geology or be served by a UPS driver who is a graduate chemical engineer.

There are numerous clannish sub-cultures of people here who revel in mountain climbing or devote themselves to conservation, wildlife preservation, painting, photography, poetry, writing, studies of plant and animal life, or other disciplines who wouldn't or couldn't live anyplace else on the planet. Sadly, economic realities have put them at risk as well, although I suspect that nothing, short of death or disease, will ever dislodge them from this area where, they aver, their souls reside.

Perhaps, despite all my breast beating, the reality I illustrate is a predictable outcome. Since the available land for private use in our exquisite valley is less than three percent of the whole, it is only natural to the system that its affordability becomes restricted to the lucky few who can pay the price. Market forces, after all, are as blind as Justice herself.

To the rest of the state, most of whose cities and towns suffer from outflow of population and a lingering economic depression, Jackson is looked upon as a kind of spoiled rich cousin who has been deliberately exiled from the "real" Wyoming. They have a point. Yet, in fairness, the political shortsightedness of the state's politicians is more to blame for its accelerating economic slide than the poor little rich guys in exclusive Jackson Hole.

For lack of opportunity, the best and brightest of the younger generation are forced to leave the state. All Wyoming citizens are complicit in this disaster, although some will tell you this has always been the case, as if acceptance of catastrophe was a virtue. Those who follow the Byzantine backroom politics of the state are well aware of the obvious, that the state is mortgaged to the extraction industry. Indeed, it is a further irony that the vast riches that lie beneath the ground are the very reason for our state's impoverishment and population outflow.

It strikes me as bizarre that politicians who preside over the affairs of Wyoming where its younger educated citizens are forced to leave the state to find opportunity, are elected and re-elected. One would think the electorate would rise up and throw the rascals out of office for the high crime of forcing the involuntary exile of the state's progeny. The travesty of sanctimoniously professing so-called "family values," then sentencing their youngsters to banishment is, to my mind, the ultimate expression of hypocrisy.

This is not to say that we are all dolts and morons to allow this condition to prevail. There are many who are content to be outside of the dubious onslaught of so-called progress, who actually prefer to be part of a backwater colony that exports its kids. It is not uncommon to find little towns that dot the landscape of Wyoming with big shiny signs that proudly hawk population numbers that barely exceed a score of souls, if that. Wide-open spaces, however bleak and wind-blown, give some among us, albeit the generation closest to oblivion, a sense of space, safety, and peace. Some might call this attitude diversity. I call it a kind of stasis.

The state figure of the cowboy on his mighty steed is more a quaint symbol of nostalgia than of present reality. Cattle ranching in Wyoming is more a way of life than a profitable enterprise. The days of the cattle barons are over and the passage of smaller ranches from one generation to another has become a taxable burden that few can afford. Real estate interests are breaking up the big ranches and selling them off as "ranchettes" where dudes can play cowboy to their heart's content on their thirty-five acre spread.

Notwithstanding, the legend lingers on. To many the "West" is a persistent romantic dream and the cowboy is a comforting image of freedom, rugged individualism, courage and independence despite the flawed accuracy of its historical reality. Much of it has come down to us filtered through the highly imaginative and expansive showmanship of Buffalo Bill Cody and the Hollywood moguls and western writing fantasists of yesteryear. Unfortunately, the legendary hubris makes our state seem more like a theme park than an environment that serves real people leading real lives.

While to some these observations may be interpreted as the ravings of some wildeyed proselytizer for a new social contract, I prefer to call it a clear-eyed view of Wyoming at this moment of the millennium.

Having what I have so sanctimoniously declared as a clear-eyed view does not guarantee the truth of my observations.

It is purely a personal snapshot. Some might characterize it as disillusion, hope, and optimism gone awry, dyspeptic analysis of what to others is a glorious sense of place, and, despite all, an unspoiled paradise.

For those who see my critique as the sour outpouring of a disappointed alien, I tender my sincere apologies. Some will undoubtedly be beyond forgiveness and offer me a one way ticket to anywhere but Wyoming. I am used to such treatment. At times I feel that if I have not offended nearly everyone, I have failed in my social critique. I have come to believe that such fulminations are an essential part of my character and I should seek forgiveness in advance.

As you can see, the novelist's eye can be a Cyclops' curse and a blessing. Yet, what it has revealed to me is that Jackson Hole and its reluctant mother, the Great State of Wyoming, contain all the ingredients of conflict and high drama. Who knows, the inspiration for the Great American Novel might even be lying dormant here hidden among the sage and the moist roots of the cottonwoods.

Tom Rea

Tom Rea grew up in Pittsburgh and has lived in Wyoming for thirty years, eleven of them spent as a reporter and editor for the *Casper Star-Tribune.* His nonfiction book, *Bone Wars: The Excavation and Celebrity of Andrew Carnegie's Dinosaur,* was published by the University of Pittsburgh Press in 2001, and won a Spur Award from the Western Writers of America in 2002.

Selected Poems

The Painter on Main Street

props his ladder two stories up
below the cornice over the shoe store
and begins climbing. Halfway up
he drops a cloth over the shoestore awning
and continues, slowly, bucket in hand,
the bow in the ladder lending him
a careful grace, until he arrives
paints white two feet of the in-and-out-cornice,
taking time. He tries
to hook the bucket to the left side
of the ladder but there seems
nowhere to hook it, and so
he moves it slowly, back to the right side,
hooks it, dips the brush with his right hand,
transfers it to his left, paints white
another foot, climbs down.
                              Climbs
into his blue van, moves it a few feet
forward — why? — to foot the ladder
against the tire?

No. His helper
leans against the van, feet on the foot
of the ladder, the ladder
all the way over against the drugstore now
so the painter can paint, right-handed,
the left-hand end of the shoe-store cornice.
Up he goes, swaying, paints, and swaying
climbs back down, moves the ladder
two feet right and again up, sway,
paint, sway, down. The world
goes by. At the high
reach of his brush his right hip lifts,
feet stay barely on the rungs,
until he's done, the unpainted
middle stretch all painted —
the sky's maintained its steady, even blue —
and it's lunchtime.

Plum

Snow can fall
softly, as if down
were its direction only
by accident, the way
when you entered a room
my great aunt Marian
would look up, eyes
bulgy and dim behind
thick lenses, the accident
of the two of you in the same room
unremarkable, if soothing.

Maybe she'd lick
a stamp or straighten
the antimacassar, not
thinking how her daughter
died alone in a room
with the shades pulled down.
One day when I'm
home on a Christmas visit
my father will give me
that same look
and say, "Oh,"
only slightly surprised,
the one round vowel
hung between us like a plum
that knows its own
ripeness, and exactly
when to fall.

The Black and the Dazzle

Some winter mornings
dawn a wild, dazzling bright
finding and blessing everything —
fence post, phone pole
brown grasses poking through snow,
brown cattail medley at the frozen marsh —
with its particular self.
The cold air holds nothing
but transparent possibility.
My daughter
beside me on the seat
chatters along of what she remembers
of summer, the races we had
in the yard on her birthday.
We pass a snowplow, coming at us
and find ourselves for a panicked second
with nothing but each other.
My father writes,
"I am deteriorating steadily and painlessly."
Again the road appears, with
mailboxes, pollarded trees around a farmhouse
and a black line of cattle
strung feeding along a line of hay.

The Bodhisattva of the Parking Lot

for Jug

With a friend I was talking in the oversized
      gravel parking lot outside the Horseshoe Bar
      June, blue sky, dust
Talked watching
      the wisps of his hair
      curve of his half-bald forehead
      edges of his eyes, suspenders at his shoulders
      all realer now than whatever we were talking about
Talked and talked with two beers and a cheeseburger
      in each of us softening the early
      afternoon glare to something
      easier to bear and at the same time building
      a binding nostalgia for the present that made it
Harder and harder each moment to get back
      in the truck and head for work
      when right then
      right over his shoulder I saw
The backhoe emptying a bucketload of dirt.
      Then another.
The grass over there was already starting to yellow
      this early in the summer and none
      of the little spruces were higher than your waist
      but they were in rows
      and this close to Memorial Day
      a lot of the markers bore flags still
      or flowers.
Little markers for the graves it was a grave
      the man was digging with his backhoe
      the dirt descending just 50 yards beyond
      my friend the Bodhisattva's ear
      onto a warming pile soon

To be moved right back into the earth it came from
        with only a slight swell
        to show where the body lies
        decaying at the speed of memory
        which is light.

The Borderlands

Yeats named himself among the last
Romantics, as if he feared his own death
would end something. Yet he opened
roads we still travel.
                              Cool water
remains. Soul and body remain
locked in their mortal embrace.
The great plate of the sea, dome of the sky
still contain us along their windswept borders.
How the past pours in. Keeps pouring.
How love, its flag a torn red cloth on a stick,
keeps scouting new headquarters.

Listening to Miles Davis Play "Bye Bye Blackbird" while my Teenage Daughter Weeps into the Telephone

What's so sweet
about longing?
What kind of love
in a muted
trumpet so
purposefully sustains
an ache
decade
after decade?

The View from Laramie Peak

Not many years ago, my wife and I and our eight-year-old son, Max, climbed Laramie Peak. It's nowhere near Wyoming's tallest. Still, it's the tallest of its range, and from the top a person can see great distances: southwest in clear weather to Elk Mountain; southeast to a horizon far beyond the Wheatland power plant; and north, though we couldn't quite make them out that day, to Pumpkin Buttes near the Converse/Campbell county line.

Heavily used and well maintained, the trail switchbacks from a Forest Service campground about five miles and 2,500 feet in elevation up the west side of the mountain to the summit. Dirt bikers pass from time to time, growling up or growling down. When we reached the top, and saw the views, we felt ourselves puff up a little, like balloons. This phenomenon I call mountaintop hubris — the assumption that, with great stretches of country newly visible, important historical and political insights are revealing themselves as well.

From the mountaintop I recalled that when Jefferson sent Lewis and Clark to explore the interior, he asked them to keep their eyes peeled for mammoths. There might still be some out there, the president hoped. Better informed but equally hopeful, the Oregon-bound emigrants making their way west up the Platte two generations later must have had an image of the mountain's great blue cone in their minds long before they saw it. They knew it would be their first glimpse of the Rocky Mountains — the Shining Mountains, some may still have called them then. From the top, I imagined seeing their emigrant wagons crawling toward me like slow, white bugs; what if I had been here before them? Would they have regarded me only as part of the emptiness? Would they have imagined my blood as red as theirs? In Wyoming, we're still arguing about what this emptiness actually is, and whether and how to fill it.

Of course, the state's already full: with sky, sagebrush, rocks, antelope, cattle. Scraps of water. Here and there a highway, a tree, a house. Once in a long while, a town. The apparent emptiness leaves room for old stories. Owen Wister first came to Wyoming in the summer of 1885, when he turned 25, seventeen years before *The Virginian* was published, making cowboys good guys forever. Wister stayed at Maj. Frank Wolcott's ranch on Deer Creek, not so far from Laramie Peak. The newcomer had only been there a few days when Wolcott sent him and a wagon back down to the railroad at Medicine Bow to pick up some cans of fish. Wolcott had ordered trout and bass for his creeks and stock ponds.

After a nineteen-hour drive and a night camping along the way, Wister and some unnamed companions arrived at Medicine Bow about five-thirty in the afternoon. The train wasn't due until midnight, so Wister ate a bad meal, walked around, and listed every building in town in his diary. There were twenty-nine, including privies. Then he slept on the counter in the store, just like the greenhorn narrator was to do years later, in the opening chapter of the novel. The next day, sun killed the trout in their cans. I suppose they were big milk cans. The bass, tolerant of warmer water, survived.

You can learn another old story from members of the Hanson family, who ranch on the east flank of the Bighorn Mountains, northwest of Kaycee. They'll tell you about Elmer Brock's paperweight. Elmer, their grandfather and great-grandfather, was twelve in 1892, when Wister's friend Frank Wolcott led a band of Wyoming landowners and Texas thugs north into Johnson County to kill rustlers there. At the K.C. Ranch they fired the house, and when Nate Champion ran out, they shot him dead. Just south of the middle of what's now the town of Kaycee, south of the little bridge over the Powder River, under big cottonwood trees, an alfalfa field now lies where the ranch house was. Picking through the burnt embers some days after the murder, young Elmer came upon a lump of lead shaped like the empty space a teacup encloses. Champion must have had bullets lying idle in a teacup. When the house burned, the slugs melted together and the teacup cracked away. The family still has the paperweight–a lump of emptiness, solidified.

When I was a newspaper reporter on the Casper, Wyoming *Star-Tribune*, I got to speak with Margaret Brock Hanson, Elmer Brock's daughter and an old woman, after the Bureau of Land Management proposed locating a seven-mile-long hiking and horseback trail along the top of Gardner Mountain, northwest of Kaycee. The trail runs on land that Brock and Hanson cattle have grazed, I suppose, since Elmer was a boy. The Hansons still hold the grazing lease, there's a chain of back disputes between their family and the BLM office in Buffalo, and Margaret was angry. The fact that it's federal land she saw as only a technicality, given how long her family has used it. Deep in her heart, she didn't even believe the land *was* federal. In any case, the question was hanging like a lump of lead inside her, she was willing to talk, and I reported some of what she said in the paper. I liked her, even though I disagreed with her; her opinions were so clear and her distress so palpable. Strangers would come in and trash the land and scare the cows; as far as she was concerned that was all there was to it.

Shortly afterwards I joined the strangers. I got to go along on a BLM-sponsored ride along the ridgetop trail. The country sweeps gloriously to the south and east from up there. South you look out over the site of the Dull Knife battle, where the U.S. Army caught up with a band of Cheyennes the winter after the Custer fight. And on the eastern horizon, quite plainly, out near the huge mines in Campbell County that employ fewer people to strip more coal each year, you can make out Pumpkin Buttes.

A man, his teenaged son and their limping German shepherd reached the top of Laramie Peak about the same time we did. At the top of the trail you meet a power line, swagging up from the south on wooden poles–and a metal building. From the building rises a radio tower. With all that stuff up there, there's really no good spot from which you can see around all 360 degrees. A rickety platform provides a vantage for the main view northward, but I didn't try to scramble over. Instead I peered around the boulders to the much steeper, east side of the mountain. A pair of hawks wheeled and cried below. A dirt road far beyond them bisected an open space my map identifies as Cottonwood Park. For two years, the man with the dog said, his sister taught school there.

"Terrible what they're doing to the rural schools," he said.

"Yes," I lied, politely. He meant our new Wyoming school finance arrangement, demanded by the courts in 1995 following three years of litigation. The details are still, winter after winter after winter, being worked out by a reluctant and insulted legislature. During eleven years on the paper, I wrote story after story about it. The more I wrote, the more interested I got.

The old system had evolved to protect rural schools — not just the tiny one-room schoolhouses the hiker was talking about, but schools in small and mid-sized towns. The system grew up on the theory that smaller school districts cost more per student to run. It was true, but no one ever bothered to figure out exactly how much more it cost. Ford Bussart, a small, smart lawyer and Democrat from Rock Springs — at 19,000 people a city by Wyoming standards — argued it wasn't fair that the old system allowed some of the rural districts three, even four times as much to spend per student as the districts in the larger towns like his. That's right, the state Supreme Court finally ruled, it's unfair, and that means it's unconstitutional. Fix the system, the court said to our two-to-one Republican-dominated legislature. Furious Republican legislators often mentioned Bussart's big houseboat, and called him "Ford Buzzard." Ford kept the boat at Flaming Gorge Reservoir, on the Green River in southwest Wyoming. The Republicans hinted the boat was paid for out of the fat fees Ford collected from the big school districts, and their taxpayers. Odd how, deep in the arid West, a houseboat became a metaphor for a blow against the status quo.

Though we are in fact a mining state — coal, trona, oil, and gas generate the highest-paying jobs and the lion's share of our tax revenues — we think of ourselves as a ranching state. We have a hard time imagining a better way to use the land surface than to provide cheap forage for beef cattle. We can't help but admire people who ranch; like Jefferson we associate land ownership with virtue. And so we vote for the cowboys, the good guys Wister admired so profoundly. We vote for the guys in big hats.

One fall, I covered the Wyoming Stock Growers Association's convention, in Douglas that year. Talking with some ranch women I mentioned that even though only about four percent of the people in Wyoming actually work in agriculture, twenty-seven of the ninety legislators were at that time ranchers. (This is the kind of thing I bring up when I'm working.) The number, I noted, was down only slightly from a few years earlier, when a full third of lawmakers were ranchers. Yes, the women agreed with long faces, it was a shame. A real shame, how the ranchers' influence had begun to slip.

One more story: The road from Kaycee, where Nate Champion died, to Gardner Mountain, where the BLM had proposed its hiking trail, turns to dirt at Mayoworth, just an abandoned schoolhouse now. Then the road cuts through upended hogbacks of red, red rock, before switchbacking up the mountain face. The red rock is Chugwater sandstone — familiar at Red Buttes west of Casper, at Red Canyon on the way up to South Pass from Lander, or just north of the mouth of Wind River Canyon, before you get to Thermopolis when you're driving in from Shoshoni.

After our long, BLM-sponsored horseback ride along the top of Gardner Mountain that day, I was riding more comfortably in the back seat of a government Suburban. Beside me was a woman, middle-aged like me, from a local office of one of our congressional delegates. Other BLM and congressional staffers filled the other seats. The hiking-trail proposal had stirred up bitter opposition from plenty of local ranchers besides the Hansons, while thousands of letters in favor had poured in from environmental and recreation groups around the country. It had been a long day on the back of Igloo, the horse. I was glad I could still walk. The Suburban's air conditioning purred deliciously. The vehicle elbowed around a switchback, now heading back down Gardner Mountain. Far below we could see where the road up from Mayoworth cut toward us through the two hogbacks of red rock. The woman smiled. We agreed how good the tawny grass, the sage and red rock looked in the late-afternoon light.

"My grandfather used to say to us 'You know why those rocks are red, don't you?' And we'd say, 'No, why?'" the woman said. "And he'd say, 'Indian blood.'"

I laughed politely, hiding my embarrassment to be laughing about dead Indians.

The red rock was in fact laid down in Triassic times — the first of the three long dinosaur ages. Iron oxides make it red. Then near the end of dinosaur times, the Rockies began rising, their granite and basalt cores pushing up the sediments that had been laid above them. The cores were hard and as a result they lasted long after the bent-up sediments had mostly worn away. As soon as the new mountains were up, though, they too began wearing down. So much grit blew and ran off the mountaintops that dirt completely filled the basins between them — right to the top of mountains like Laramie Peak, and mountains far higher. But wind kept coming, and rain, and snow and frost, scooping out the softer parts again until we're where we are now, living with mountains and space, great stretches of scooped-out space and then more mountains.

Time eventually grinds everything to dust, the hard rocks and the soft. You could call it a lonely feeling, but it's something more important than that. What's important lies in the meantime. What's important happens now and happens here, as we decide exactly what to do.

B. J. Buckley

B.J. Buckley was born in Cheyenne, Wyoming, in 1953. For sixteen years she lived on the 7UP Ranch between Arvada and Leiter, Wyoming, and considers the Powder River Country her heart's home. In the early 1990s, she moved back to Montana to be with her sweetheart Art Anderson, a blacksmith and tool-and-die maker. They live with their dogs in a cabin in the woods south of Lolo, Montana, with no electricity or running water. For more than twenty years, Buckley has taught in poetry-in-the-schools programs sponsored by state arts councils in Utah, Idaho, Montana, South Dakota, and Alaska. Her work has appeared nationally in many little magazines and has been anthologized in *Leaning Into the Wind* and *Woven on the Wind*. Her first collection of poems, *Artifacts*, was published by Willow Bee Publishing in Saratoga, Wyoming. She is the recipient of many literary awards, including a literature fellowship from the Wyoming Arts Council, the 1999 Writers Exchange Award from the Poets & Writers organization, the Robert Penn Warren Narrative Poetry Award from *The Cumberland Poetry Review*, and the 2003 Rita Dove Poetry Prize from the Center for Women Writers at Salem College in North Carolina.

Selected Poems

Living in The Other World

This is how you must live in The Other World:
never kill a frog or a toad, not even by accident.
Out of who knows what weariness, or joyful play,
or the pain of being too separate from the mud,
or the wish to go on singing without the burden
of engendering some new cosmos with every turn
of melody, one of the Holy People became a frog.
But no one knows which one, which fat amphibious
body holds The Bringer of Rain, The Water Carrier,
and which is just frog-self, dreaming only of
dragonflies and river and the wet hot clasp
and the sigh of wind and egg-jelly floating in the weeds,
dreaming only of warm and wet in its sleep grave
in the sand all winter, buried by snow and memory.
At the back of a dead-end canyon under Navajo Mountain,
a spring higher up in the rocks spills first into a pothole
the shape of a moon not quite full — fills it,
runs over the lower rim tipped towards the canyon,
flows flat down the rock face trailed by moss

slick and green as frog flesh — falls, at last, exactly
like a soft perpetual rain, musical and unhurried,
into a deep pool which cuts back into the Moenkopi
sandstone, makes a curved cavern, a bowl over the water —
black as heaven before Coyote scattered the stars
all haphazard across it, black as a ceiling soot-stained
by four thousand years of the fires of the people,
black from iron leaching out of the rock. From the shelter
of this canopy the pool creeps outward along the canyon
floor, laps at the ragged skirts of drought, stains
its hem with the scarlet flame of paintbrush in the shadow
of parched sage, with something green and weedy
braided into bones — mouse? Some songbird come at dusk
to drink? — small bones, needle-quick, stitching themselves
into this wet new body. And on the surface, far back, two
desert spadefoot toads float on their bellies,
arms outstretched, legs, broad webbed toes shimmering
like the petals of flowers; and sometimes they lift
their heads to sing, deep and burpy and resonant
in the singing always rain. Closer, at the shallow end,
under only inches of water, a third toad sits, and in its mouth,
half-swallowed, sits another — together, too heavy,
they sit calmly looking upward into the light, alert
and quiet. And the swallowed one, too, is singing,
underwater and wild and silent, singing, singing!

Bear, in a Tree with Apples

We saw him first in a great pine, asleep body-long on a limb,
        snout to trunk, belly to bark, all four feet dangling,
deep in dreams — there was a wind — of flying. Under the
        apple tree where we'd scoured the lawn of dead fall
every morning, tossing the bird-pecked or worm-wracked fruit
to the horses, keeping the best to be baked at dinner, apples lay
        half-eaten, fallen from the weight
of a bear in the branches. The weight of our staring woke him —
        the ears twitched first, the head turned, wary
– and he looked at us, knew us for neither dogs nor climbers,
        turned then and curled in perfect balance nose to
belly, though it looked so precarious, that rough cradle,
        twilight come
and the wind rising. Sometime later in the dark we heard the
        quick rasp of claws, saw the butt —

scoot of shadow into the aspens.

Morning brought us furred fruit in the tree, cider-musk of bear
        pelt and apples ripe for
the plucking, and that audible *crunch*, teeth in firm flesh, claws
        raking through branches, *more*,
more, the muffled thud of fruit shaken loose by this dance of
        appetite. Each little while
the kenneled dogs would catch his scent, and bark, hurtling him
        down in a mad rush and up again into the safety of pine,
though as the morning wore on his ascents lost altitude —
        he was executing a courtesy, interrupting
his hunger, little diplomat in negotiation of dignified retreats.

For three days our faces, pressed to the glass, were so close to
                              his that we saw his lips lift,
his tongue curl, his nostrils open like flowers to bee-scent of
                              sweetness, our bear, growing fat
and sleek before us, whose ribs when he came had been visible,
                     yearling cub cast out to forage
for ghost berries blackened in bloom by late frost. No food,
                              nothing, and the bears had been
coming for weeks down into our yards and driveways, walking
                     like men to peer through screens, starvation's
ache precluding caution. We knew a neighbor had shot one
                              already, hustled
the corpse to the taxidermist — God help him if he doesn't
                              use the meat.

Day after day our harvest brought in, stored in a barn of bear
                     fat, we watched him, how little different he was
from us when he stretched for the last and most crimson globes,
                     when he tiptoe reached for the highest branches,
such slender branches, how could they hold him? Acrobat,
                     gymnast, he walked the limbs more gracefully
than ground, weightless save for sleep's heaviness gathering
                     him up, late afternoon heat and his bed in the pine,
how he yawned and nodded and fell away from us.

Tomorrow he'll snuffle the naked grass, look one last time to
                     the emptied branches — as if the pain of desire
could fill them. If I were the answerer of prayers, I'd fill them.
                     He'll go down hill to the broken orchard, apples
sparse and bitter but better than none. The bulls will chase him,
                     and the thick magpies carry every dropped bite
away. He'll eat what he can against tides of hunger, and soon
                     enough, the cold will come.

Grace

It's like coming out of the trees and into
the rocky meadow, careless and noisy and your mind
not where it should be, not *here*,
so you trip on stones and the supple willows
whip the backs of your legs and you swear,
awful words you almost mean. But the deer
only look up startled at their fellows,
blink six pairs of chocolate eyes to clear
their vision, and they don't run away; they find,
these lovely beasts, that after all it's only *you* —
and they don't run away. They bend to the sweet grass
as if you were not the enemy, as if with your distractedness
and your clumsy body and your anger you were
as integral, as whole as they are.

Mad Alyce In October

I. Altars

There was a hard freeze in April, and the blossoms fell,
ivory coins of fragrant, silken snow; and again
in August, so this year's crop of apples comes to us
brown-blood-red and small enough to clench
inside a fist. But sweet. The way we used to sink
the stems of white carnations into colored
water — that's how wild crimson seeps
into the butter-hue of maples. The tamarack
are goldgreen and when the wind blows, their soft
needles rain, and longer brown ones
from the drought-starved pines; and cones blow
down, too, crash and rattle loud as bombs
against the cabin roof. I burn them. They explode
inside the stove and the room smells clean
as when my grandmother once washed down
her walls and floors with Pine Sol against
the tomby odors of the cold. Aspen, alder,
willow, poplar, all gone gold
along the hillsides in the deepest
folds of soil and stone where water
flows most easily, sinks deep. Out of those
same channels in the earliest morning
mist smokes up to clothe the trees in silver.
Underfoot each step's crushed crystal —
grass so stiff with hoar it breaks like glass.
Where you can't see them, hunters have already
sent lightning up to pluck birds from the air,
gutted the first small deer and left its entrails
in a steaming pile — an offering to the magpies

and the crows, it's only right — so few gods
are left that we might gives things to, bone
and blood, things we'd know they wanted.

II. The Lovers

It was in a field like this, the grasses a gold
tangle of barley and timothy and bird-sown
weeds, worn fence posts leaning against the blue brisk air, strands
of broken barbedwire as insubstantial in their
support of anything as memory. Here and
there were wild roses ruddy with hip fruit, and some
low shrub so fiery orange it burned your eyes if
you looked too long. Late meadowlarks and goldfinches
called out so sweet that summer almost answered. Then
suddenly the shell of sky cracked open — a hawk
fell like stone, air whistling through her tight feathers, head
first until the last moment when her talons whipped
out — and then she hit the ground, screaming. And was still.
I'd heard no gunshot, the sky was cloudless — no god
cast thunderbolts at this bird who, living, claimed all
heaven home. She raised her head, then, breast soaked bloody,
and clasped close the rabbit she had struck clean in half.
The rear legs twitched, a dream of running caught in the
severed tendons; but its head lolled against the red-
tail's downy breast, the nervous ears quiet, the bright
eyes closed. Mantled by soft wings it rested; it had
never been afraid. Her hooked beak bent to its red
task — she ripped fine ribbons of fur away to reach
underlying muscle, broke those quick bones for the
marrow. Hunger married them — hunger's always at
the root of consummation. When it was done, the
hawk preened her feathers, stretched a crook out of her neck,
spread gorse-gold wings to catch the damp wind rising out

of the river. And she was a little clumsy,
fat, the load of flesh and souls in her belly not
quite balanced — rabbit leap was in her heartbeat, some
part of her still hurtled wingless towards the stones. The
grass had parted like a yellow sea for her! Blood
wedding music rang the chambered hollows of her
bones. I watched until she found a roost in the high
dense branches of a fir, until they and darkness
closed over her. The field was quiet, save for soft
whispers of mice, bird clatter in the chokecherries.
A poor-will. Larks cuddled in their nests. Rabbits crept
out to feed in the purple dusk as though nothing
had happened, pink noses atwitch with the heady
fragrances of clover, long ears listening for
fox fall, weasel foot, owl wing white against the air.

When Asked if I am Married. . .

When asked if I am married, I say no; I have a sweetheart, a life-companion, but there are no legal documents between us — and so my answer is a true one. But it is also a lie — I am married to dust. I am a polygamist — I am married to wind, to bitter winter, to the smell of sage after rain on the breaks above Powder River, to cattle struck by lightning and the coyotes who feast on the carcasses, scatter the bones. I am married to voices I have not heard in nearly a decade, to hands cracked by weather, to faces screwed into a perpetual squint from sunlight brighter than heaven. I am made one flesh with gnarled cottonwoods and stones and sheep, and I have swallowed earth so that the grit of the country around Powder River would stick in my cells, would never leave me, would pull me back to it if I went away.

I was born in Wyoming, in the southeast corner, in Cheyenne, a city child with the luck to have large yards front and back, a park within walking distance, a cemetery across the street where I learned to walk, to ride my bicycle, to cool my body against carved stones.

I had a house, of course, but I knew early on where I lived — in the grass. Under the graveyard pines. At the edge of a pond catching crawdads with bacon on a string. I also lived on paper, with a pencil in my hand. But the page and the place were never truly separate — I was in both at once, always.

There are people — most people, perhaps — who do not feel this sort of connection to a place or to any place. That is not to say that they do not feel at home — they seem, from my perspective, to have some kind of home inside them which they are able to unpack at any given destination; or else to have the ability to be everywhere at home, to quickly send out tendrils and grow into whatever country they arrive in, almost as if they are native to it.

I have left Wyoming numerous times — twice for two or three years to attend universities; frequently for weeks and

months at a time in my work as a poet-in-residence in schools
and communities throughout the Rocky Mountain West. I found
that my linkage to place was to some degree extensible. It was a
way of being in the world; and if I entered the doors to canyons
or walked out in search of the buffalo herd on a tiny Alaskan
island, I did not feel myself an interloper or a stranger. I had a
place of reference, and I had the growing landscape of the pages
on which I wrote; and I had books by other writers whose true
homes were the places I visited, and was by that means lent eyes
and ears and voices of welcome. And there was this: I always left
with the intention of returning. I was a traveler, not an exile.

The place I came to know most intimately in Wyoming
extended east and west along Highway 14-16 between Gillette
and Sheridan, north to the border with Montana, south past
Arvada and Buffalo: Powder River Country. For sixteen years I
lived on the northwestern end of Bob and Connie Moore's 7UP
Ranch, more as guest than tenant, so small was the rent. It was
there I learned that place is more than land and water — it is
faces, voices, people whose whole lives, and often the lives of
parents and grandparents, had been spent on the same acres. "A
hundred years of the same damn hundred miles of fenceline and
it still ain't fixed!" was how one of my neighbors put it, showing
me how to fix fence on my own.

I was the recipient there of a miraculous grace — I was
allowed in. I helped brand, dock sheep, look for lost stock. I got
"set up" on a tricky cutting horse, laughed at when we parted
company, was dusted off and shown which way to lean. I sat at
Joe's Place and played cribbage, I worked at the school and the
tiny post office, and everywhere people told me stories — gossip
and history, geography and sorrow, trusting me to keep them, to
be a link in the chain.

The links I forged were poems, and these people who rarely
read, except for newspapers, read them and explained that I had
Pumpkin Butte in the wrong place, or asked, "How is that a
poem if it don't rhyme?" But at the next branding, someone who
didn't know would be admonished that "She ain't no hired hand,
she's a writer." I imagined never leaving.

But I did leave. In the early '90s I moved to a tiny cabin in the woods twenty miles south of Missoula to be with a man I loved. It was a different and difficult transition, because returning was not a part of the equation. We laugh now over the filthy temper I was in the day I finally had to trade in my Wyoming license plates, or my tears over the trees being in the way of the stars. "So buy 'er a clearcut!" was the solution offered by an acquaintance. Although not totally ignorant of the variety of Rocky Mountain flora and fauna, there were too many — to borrow from a poem of David Romtvedt's — "flower(s) whose names I did not know". And I found myself, for the first time, silenced — I sat down to write and was unable to. I felt cut off, disconnected, displaced, a stranger and unable to speak; and every blank page was an alien country I no longer knew how to enter.

A lucky thing happened, though it did not seem so then. I was unable to find work. So I stayed home — alone at first, and soon with one dog and then another. Not all of the ten-acre plots in these woods are occupied by houses, and some that are have friendly neighbors, and so I walked them. I became an addict of field guides, a taster of a profusion of mushrooms that mostly didn't look poisonous, a moss sniffer, a helper in the felling of trees. I learned the different snow the woods quite literally filled up with, and I began to distinguish birds from branches, to call owls in at twilight to the snag across the meadow. My mimicry was imperfect, but they came to the longing. And suddenly — it seemed suddenly — I was writing again. The unfamiliar forest crept into the ink, the paper smells of leaf rot and apples, and this place began to seem like one of the attic rooms of home.

So it should be no surprise to anyone that my writing is considered regional, both by myself and others. There are some in the writing community who consider that term to be a derogatory one, synonymous with "limited" or "not as good as" writing or writers that seem, at first glance, more general in their contexts. But to me the "regional" has always, in the intensity of its detailing of the particular, struck that resonance in me which I cannot help but believe that all writers aim for: it spoke to me where I lived, in my prairie-entangled heart. I recognized Miss Welty's characters at the Arvada store, I knew cottonwood and box elder as Faulkner knew live oaks; more recently I have found Frost's woods in my own.

It's both humorous and ironic that many of those who espouse that diminished opinion of regionalism are those who jumped eagerly onto the bandwagon of "The West" and the marketing of the heavily romanticized and often outright false images and concepts of it prevalent in American popular culture. "Western" writers were suddenly quite the thing, and more than a few of us got published by fortunate accident who might not have been noticed otherwise.

The literary world is also fortunate in that most of those writers were out to set the record straight, to rip off those "riding-off-into-the-glowing-sunset" colored glasses and make readers take a look at a way of living and a beauty that were harsh and dangerous and not at all romantic. Out here, winter can kill you. So can your most beloved horse. Children slip into grain bins and suffocate. A bum lamb runs to the farm house, bleating and carrying on until the wife comes to the door of the kitchen, sees her husband lying in the field. A heart attack. (He lived. That lamb they may not butcher.)

C. L. Rawlins

C. L. Rawlins, a native of Laramie, Wyoming, has been featured as a poet in various journals including *Ploughshares, Poetry Ireland Review, Poetry Wales, Chicago Review, Cumberland Poetry Review and Quarterly West.* His first book of poems, *A Ceremony on Bare Ground,* was followed by a Stegner Fellowship to Stanford University. A second collection, *In Gravity National Park,* received the 1992 Neltje Blanchan Memorial Award, a 1996 Wyoming Arts Council Literary Fellowship, and the 1999 regional book award from the Mountains and Plains Booksellers Association. He is the author of three nonfiction books: *Sky's Witness: A Year in the Wind River Range; Broken Country: Mountains and Memory;* and *The Complete Walker IV* with Colin Fletcher. He has two books in progress, a natural history of mountain streams and an essay collection. His prose has also appeared in *The Bloomsbury Review, North American Review, High Country News, Northern Lights, Sierra, Hungry Mind Review,* and *Western American Literature,* and in anthologies such as *American Nature Writing,* 1998. He has worked as a firefighter, range foreman, range rider, field hydrologist, editor, and teacher.

From *In Gravity National Park*

Eleison

You could go mad in these pines.
Trappist lodgepoles, crowded,
shift, and only moan or sigh.
Stand, standing, never waiting,
not in judgment nor in resignation,
with their dead all barked and bleached and mulching,
heaped like wheatstraw coarse about their feet.

And the wind breathes hard,
shovel-cold, uncomforting,
with no familiar reeks and memories,
hollow boxcars down the snowfield
in a flood of nothing. Clouds tear back,
above, cathedrals, granite wings and spires,
walls in which are cracks, no doors,
which only lead you up, across, along,
to lose you in the sky. Holy water
bleeding from the glacier, murky,
runneling through scree and shattered gravel
swells and freezes every clot of moss.
Wet boots, summits drowned
in roaring cloud. *In excelsis Deo.*
Cold enough to kill up here.

Huddled in this broken field, *Kyrie,*
the crevice seeming warm, though only still,
under talus big as houses buried in the wind;
the goddamn years it takes to lift a mountain;
in these bodies, mine and yours,
how precious little heat.

— *Mount Bonneville, Wyoming*

In Rock Springs,
There Will be a Reading

on the equinox. I take the poems that I'll return
to a writer just divorced, whose mother died
last year. She broods on youth and disillusionment.

The first hour, north of Eden, the desert folds like memory,
holding remnant snow on sheltered slopes; all else is dry.
The road's black curve is long and slow, the sky recedes,

blue ebb along the horizontal coast.
On the peaks, the snowline's high for March. Recollection
says late April, even May: an augury of smoke,

forests rising up in flame, and losses counted high.
My tires trace the asphalt line between small towns
with smaller reason to be here, maps of wish and lie.

The road's fenced — for every mile, three hundred posts,
four braces and one gate. Barbed wire glistens and the ravens
scatter as my shadow flies above their carrion smear–

a red blot with a jutting leg, a rabbit's ear. Cretaceous sand,
and yellow shale and gray, the Mesozoic beds of coal that hump
high to the east, the Rock Springs Uplift, pierced with mines,

shrugs the highway down its bellyseam. Of soda ash,
methane, oil, uranium, the troubled harvest of all things,
this urge, my going where I will, an envelope

of poems upon the seat. Divorce, democracy, and doubt.
Land where my father died. Of thee, and not alone, I sing.

— *Boulder/Farson/Eden/Rock Springs*

Drinking in the Space

I come here for faces,
voices, glances, bodies full of blood.

All day aspens emptied out the sky,
gold tatters spinning down 'til only twigs
were left to finger the impending blue.

Clouds breathed one word: snow.
You could clamp the taste of storm
between your molars, wind

kicked willow leaves, bruise-brown,
across the sand to nest in shadow
under sage, a pillow for the cold.

The house, a vacuum, darker
than the space between two stars, atmosphere
too thin to hold an echo or a wife

says: you don't live here
and you never did, and I know nothing
of your history, your life.

Twelve miles to church
and two miles to the bar, I worship
close to home, a being

I can touch, a god who
goes to work each day,
a goddess, bourbon on her breath

who has strong wrists from bucking hay,
who raises sparks from wornout denim, nips your earlobe,
draws you from the close and smoky temple,

from the brief embrace of light, urgently
out through the bootscarred door
under the hovering storm, into the night.

– Boulder, Wyoming

Grace
for Leonard

The kids endure him,
better now than he, himself.
He won't disclose how old
he's grown in pain, what each breath costs,
the shame; can't tell his secret
any more than a leg-broke horse
could tell him.

He's seen it a thousand times: the gelding
butchered in the barbs, head bowed
to the bloody grass; the cow far gone,
heaving at a dead breach calf;
blue heeler kicked by a broody mare,
dragging dead legs.

What doctoring won't save, you spare
indignity: coyotes circle in, the ravens
peck still-seeing eyes. Can't make it good,
that awful patience, when a bullet
is the only gift. Death looks
to him as he must have looked
to any animal in pain: sudden,
looming black against the light.

He's read a book or two, named his rifle
Misery Cord and hefted its cold weight,
flinched at the blast, at his image fixed
in the mirrors of those eyes,
the shock and then the cloudy calm —
how many times? Seen
that last, quivering breath fly off,

and silence beckoning
beyond the deed.

                                       – Boulder, Wyoming

Solvay Trona Mine, June 30, 1994

The cage drops fast, through zones of deposition
hung on humming steel rope in squared-off dark.
As underfoot, through steel grate, a light
glows yellow 1600 feet below the ground.
As we fall towards the earth-remembered sea
and hear in shouts, the customs of the mine.

The dustman, with a dust moustache, has mined
gold, coal and trona — intrusions and deposits.
Clotted magma, crystallized rot, evaporite seas,
slow-processed wonders in the heavy dark,
each age pressed thin and carried underground,
laid like quilts in bedrooms without light.

The cage cries out and stops. The yellow stranger, light,
does not belong, nor we — tourists in the rumbling mine.
Our eyes are stung with glare and crystals finely ground,
salt and carbonate from shallow oceans, dried, deposited,
welded like brown glass, the content of earth's dark.
We board a red jeep diesel truck to sail the buried sea.

He drives, too fast. "Two miles," he shouts. We see
cables writhing overhead, roof-bolts blurred, lights
boring, tunneling the hot and powdery dark.
Eyes. He backs into a side-cut as the whole mine
roars. A tractor forks a steel knuckle by: "Deposit
for the welding shop," he says, "here, underground."

"The miner's law," shouts Moses in the underground.
"Take too much, and the roof falls in." And ancient seas
rush back. We follow a tunnel through the brown deposit
into mayhem: a shuttle swerves and barges into light
to puke on the howling belt. I catch a fragment — mine —
and bow to these machines, assembled in their self-made dark.

Pulsing dust, the thing he calls *The Miner* chops raw darkness,
guided by red laser beams, two tall discs harrowing the ground,
it booms and spews its broken harvest back to the mine,
boring a double circle, **OO** , carving a floor with chain. Y'see
that cable? There. Step *on* it when you cross. *Never* shine a light
in a miner's eye." "How far," I yell, "does it run — the deposit?"

"Farther than you'd wanna go," he says. "This old deposit
might outlast us both — years down here." We breathe their dark,
and shrink into a drift as a shuttle hammers by. He goes. My headlight
dims, then dies. I fumble with it, far from my home ground,
as they walk away and turn a corner, go. Then, I smell the sea:
salt and carbonate, fear and methane, ocean's mind.

My light is dead. I stumble through the mine
dismayed, imagining fish eyes in deposition,
shuffling on a dusty floor no longer seen,
under black-nerved cables, as the hot, impounded dark,
floods back to claim this pillared underground —
and long for sharp, sweet, windy, burnished light.

Every miner learns the lack of light,
how long bones yearn, more gravity than mind,
for mineral bliss — the estuary and the deepening ground,
the comfort of all clumsy form deposited,
all dread and hunger given to the dark.
Earth-locked, I smell the rank breath of the sea,

And run, and corner blind towards a voice and see
legged silhouettes, a lurching porcupine of light;
as at my back, in sweat along my spine, darkness
calls the black eventuality that's mine,
black puddle with a leather glove deposited,
all memory in the hard and holy ground,

Broken, belted, hoisted, fired, and ground
for soap, toothpowder, soda, glass, and wine. See
the jeep? See us crowd in tight? The air's deposit
stings our eyes, haunts us as we roll toward the light
and tongue dry lips, taste blood, the blush of mind
in mindless ages, moving through rich days and darks.

Braced against ourselves, in stiff, dark
coveralls, we board the cage, fly through the ground.
But the miners say you never leave the mine.
Its ore spins in your blood; under sky you see
rock walls and feel earth's burden, cherish light
in passing, love as air; know death as a deposit.

All joy and pain deposited, and married to the dark.
O house thick-thatched against light's rain. Powers underground!
We rise from the old sea's mouth.
            A cloud floats free above the mine.

— Little America, Wyoming

Note: Six months after my visit, on February 3, 1995, nearly one square mile of the Solvay Mine caved in. The shock registered Richter 5.3, and according to the U.S. Bureau of Mines was "one of the largest mining-related seismic events ever recorded." Fifty-three miners were on shift and ten were injured. Two were trapped for several days before they were found and one, Michael Anderson, twenty-six, died before reaching the surface. It was later reported that for several years the support pillars had been decreased in size, or "shaved," to increase production.

"Enter My Dreams, Love"

after a line by Czeslaw Milosz

In our slow-growing year,
with frost in every month,
I left the grass unmowed,

let the narrow forage build,
moon by moon, watched
seedheads form. Refuges
are few in this cold light,
our history, the close of sky
with low, blue cloud, a storm
that will not stay. Thin flakes
hold the air, hide mountains,
senseless, repetitious power.

As snowbacked heifers gather
to the fence, crop the tawn thatch
softening with fallen sky,

sleek and shaggy, rust and black
and cream beneath the white,
a cottontail comes under the wire,

under the low pine rail, stops
and settles, sees the inner yard
for what it is: grass, uncut and free,

small courage spared the whirling
knives. In other years, less hard,
I kept it neat, watched rabbits starve,

kept mine and winter's count.
In love or dream the world,
if we are lucky, is begun;

in snow or unmown grass,
a wish that one thing live
for one thing left undone.

– Boulder, Wyoming

Staking the Ditches

The patch of earth is seven paces wide, and sixteen long. The old furrows ran the wrong way, down the hill, and when we turned the water in it flowed fast, making little v-waves. At the bottom of each row it left sand, scalloped with black organic soil.

Since my family came West, in the 1840s, irrigation has been closer to our lives than politics or religion, so the second year I wanted to get the ditches right. The object was to dig new rows across the fall of the slope so that the water would lie slack. On the northeast corner, I drove a stake with two lines scribed a foot apart. I tied cotton string at the top mark and knelt on the grass, by the windbreak hedge of wild rose.

I took a line-level, a little tube with a bubble and two hooks, to suspend it from the string. With three wraps around a willow stick, notched a foot from the end, I pulled the string taut. Then I moved the stick downslope until the bubble centered on the line: Good. I reached for a stake and whacked it in, to mark the first row.

Resetting the stringline for each row, I dug and raked, feeling the sun on my neck. The ground was dark and moist, but by the time I reached the end, the starting point was a lighter color, already dry After it dried, I raked it again to break up the clods and then planted, and turned the water in. As it filled each row, I set old bricks and glacial cobbles into little spillways until the current slowed and the water formed a mirror for the sky.

Where did I learn this? I can see my father, in jeans and a white, broadcloth shirt, staking a ditch in just this way. He had a slight, intent smile that made me think: *this is the heart of something. Remember.*

For settlers in the arid West, staking ditches was the first step. In the 1840's Harvey McGalyard Rawlins and Margaret Frost turned water out of Big Cottonwood Creek where it issues from the wall of the Wasatch Range. My great grandfather,

Harvey Mack, Jr., was born there, December, 1851. He moved north to Cache Valley, married Rebecca Lewis and staked his own ditches in Shoshoni ground. Like water, memory has flow and direction, and the power to carry the various fractions of what we come to know as ourselves, or on the other hand, to silt them over, out of sight.

Despite the time and care I've given to this ground, I don't own it. I rent this place from a rancher. In curious fact, I have a fear of owning land, and that is memory, too. In 1921, my grandparents owned several tracts of farmland and ran large herds of cattle and sheep on range in Utah, Idaho and Wyoming. That same year the market plunged and they lost all but the home place. That may be what turned my father away from ranching and farming and into cynicism and reaction.

In American memory there likewise runs a deep and turbulent current of dispossession: of European homelands lost or taken, of the Enclosure Acts, of transportation and indenture. Because England saw its colonies as dumping grounds for English felons, most of them impoverished thieves — there is a fierce craving for property at the very root of our selfhood.

A century ago, Frederick Jackson Turner wrote:

> " . . . the frontier is the outer edge of the wave — the meeting point between savagery and civilization.
> "The existence of an area of free land, its continuous recession, and the advance of American settlement westward, explain American development."

Historian Patricia Nelson Limerick said recently that, "Turner, in 1893, seemed to have the field of Western American history fully corralled, unified under the concept 'frontier.'" In *The Legacy of Conquest,* she writes:

> "Frontier, then, is an unsubtle concept in a subtle world. . . . If we give

up a preoccupation with the frontier and
look instead at the continuous sweep of
Western American history, new organizing
ideas await our attention, but no simple,
unitary model . . . Reorganized, the history
of the West is a study of a place undergoing
conquest and never fully escaping its
consequences."

In this high, cold, arid basin, the rectilinear yeomanry of the Homestead Act was an immediate failure. The many failed ranches were taken over by the most aggressive settlers until they were large enough to include a working mix of irrigable stream corridors and rangelands.

But even this patchwork of fenced properties exists at odds with the grassy, windy country itself, which is best suited to free-roaming herds of bison, pronghorn, and elk. Some ranchers, ingenious and lucky like our landlord, have done well. But others struggle terribly to maintain possession through ranching, of a land which does not favor it.

The log ranchhouse was built by a family named Bergen. Their first cabin burned and they used the scorched logs to support the floor of the second. When I go to the cellar, the charred joists are an elemental reminder of loss.

This garden patch, says the landlord, grew truck for local stores before the time of all-weather roads and semi-trailers. His youngest son and daughter-in-law lived here. "We put tons of manure in that ground," she said. Outside the garden, it takes a steel bar to dig a posthole. Inside, we can dig potatoes with bare hands. This year we planted three kinds of potatoes and four of lettuce, onions, garlic, peas, carrots, beets, kohlrabi, cauliflower, kale, spinach, and chinese cabbage: plants that will stand a summer frost. The greenhouse, scratch-built, holds tomatoes, peppers, and herbs. North of the house, the Boulder ditch follows the base of the hill, giving out into smaller ditches that flood the meadows of native grass hay. Since I've been able to choose, where I live has meant as much as life itself.

"Turner's frontier was a process, not a place," writes Limerick. "In rethinking Western history, we gain the freedom to think of the West as a place. . . occupied by natives who considered their homelands to be the center, not the edge."

The earliest human sign found here dates back twelve thousand years, perhaps a shallow estimate. About 1,500 years ago the ancestors of the Navajo and Apache may have passed through on their way south, since ceramics in their distinctive style were found nearby. But if the basin of the upper Green belonged to anyone, it was to the Shoshoni, who keep a reservation on their old wintering grounds in the lower and warmer Wind River Valley to the east. Extreme winter cold and capricious weather made the upper Green River a risky spot for hunters and gatherers.

Irrigation and the rifle, among other tricks, make it easier to stay here. On the east slope, the Shoshoni also irrigate and hunt with rifles. Sixteen years ago, I spent a summer camped out with a Shoshoni crew, building log fence on the national forest. We worked hard, cooked frybread and stew, and joked, but there was an underlying tension that will persist as long as memory. By virtue of conquest, I live on land that once was theirs.

haven't hunted for a few years, since the deer and antelope were scarce, but now the herds are growing and a wet spring has greened the desert. This is the other part of my memory, my other link to this place, which has given me not only potatoes and greens, but wild meat. From the house we could walk to the spots where I hunt: I remember each animal, alive and dead, and the place I found it. And I remember, as one thing, the land and the life we take from it.

Not all of my people were ranchers or farmers. My mother's father, Frank Christian Torkelson, was the son of a Norwegian immigrant who became a mining engineer. His first job was at Goldfield, Nevada, now a ghost town. He married Mabel Reed, of English stock, an alto in the Mormon Tabernacle Choir. When he started his own business, he kept notes in a leather covered fieldbook and used a fountain pen with a fine point and black ink to write, on the first page, "F. C. Torkelson, General Engineering, 159 Pierpont St., Salt Lake City, Utah."

On the second page is a date, "June 1, 1924." Below are sketches and labels: "Crude ore bin 7"x11" Jaw crusher. 10 — stamps. #54 Ball Mill." The page is divided by four dots, three lines. Then, "Ore : 0.4 oz. gold, 20% Pyrite, grind 70% — 200 mesh, 36 hour agitation 2 to 1, 50 ton plant."

There are names and addresses in Los Angeles, Vancouver, London, and Oslo. There are diagrams, equations, dates, and prices. Between the last pages are two red three-cent Canadian stamps, unused, with a king's head in profile. Near the end, I read: "The only real joy of possession is the power which it confers for a larger life of service. Sir Wilfred Grenfell."

My mother, Helen, was born in Anaconda, Montana, in the shadow of the huge brick stack, and she grew up in mining towns all over the West. My grandfather, an apostle of boom-and-bust, wore a gray Homburg and a vest with a gold watchchain. He also read, fished with a split bamboo rod, photographed deer with his Leica, and gave every indication of kindness. For him the verbs of mining — dig, blast, bolt, load, crush — reached their apex in words like joy, power and service. It no longer seems that way to me.

Years ago, I went to a meeting in Jackson Hole on the fate of the West. In our company were writers and thinkers — Harrison, Hogan, Kittredge, Limerick, Lyon, Matthiessen, Merwin, Lopez, Nichols, Ortiz, and Zwinger. The expenses were paid by a private grant. The woman who poured the wine had flown in from Santa Fe.

My bad back — the legacy of horse wrecks and eighty-pound packs — woke me early, so I walked. In the halflight, under pines, I saw a strange flower. I hastened up the slope, only to find red survey flagging on a spike. The forest was ready to be sold.

Later, we talked about the frontier myth. I remember asking how we might change some of our ideas — frontier, enemies, and money — while preserving what binds us. There was a moment of silence. Then someone changed the subject and we talked on, a comforting herd-sound. The scent of lamb and rosemary drifted from the kitchen. And outside the window, in the pines, the red plastic flagging rattled in the breeze.

I take refuge in what I see: the water flowing in these ditches, falling over impediments of rock and scarred brick, some soaking in and most proceeding on. Yet the substance of memory is not so much like water as the sediment it moves: dark incidents, faceted grains of experience, hard fragments cracked from the human bedrock.

When I first wrote to Patricia Limerick after reading *The Legacy of Conquest*, I said that her version accorded with the late-night tales I heard, my child's ear pressed to the crack under the kitchen door. In daylight we all nodded to the faith-promoting legends, but by night I heard of the failures, the bad uncle who hung himself from the hay derrick, the embittered wives who'd been set aside, the hidden deposit of our frontier life.

My first summer in the mountains I was obsessed with water — the sudden pulse of snowmelt, the splash of rain from broken limestone, the gather of rivulets, the brawl of steep streams over toppling beds, and the calm dark of mountain lakes. The mountains were dangerous, but they never lied. And I learned to trust the water, and the way it goes.

Water is the universal solvent and gravity the universal tug. And these aspects of memory — its fluid nature and its momentum — overpower our grasp of specifics. That is, all memory is not necessarily true, nor is truth necessarily memorable.

It's a problem I can't pretend to solve, but now I know this: all decisions are personal. And that's why I write, and how I write. It's like staking these ditches and planting and turning the water in; I try to hold a little back, and then let it go.

Part Three

No West

"Because he lived in an arid locale where the nearest water was a day's ride away, many of his daydreams concerned the ocean, which he had never seen."

– From Will Murray's unpublished biography of pulp-fiction writer Lester Dent, who spent his formative years (1912-1918) as an only child growing up on a ranch in Wyoming's Powder River Basin.

Vicki Lindner

Vicki Lindner is a fiction writer, essayist, and journalist. Before joining the English Department of the University of Wyoming, where she is an associate professor and director of the visiting writer program, she worked as a freelance and fiction writer in New York City for twenty years. She is the author of the novel *Outlaw Games*, and co-author of a nonfiction book about the psychological relationship of women and money, *The Money Mirror: How Money Reflects Women's Dreams, Fears, and Desires*. She has also published short stories, essays, travel pieces and articles in a wide variety of magazines and anthologies. Her award-winning short fiction has recently appeared in *Ploughshares, Fiction, Witness, Chic-Lit:Post Feminist Fiction* and *The Kenyon Review*. Her essays and travel pieces — many about the west — have been published in *Northern Lights, The South Dakota Review, Grand Tour, Frontiers: Journal of Women Studies, In Short: An Anthology of Short Creative NonFiction, The American Literary Review*, the *Sonora Review*, and *Gastronomica*. Her essays and fiction have also appeared in Web literary magazines such as *Terrain* and *Web Del Sol*. Lindner has received grants for her fiction and non-fiction from the National Endowment for the Arts, New York State Foundation for the Arts, and the Wyoming Arts Council. Her work has been selected for the PEN Syndicated Fiction Project, featured as "Fiction Premier" in *New York Woman* magazine, and cited by the Pushcart Prize and *Best American Essays 1995*. She has taught writing workshops at the Ossining Correctional Facility, the Naropa Institute, the Brockport Writer's Forum, and to teenagers and adults throughout Wyoming.

Lonely in Wyoming

Last October my neighbor moved away. She stored her valuables at Mother's, had Norb drain her pipes, took her swishing Pomeranian and the accordion she played at the Cake Auction down at the bar. She was headed for Nevada to get back into gold mining. She showed me a photo of the square-jawed machine she knew how to operate. Trained men to operate it, too! She said she'd be back every chance she got — this country was home. That fall her mint-colored house, blankets nailed over the windows, shared its blind non-animation with the summer cabins overlooking the Big Laramie River in my rural community, twenty-nine miles from the nearest small town. I barely knew the neighbor; we had chatted only about pets and houseplants. Yet, with winter in the margins of my forty-eighth year, the smokeless butt of her frozen chimney made me feel more alone.

For most of my life I have lived, worked, and traveled alone. My solitary state, atypical for females, has always evoked astonishment. Once, in an Ecuadorian museum, a family of five stared, then cried their dismayed question: "*Sola?*" Alone? Believing binges of seclusion nurtured novels, I wrote three on Sunday mornings while civilized New Yorkers communed at brunch. For dues, solitude has demanded some fearful moments:

In 1982 I wrote in an eight-room North Carolina farmhouse, known to locals as a "cold block." When the honeysuckle bloomed, a stranger, who, it turned out, had just murdered a drug dealer, rammed his hot rod into my bumblebee-ridden porch, hollering, "C'mon out, Jimmy, I'll take you to the Cyclone!" As I brandished my ax behind the rotting screen door, I remained aware that my life was unique. New varieties of aloneness have proved educational. Thus, my first week in Wyoming I drove, unaccompanied, to a remote canyon called "Outlaw Hole" and crouched out a lightning storm under a low bush, as *Adventuring in the Rockies* suggested I should. Of course I never married. Marriage, said the writer, Alastair Reid, is for people who prefer any irritation to being alone. Until recently I agreed with this: Alastair never spent a winter on the Big Laramie River, watching dogs chew up a mule deer trapped in the ice.

I was comfortable with solitude until I found myself in Wyoming, lonely as well as alone. Although I lacked the endurance for family life, I thought I possessed sufficient flexibility for multiple friendships. Before I moved West, I made friends, capable of a deep-cutting, explosive intensity, the way some fall in love — at first sight. In New York City I always had between eight and twelve close confidantes. Some I had known twenty years, others a few months. Most were women, as men tended to get sidetracked by more possessive liaisons. Our conversations would begin with trivia — our haircuts, our hassles — then progress straight for the bone. No question or confidence was impermissible. In spite of highly-scheduled lives, our expectations of human society would have been breached if we didn't telephone each other once a week, meet every two or three. Occasionally our conversations, so hotly intimate, festered into arguments. I was not on excellent terms with all my soul mates at once, but rapidly replaced fallouts with vivid new blood.

It isn't so easy to make friends in Wyoming. The fabled Western space stands between people with the inflexible fortitude of China's Great Wall. If you want to see a contained

Wyoming face deconstruct into fury, bump into its body on the street, or knock it with your purse as you squeeze into your rodeo seat. The extra-wide proximics Westerners demand include emotional distance. And they give you the space they expect to get back.

Two years after I moved to Wyoming, a year after my mother died of breast cancer, the radiologist spied an egg-shaped shadow on my mammogram, that no doctor could palpate. Having no sense of privacy and only two secrets, I immediately telephoned the bad news to all my old friends and apprised every Wyomingite I knew of the "phantom tumor." As the tests, trips to the Denver specialist, and anxiety progressed, no Wyomingite ever inquired about my breast, whereas every day I got a commiserating call from a New Yorker. Finally I told a Montana-born woman, who had helped me paint my bedroom — a more tangible gesture of friendship than most cerebral New Yorkers would make — "It looks like I don't have breast cancer after all." She was so glad to hear that, she had wanted to ask, but didn't think she should invade my privacy, she said.

One Laramie friend would do anything for me. Psychologically astute, she provided (requested) advice that enabled me to leave one man for another. On my birthday she sent me a single rose. When I give a lecture or reading, I can count on seeing her receptive face in the audience. If I was dying she would be the first to bear soup. But she would never call just to tell me her news or to ask how I am. What I can say and what she will say in our biannual lunches is circumscribed by her birthright — the prairie's obdurate space.

At first I thought they didn't like me because I was an outsider, because I didn't have children, because I wore black clothes and magenta lipstick, because I complained, said what I thought. Then I realized that whether or not they liked me they didn't subscribe to the Easterner's unspoken rules for female friendship: Consider friends as important as men or family members. Always inquire about the other woman after you've talked about yourself. Pursue conversations to their extreme conclusions. Don't cut off a friend because you fear she might say what you don't want to hear. Listen, and if you feel so inclined, shout, "Shut up, bitch!" Call even if you are busy or depressed. Talk about sex! Minus these rules, women I had deemed insiders were as lonely as some of us outsiders. Western friendships, I learned, did not require risky mutual confidences or consistent contact. In Wyoming you can have a friend for twenty years without knowing the details of her personal life. A "friend" can be a woman whom you lunch with every three months. Most astonishing, for many Western women, one really intimate friendship seems to be enough.

In February my neighbor returned from Nevada to check her cabin. Richard, who had taken advantage of a break in the weather to drive the 180 miles that separate his house from mine, and he and I were theoretically taking a nap, when she burst through my door without knocking, crying distractedly that her little dog was lost. We arose from our *in flagrante delicto*, helped her beat snowdrifts in search of the missing Pomeranian, calling, "Honey! Here, Hon! Honey Lee!"

"She would come if she heard me. . ." the neighbor's voice broke. I was sure the dog had been gobbled by a raptor. "After all I've been through. . . I just can't leave without her!" Her gold-framed glasses mirrored her tears. Finally she found the trembling pet, trapped in a garage. I put my hand on her arm. "I felt for you," I said.

I did understand my neighbor's despair over losing her dog. I would die if anything happened to my cat. I hated cats before I moved to Wyoming. Now, this tensile, marshmallow-colored creature with acute chartreuse eyes is the only sensibility between my self and the wind shattering the icicles. I talk to this animal more than I care to admit. I don't like to be away from him for long. When I return to my cabin on the frozen river, only he waits behind the double-paned glass.

Perhaps I moved to Wyoming because I wanted to experience a more challenging solitude, although I was not conscious of that desire at the time. After two years in the constricting university town, I opted for a shack in the country.

Since the academic dinner parties, where mostly "The Department" was discussed, non-confiding lunches, friendships that began but never progressed,were not satisfying my need for intimate companionship, I thought I might try the spiritual connection with nature, forged in solitude, that is one of the West's fundamental myths. This theme appears in most contemporary Western personal narratives: man or woman, voyaging through natural space, ostensibly by him or herself, unites with a magnificent, threatened, or threatening environment and, in the process, with an essential aspect of him or herself.

I first encountered this myth in the "Western" writer New Yorkers read first: Gretel Ehrlich, a Californian who lived in New York, finds the West's open spaces a solace after a lover's death and while recovering from pneumonia alone on a remote ranch. In one essay she portrays herself setting off on a journey to the source of the Yellowstone River. At first there seems to be another human along, as her sentences include an unspecified "we," but her "we" shrinks to "I" as the Absaroka Mountains' inspirations increase. "Isn't that why I've come here to seek the wildness in myself, and in so doing, come on the wildness everywhere, because. . .I'm part of nature too. . .." Ehrlich doesn't have to ask.

This romantic concept of a personal connection with nature, resulting in a comprehension of self, informs the work of more authentic, subtle Western writers, too. In his book about Wyoming's Wind River Mountains, *Sky's Witness*, C.L. Rawlins declares, "All the real things that make up this place, even the threatening wind, slowly have become part of what I call my self. I don't contain them, since they go on without me, but they have become the vital organs of my thought." And the author of *Refuge*, Terry Tempest Williams, describes solitude in a natural setting as ". . .what sustains me and protects me from my mind. It renders me fully present. I am desert. I am mountains. I am Great Salt Lake. . . We are no more and no less than the life that surrounds us." In Williams' vision, it is intimate connection with the natural environment that obliterates human loneliness, provides the instructive metaphor for harmony with family and community, and, ultimately, acceptance of her mother's death.

For me, an urban outsider, beating through untrammeled sage into selfhood didn't work. Habitual solitude has metamorphosed into isolation, which is different and worse. Isolated in what I see as a wilderness, I have grown progressively less connected to myself, let alone anyone else. I don't reach for the phone, but jump with suspicion when it finally rings. Has my roof caught on fire? After being alone and silent for days, at first I find it difficult to talk. Then I talk too much, or too loud, telling secrets, which makes Westerners uneasy. Isolation makes it problematic to invite an acquaintance to dinner, even assuming I could bribe her with homemade *i ravioli con lo stracotto* to drive fifty-eight slick-in-spots miles through blowing snow. I look up her number, then ask myself if I like her enough to let her into my locked open space. Given our different takes on family values, what will we talk about? I'll surely have to watch my big mouth, be circumspect, tactful. I mustn't complain about being lonely, as that, I've found, turns would-be friends off. I thumb through *Refuge* again, looking for tips. I wonder if Terry Tempest Williams, who acknowledges countless loving friends in the back of her book, has lived alone in the country for more than a month. I'm irritable, tight-headed. I phone Richard obsessively; I pick a fight, argue with his image, then with myself. It becomes obvious to me, if not to researchers, why there are more suicides in the Rocky Mountain region than anywhere else.

The beguiling Western myth provides no consolation. Not only can't I connect with nature, I can barely escape my fevered cabin. From C. L. Rawlins I've learned that it's dangerous to cross-country ski alone in the Wind River Mountains; my dentist's wife has warned me not to do so in the nearby Boy Scout camp. The trailhead to the purple humps of self-absorbed Sheep Mountain is blocked by drifts, and a seventy mile-per-hour gale prohibits a less ambitious, unifying walk. In any case, the neighboring rancher, furious because his cattle bunched up to follow me after I squeezed under his barbed wire fence, told me to get the hell off his splendid private property and stay off. In the dry, crackling sky I see an eagle, an immature golden? Inspiring, but it might eat my best friend, the cat. If you don't like it here, why don't you go back to New York?

Because, for better or worse, you are not exactly a New Yorker anymore. Your isolated confrontation with space has transformed you into an emigrant with no territory to defend, as uncomfortable with the frenzied yipping of coyotes as with caterwauling sirens on the shoe-worn concrete. I have become a woman who talks too much, yet who carries the silence of winters in a wood-heated shack inside herself like a fertilized seed that might sprout in a season of greater patience. Because when my New York visitor, hanging her damp underwear all over the house, described how the jagged contours of her boyfriend's anatomy had mangled her insides on their camping trip, before I began to feel delighted, I felt a little shocked. Almost invaded.

In Wyoming, a boom and bust state, friends depart, taking with them the betrayed desire for friendship of those who remain. Since I moved here in 1988, Sheila left, then Diane, as those intimacies were about to blossom, and last summer Laura, who had made the complex transition from student to friend, finally left, too. As we said goodbye I, who weep only when angry, surprised myself by breaking into uncontrollable, honking sobs. I had taken her — perhaps all the friends I'd ever had — for granted; I couldn't imagine life without her quirky revelations and tireless receptivity a local call away. Here, maybe anywhere, she could not be replaced.

Now, most of my Wyoming friends live in other parts of the state. In the void of daily confidences, which female friendships require to take root, distance does not necessarily make our hearts grow fonder. After months of non-contact, we sometimes have to start from the beginning. Did we really like each other the first time we met? On the other hand, the longer I stay here (and the more I mutate), the more I am privy to a cautious trust. Just as I resigned myself to life without what I think of as friendship, the confidences of women I've known for five years are thrown down like medieval gauntlets. ("I'm

writing a novel and don't you dare tell a soul!") And —
something new — I have useful friendships, occasional but
intense, with married male writers.

In June the neighbor reoccupied her cabin. Along with
her guitar and the bouncing Pomeranian, she brought back a
man. Having almost mastered Wyoming reticence, I asked no
questions, but I gathered that gold mining in Nevada hadn't
worked out. Soon the man rode out on the horse he rode in on,
but that, you bet, was none of my business. One fall day the
neighbor summoned me in. "I'm only telling you. . ." she said in
a thrilled whisper, then confided that the Nevada job had finally
come through! I responded like any New York woman
well-trained in friendship — with pleasure and excitement, as if
her good news was my good news—aware, as I did, that the
neighbor would soon be gone and I would never get to know her.

Now the neighbor's windows are blinded by blankets
again, and by the time she returns to check her cabin, I will have
abandoned this isolating wilderness, too. Yet, that fall night,
flattered, a bit bewildered, but hopeful in Wyoming,
I replayed her words, I'm only telling you. . .

What Am I Doing Here in This Ghost Town?
A Cautionary Tale for Writers About Place

After I moved from New York to Laramie, I began traveling to ghost towns. For three and a half years, that's all I did. When I wasn't on the road — in Wyoming, Nevada, Colorado, Arizona, New Mexico, Idaho, Montana, and finally, South Dakota — I was reading about the history of mining towns that now ranged from stone heaps in the sagebrush to boardwalks lined with phony heliotrope shops. The urban names of these intriguing old camps — South Pass City, Silver City, Virginia City— brought to mind the multicultural metropolis I had lived in and loved for twenty-two years, and excited my wanderlust. I thought of these towns as "ghost towns" whether they were populated or not; and it was true that at some point in the last hundred years these ruinous outposts in picturesque mountain passes had burgeoned, then were abandoned, or almost.

Why did I, a stranger to the West, become obsessed with ghost towns? The answer is complex. At forty-three, I had accepted a job as Assistant Professor of Creative Writing at the University of Wyoming. A freelance writer, who supported her fiction by churning out schlock, I initially refused to admit that I moved because I was now middle-aged, and needed a salary, and employment that would exercise my nurturing instincts. I did admit that I needed to escape the carbon monoxide fumes that had afflicted me with a permanent flu; plus, the university offered dental insurance, and all my teeth needed root jobs and caps. Like other emigrants to this region, I was by no means immune to the lure of our nation's least avoidable myth: that by moving West I could reinvent myself. Although I hadn't thought about the West since the age of four when I donned a cute red Stetson and fired a cap gun, I now imagined that I could relocate to another part of my country and become someone else. My notions of metamorphosis centered around the new writing this legendary place would inspire: I would become a Western Writer, I declared to myself, imagining this was an original thought.

My first year in Laramie was not very inspiring. I came to rest in a tight green cottage on Eleventh Street with a trim bluegrass yard and a view of the university's engineering building. The windy college town with its U-Bake-Em Pizzas, K-Mart, trafficky intersections, and middle-class family atmosphere wasn't my idea of a place that could fuel a reincarnation. But the realities that the real Western writers tapped to create books — nature, and the colorful characters who worked on ranches — seemed unavailable to this Manhattan transplant. The one and only cowboy I met was a Fundamentalist Christian who hadn't had sex since the age of eighteen, except, he blushed, for a "special treat" on his birthday. In the wide open spaces I became disoriented; reeling among strange birds, rocks, and flowers, I believed I was lost.

Yet I soon found myself entranced by a nearby attraction — the defunct town of Bosler, eighteen miles northwest of Laramie on the Old Lincoln Highway. In the lopsided yellow library and faded, see-through house, clinging with peeling fingernails to a bowl rim of sky, I saw a compelling romantic image of a place whose present and used-to-be were existentially combined. One day, I interviewed the owner of Bosler's second-hand furniture store where I had bought an antique brass lamp. (Only twelve bucks, but it needed rewiring.) "Doc," a former sewing machine salesman from Pittsburgh, I learned, had relocated to Bosler after surviving a tornado that had rolled his vehicle, then opened a popular nude discotheque. The "gods" in Laramie had shut him down, he told me, and he'd done jail time for serving drinks without a liquor license. Now, having transformed the disco into a furniture warehouse, Doc was constantly harassed by police who "refused to believe that a man could make a living in the middle of nowhere without selling drugs." Hail, wind, and the freight train's boreal hoot competed with Doc's raspy voice on my tape. This guy stored his own shirts in the dressers for sale, and parked a gold limousine amongst the second-hand couches! I nicknamed Doc "The King of Bosler," and thought I had found the perfect location to launch my career as a writer of place.

A real Western writer would have moved to Bosler, and gotten to know this windblown strip well. At first, I confess, I wasn't looking for true literary material as much as a boondoggle that would take me away from Laramie and the inexorable security of the tenure track. An adventurous world traveler, I decided to revisit the derelict sites listed in the ghost town guides I had inherited from a Colorado aunt, and interview the colorful characters living in them now.

My New York literary agent was excited by the idea ("I will sell this, Darling!") A big publisher called, requesting an "exclusive" on the proposal. Wyomingites, by contrast, groaned at the prospect of yet another ghost town guide. My academic colleagues, implying my thesis was superficial, recommended a deconstructionist scholar's heavy tome on the meaning of tourism. Ironically, the university I was trying to escape provided me with a generous research grant.

Thus armed with mixed messages, I set off in June 1990 for South Pass City, once an 1860s gold rush town, now a Wyoming State Historic Site, where a century-old dance hall had just been flattened by a runaway cement truck. I bunked in a trailer with young volunteers and, between designing and executing a tourist survey, ran around with my tape recorder, interviewing every colorful character I could find.

This small, briefly rushed camp in a dusty depression on a cold mountaintop in west central Wyoming, had become a museum, displaying a hodgepodge of false-fronted log buildings from different eras that had been moved, reconstructed with modern materials, and reinterpreted by a variety of curators. Yet, this artificial town incited conflicts and passions that were difficult for an aspiring Western writer to understand. (Why, I wondered, was everyone mourning the death of a dance hall that had been equipped with new windows, a concrete floor, telephone, electricity, pink fiberglass insulation, and used as a workshop?) Everyone involved with South Pass City — the present curator, a year on the job, a California volunteer with ancestral connections, and Minnie, a former owner and history buff, who had reinvented the gold camp in her own image then sold it for a profit to Wyoming — wept when they spoke of their emotional investment in the idea of the town. Minnie, ill with cancer, refused to visit the State's current version. "Dammit, it hurts. . . . It hurts to see the way they've changed things," she said.

South Pass City's first curator, assigned to the site in 1966, despite a degree in Animal Husbandry, was indignant because his efforts to invoke gold rush history, including building from scratch a Variety Theater that had never existed, had been discredited. ("There was a pharmacy! There was never a hat shop!") This amateur historian's three-year-old son had drowned in the creek that parallels South Pass Avenue. Did the tragedy color his feelings about the years he'd spent in South Pass City, I asked tentatively. "Having lost him there, I feel South Pass City belongs to me . . . . I bought it with his life," he told me, eyes glazed with tears.

I soon learned that no one could live in this fake town for long without despising everyone else who had ever lived and worked there. Territorial conflicts over historical interpretation — what had really happened in South Pass City, and how its present manifestation reflected that — were bitter and rife. One curator, an authentic historian, who fought to interpret the shuffled site as "a study in the history of change," and nobly defended its thousands of artifacts from state employees who were ripping them off, found himself embroiled in a vendetta between rival government agencies. He was fired, wound up in court. The state ordered him and his family to vacate his cabin in a blizzard; his telephone wires were cut. During his reign, he said, a tourist visiting the Hotel (a new replica, containing not one splinter of the 1867 original) captured an image of a ghost on a Polaroid print. The spirit, summoned by a storm, appeared as a woman in a Victorian gown, standing by a window in a room filled with light.

I should have stuck with South Pass City, but hooked on the excitement of the ghost town trail, I continued on to Colorado — Tin Cup, Gothic, and, finally, Cripple Creek, once "The richest gold camp on earth," then a "Graveyard with lights," destined to become a casino strip.   Those who had fought to legalize gambling in Cripple Creek and Central City had sold the initiative to the Colorado voters in the name of preserving historic brick buildings, a heritage supposedly about to crumble. The day the Johnny Nolon Saloon opened in the high mountain town (a major event in New Western history) I was the only writer on hand not working for the media. I stayed for ten days, first in a frosty campground, then in a tin can of a trailer, moving through hordes of "quarter rushers" — gamblers, real estate agents making a pile, hustling old timers — eavesdropping and brandishing my tape recorder.   Fascinated, I returned many times.

I learned that the new industry, introduced to preserve Cripple Creek, was literally destroying it. In order to transform fragile old fire traps into buildings sufficiently safe and sturdy for slot machine traffic, contractors had to gut, then reconstruct them. (I took photos of historic facades braced by two by fours with nothing but vacant lots behind them.) As a result, the original owners, who had envisioned "mom and pop" blackjack tables, could not foot the bill to satisfy new building codes, and were bought out by strangers and corporations. On my last trip to Cripple Creek, an entirely different town than the one I'd first visited, I saw a crane, armed with a wrecking ball, demolishing a late nineteenth-century Masonic hall.

As in every occupied ghost town I visited, political and social conflict prevailed. In the new Cripple Creek, where millions changed hands daily, residents with different ideas about what history meant were ready to murder each other. One councilman, a proponent for small, unpretentious casinos, had been deposed in an unethical election. A young historian, who had politicked for gaming, then, later, as Historic Preservation

Officer, opposed the onslaught of Vegas-sized casinos, was targeted for death threats.

I should have moved to Cripple Creek on my research semester and slung hash in The Golden Eagle Casino, but instead I moved restlessly on to other ghost towns in other states — Rhyolite, Bullfrog, Bisbee, Tombstone, Gleeson, (where a one-armed man once played the banjo day and night), Elkhorn, Pony, Comet, Granite, Atlanta — to name a few destinations of my amorphous quest.

It was on my second trip to Basin, Montana, that I realized I was in over my head. On my first visit, interviewing arthritic senior citizens taking Radon Cures in abandoned gold mines, I had learned of a lesbian group that had occupied the camp in the late nineteen seventies. These women, like other counter-cultural newcomers to old Western towns, fantasized that they had discovered a funky commune; they bought brick buildings for diddley and fixed them up, then worked hard to support and enhance the dying community just north of Butte. Disturbing changes soon invaded. A highway to Helena went through; an architect called a meeting to discuss historic preservation. Other lesbians, traveling cross-country on motorcycles, stopped to visit Basin friends, and kissed in public.

About this time, Marilyn, who was raising a son with a female partner, opposed the new Nazarene preacher in a school board election. The preacher campaigned door-to-door, saying aloud what was known but not spoken — that his opponent loved women. Thus incited, the Basin old timers, already unnerved, began harassing the lesbians, scrawled CuntLesboLickBitches on their houses, pissed on their doorsteps, and finally shunned them. Some women feared they might be burned out, like a group of unsavory bikers before them.

This had gone down in 1982. Now, twelve years later, the lesbians had agreed to tell me their story and videotape our encounter. They seemed to feel that revisiting the disturbing persecution together would help them find closure. Melissa, a novelist, had traveled from San Francisco for the reunion. In a charged, four hour event, so moving, so dramatic, the women, one by one, recounted their Basin stories — about coming out and falling in love, about surviving financially, about fixing up trash-filled houses, about the terrifying transformation of their ideal community. One, from a Butte mining family, said she had thought that she was the only lesbian in all of Montana until her therapist laughed and told her about Basin. Most of these articulate, gifted women, writers, film makers, musicians, health professionals, had left the town and prospered.

Before I met with the group in one member's renovated loft, I had visited the Nazarene preacher's wife. (He was out of town.) It would be fair to hear her side, too, I thought. She told me that her church opposed homosexuality because it was a "hate crime" against the opposite sex. She had said that she had wanted to leave Basin when she learned that "reprobate" lesbians were there; she was afraid they would want to have sex with her or her daughter. Her husband, a cancer survivor, had fasted and prayed, received word that God had sent his family to Basin, and He would protect them. She had never wanted to be a minister's wife, she confided; she was strong-willed, enjoyed working for an LA insurance company. When her husband had asked her to give up her job, stay home, raise her children, she'd submitted reluctantly, as God had willed her. Now she knew her decision had been good.

The interview was often interrupted by the preacher's sullen adopted son, head shaved, who unequivocally hated his father's guts. The preacher had restricted this boy severely — forbidding him to play with other kids, including his best childhood friend, Marilyn's son. He had been beaten, sometimes in public, for his "own good." Isolated from his peer group, he had been home schooled for years because his parents didn't believe in public education. Finally he had become so miserable, so rebellious, that the preacher relented, sent him to high school in Boulder, although a teacher there had been busted for sexually molesting male children. Just the week before, however, the boy had been forbidden to attend his senior prom, where drinking was prohibited, because, according to his father, to prohibit drinking suggested that drinking was possible.

To the preacher's credit, he planned to pay for his son's education at the university in Missoula, a den of iniquity if there ever was one. "We have covered him with prayer," his mother told me. "He must do as we say until he leaves home, but then he can make his own decisions." She predicted that the boy would return to God, and I feared she was right. The debate, often degenerating into a shouting match between the desperate child and his mother, playing intermediary between her son and her absent husband, ended when the resentful young skinhead stomped out of the room, muttering, "It's your interview; you give it!"

At the end of this day, I parked next to a disintegrating bed frame in a torrential rainstorm, confused and upset. I had intended to write a tale that would avenge Basin lesbians; now I wondered, who were the real victims in this awful old place? So many ghost towns, so many stories, none of them mine. How would I, a pretend Western writer, make them cohere? Soon after that I became the first professor in the history of academe to return a chunk of her research grant.

Whatever happened to your ghost town book? People still ask. To make an embarrassing story short, two different proposals — longer than some novels — were rejected by more renowned editors than I care to count. One, famous for publishing works about nature and cowboys, read my unfocused sample chapters about conflicts in historic towns and stated, rather grandly, from her Park Avenue desk, "This isn't my West!" For a long time, when I glanced at the file cabinet stuffed with hundreds of pages of tape transcripts, notebooks, slides, pamphlets, books, newspapers, maps, and rough drafts, I felt as if its weight was sutured to my heart.

In the end, I don't regret going to ghost towns. My travels provided a crash education in Western geography, history, and culture. A phobic driver when I moved West, I had mustered the courage to inch my car up boulder-strewn tracks, through icy passes, and camped alone in deep forest campgrounds, once, cheek by jowl with a mother moose; feeling like an impostor without a book contract, I had approached and interviewed hundreds of strangers. I had photographed fragile houses, barns, and burned union halls, the architectural remains of Old West civilization. I learned some reporter's secrets — such as, people lie to you if you use a tape recorder — and, maybe, what kind of writer I'm not. And I was happier going to ghost towns than I've been ever since. I also believe that I was on to an important story, one that I didn't have the depth of knowledge? The educational background? The imagination? to tell. The story takes place in a small town — seldom a setting in the literature of place, although most Western writers live in one — where conflict reigns, and where myth and reality are two different things.

Dainis Hazners

Dainis Hazners is the recipient of two Wyoming Arts Council literary fellowships, a Neltje Blanchan Memorial Writing Award and a National Endowment for the Arts fellowship in poetry.

In Memory of
Elza Veronika Bundza Hazners
June 28, 1911 — March 21, 1998

◆

not even tracks in snow
mar imagined passage —
mouse & mole, the weasel's

wormy burrow through
drift — in the creekbed, pebbles
begin to click, roll

through sludge-thick
clasp — mass, brute
silence, freeze — who —

in the hours of wind
and vernal bight, St. Kevin
ascends from the basement's

barmy deceits: gloom
and dungeon, bludgeoned
delight — pate prickly

though freshly sheared,
shaved — he shakes
millipedes from the folds

of robe and steps
rough-soled, blood-
heeled into thaw, drip

and light: it blinds,
harsh after quirky soothe
of habit, dank years, crusts

and gruel, the bowl of turned
wood, carved spoon, cup — comforts
of return and routine, chant,

prayer — how having
nothing tenders ephemeral — his
shrunken belly

grumbles as he drums
skeletal wounds, wrist
on ribs — plays at first

dirge tunes, somnolent
harp-thrum, measured
gallop of heart — hums then

resonant air,
jig, cheekbones buzzy
with mucousy sneeze: hatchoo!

to the birds that bolt
from quick-scratch and thicket, dry
thatch raked and clawed —

with hulls in their bills and dearly
chittering, now hop and bobble, paired
on swelling branch. . . he finds

in his pocket seeds
which lifted towards bright
perplexity, seduce

and attract. . . after,
in the fall and falling,
St. Kevin will linger —

how faith never wobbled, knees
on hummock, thistle
pricklish on thigh, blooms

pallid within
tent of cassock — rains, scent,
clouds on his outstretched

arms — blister, burn, stars
he sometimes slept through —
twigs and down, scavenged

thread, feather —
the immense lightness
as they came and went

malodorous-marvelous
bloom — the pulpit's bid
spadix and spathe, a saprophyte's

herby, sexual, upthrust
pipes — peony, poppy, lily-
spear, lanceolate leaves — muck-split

scent of a season's arum,
the cabbage's deleterious rush —
everything opens: throat

of robin, lark, ribs
and heart, mouth and the means
of meadow: falls,

froth and returned: the ouzel's
gorgeous racket — steep-crazed creeks
lean and meander into

slow-spill-pools, slough and edges —
riparian bric-a-brac, shimmer
stick-click breeze, draw-muddled

root, wood, the sap-course
pulse-engorged: white pith wrapped
in flexing pewter — sun-flux struck-

skin, scar-marred bark —
even rocks as marmots
sprawl and dozey, warm

to a dense, unlit core — what
sorrows we keen to, hammered, halve
crystalline: flint-fleck knapped, spark

— plangent appellation
within hubbub surround —
pall and mauve

assemblage — chandelier, smoke,
box and damask — silences
proceed, ascend —

then we begin
with and without prescience,
plot or denouement — presences

intimate/elude
illusion and evanescent,
sustain — wind-

struck whimsical — reagent
rearrangements, variations
on a four-note theme —

string, hymn —
dirge and drum — the under-
drone scarcely

heard — ineluctable,
intractable — entranced —
consumed entire the known/

unknown, brushing
vaporous surround, thin
transluce, ephemeral

shiver — deaf
to praise — transcends
delight, omit/inclusion

in/after crepuscular
transits — draught-drouth
of dream — vapid, forgotten,

ignored — awakened from outside
ground — who couldn't pity
what speaks, what raises

damp nape — shiver —
shock-hour sweat — gives
shrill address to sleep-

smeared ear — dread night
fragment — severed tangent of plot,
mind-meander — clots,

thickens but for sound —
strident arc of glottal
cord-twang, shriek —

breaking the wet
wind — hesitant eddy —
a final plash

in high ether — flowers
in the yellow sphere — again,
wandering — whatever

it was/is —
isn't — now farther beyond
barn-cluck, fear-

gurgle — raw-
eyed brawn — even cold
water — soothe, elixir —

sweet recalcitrance,
divergent — watch
the resistant, forward

lope — how horses lunge
from the plum-slope —
frost-bottom

pond, the till —
sludge milkiness of flood-
briar and bud — snarled

manes and burdock
knotted — to a feisty
toss of light before

the rein — huge
check-wheels — dark
lipped, muzzle-nuzzle,

long-toothed
chew — how their clean
hides glisten, lean-

flanked as they clamber,
thrush-clear, frog-
pattern, pastern

flex — sleek slinkily
monstrous, ponderous — plumed
fountains of nostril-

flared breath — wither-
nicker, saunter laggard
to hand — bow-

necked blonde and palomino,
the bay the black and one
more — crop cut,

roped, who rears
on slashing, dew-smudged hoof,
sack on blaze —

grackle — gives fractious
display — indigo crown
shimmer, chocolate

saddle hackle — huff —
feather enlarge —   kireee kireeh!
tscii-wit — resume

mild palaver — rock
clatter — crossing mossy
salt-trickle, glacial pock —

riffle, jewel slope, talus,
lichen moraine — massed
dialectic of stone — magpie

precarious/gregarious,
bold-black — loud — of craven
raven-bill gawp — straddles

hawthorn, white
arc bow — bloom — floats
on scent, gust, to eye

meatcage — mouse & sun-
sprung sternum, frayed rib — tallow -
marrow blood cave — tunneled

vertebral burrow beneath
lodgepole, cloudpull, moon — dog-
tooth violets flashing gloam

& light — glory —
glory-glory! splendiferous
exalt — transitory

step through this disc —
circular, silver — tongue
luster skin — every

mole and freckle would luck
beneath mouth-hum — every star-
struck scar — find

scapula, rib
to match — recumbent
line, thigh, tender

kneepocket, slim
achille, musk-redolent
arch — sock-fluff — pure

lure of love's refulgent
crave — but real — silhouette
same, my other

sings, so
sweetly in fragments
of tree

and light — betrays
the bullfrog's brag — on racked
stub of burl, rail —

humble, shy
of bone-jut, waits — rare — how
-who would imagine refine?

blood in the brook, stone
on end — haphazard
recline, starling

— darling
unseat me, master
the sweet-dank, trembly — gloam

come farm-pond preamble —
slow/quick stir — plinked
splish from brittle reed, lush

rush — rose in the borrow,
sage on bench, yarrow,
penstemon, salsify

stand in the weed-dock —
gust — grassy wind-lisp — drone —
everything at once — nervy

dither — the caul sack torn,
devoured — ribbed web, net — twin
slippings glistening — afterbirth

dangle — drag
of gravity's certain, companionable
drawl — good

morning little nubbins —
welcome — welcome! — resist
lazy phrase of recline — up!

spring into day-old day —
greedy guzzle-nuzzle — but dawdle,
dally summer-wile —

◆

tin-tinnabulation/ululation
o-so-gorgeoso
recitative ring of wren —

from throng & meander —
how will you — wary — yearn? —
from fashionable

bog — known-drone
of the righteous sound —
weary — RUN —

swallow-lifted
sun — dear — dun-flank, shiver —
twitch — sheen — diffident,

unrenown, leave
fray, obscure — abandon
niggle — doubt burr — dissolve —

mirror dresser divan — charcoal
chiaroscuro smudged in the undefined
edge of darkened room —

blondely divine, the dozens
have assembled — blood of blood, all
kin of fevered coursings — pulse —

perched on ladder-back chairs, plump
cushions of shadow — palms
clamped between bare knees —

in louvered light — mote-flit
trick-sparkle — hushed, flushed
from sword-play, bout,

joust of lance and stallion —
gored, intestinal loops drag —
dangling dust — the Prince of Darkness

pierced, gorget creased, cuisse
askew, is hobbling towards the block. . . how small
their chevelure glow, enlarged

eyes black with pupil — expectant —
tense, defenseless — the near-oldest,
barefoot — how clean, how white,

unmarred the soles — speechless, rises
in greeting — scrap of message — confession,
declaration — adore — penned

in soluble ink — passed,
catches on a slat of light
blazing in the burn —

More Light! More Light!
the angels cry, and burst
into thunder, lightning applause

chirr-birds stir —
sculpt the loved one's
broad-backed

alabaster disregard —
touch the cuffed skull
closer — tenderly —

whose hand
holds it — not mine — surely
commands — fingers

laced — palm as
bowl — cup what's scoured,
transformed —

— except for the roaring
which obscures, abhors. . .
shifty, blue — rubbed

with ash, stench-scent,
pall — haze veils the changing
light — extravagantly

red — swift coalesce
brushing brow, knobbly spine — enters
the mouth, its acid

pits the tooth. . . unknown
in the wraith and tangle, humped,
rasping — methodical

among hot rocks
hissing, crowns
of ponderosa exploding —

what's left
but pressured fizzle? — thought
fractures, dissembles —

language enraptured,
ruptured in the concrete
spillway, torn,

tattered by venturi —
prismatic — splits once-
clear air — murky

slivers, rainbow —
shards — what's left blisters
flesh in fistfuls — my —

entranced, askew — mine
in its soft spin pedaling
fast — fractured

enraptured — arisen,
on his dirty feet he leaves
the room on leaves,

duff, tinder, green
pungent wonder — the long
light thumping

bony — gold streaming
from scapula skin — wispy
cape of rippling

◆

— ethereal
plane — yellow bloom on
still pond — ring

of the rise — red
moon fasting over — the fat
brown hen pronouncing

pwaauck! announcing
aspen glory-gold leaf-clutter — breeze —
introducing my fur-four —

cleared, in tune —
humble — resume their wondrous
cud-humming

rhymes — among
frost riddled rock, russet
currant revise — as if — except —

drift — ooze
of false summer — mud and its slick
raconteur accomplice. . .

his hand thickens
breadth-breath, drek and disabled,
tangent — passes

over — ruffles,
muffles crumpled — o. . .
the glory days are nearly

here/dear-&-done — the littlest
assembling on wind-raked limbs,
clack-twittering — & nights

too long to sleep — upon us — pristine,
steely — glazed — glittering
suspension — deep still

of place — slow/
quick pulse, the darkening
coagulate vein

◆

— surreptitious — tink —
released from limb, juniper
berry breaks frost—

flower skim — clear
glimmering — rainbow refract — too
small for fish

& bug — eyed
right magnifies moon and all
that beloved, behold

it — little pool
I lip with eye — on
knee, like any

other sky — wind —
tossed bell & curve
of cloud — clang

cliff-clatter, pebble-
roll — rung — as something else —
thirsting — passes —

moth-shushering
drone from wall-corner,
ceiling interstice —

voice — powdery
sift of the unseen mote-
flower — hand

in mine, or mine —
yours — shot
bird trembly in its last — o —un-

humble under-
tone — fraction/reflection — without
gleam-oval, window,

door — obscure on thread-
mat, plank — on my knees
in opulence & fringe —

without shiver
of light — led towards/
away — followed —

following smooth
plumed flesh — breath — pianissimo,
whispery, recites —

◆

permitted. . .
in the hall of the weird, where,
marginal/exorbitant

the extreme assemble
and watch with awe
the peculiar antics

of droll & divine:
the disc that suspends
itself, the empty sphere,

my body floating
on air the air
on water — this great

thirst — waiting for some
thing larger — immense — who
pressing, crushes. . . breath,

◆

another sleepless,
speechless rue, re-
ductive ramble —

why? — mutter: wherefore long-
lingering, monstrous/preposterous, grim
care — who. . . therefore. . .

in the pulse-knocking
round of hours, the lovely
day draws never

ever nearer with its clear windless
light, happy
demarcations of spoor,

sign, the claw-tipped print
filled now with spangly sphere-
frost, rime —

o they are waiting
o they are turning
o my poor beloved

hollowed bones
by the wilted, in the bed,
in this thin, papery,

airless air. . . this. . .
perfunctory. . . these
perignations —

                        this body's
dull dereliction — final,
acute — attendant-

resplendent they are turning   o
they are turning my vague
and shadowy — translucence

unreproachable
dark — bilious/oblivious —
the black divine

in cape & tails —
in the plume-dark
feather-trust, embark — ignore

snore-cold of nostril —
clogged breath, fire
in its ash-banked coal,

the faceless/blameless preceding
unnamed intention/
dictate, infinite premise, half-

uttered prayer — what one
meant — what's wasted, forgotten —
cruel gruel —

recriminations, perignations, circum-
ambulations — proof/reproof. . .
lie down now,

rest. . .
          in this
room without window or door

I lie in my bed, kneading
knuckles, polishing bone, excrescence,
unconscious and wait. . .

swallowed disc
of moon — wafer of light
in the deep blank: revolve

The West, If You Will

This place — the West, if you will — though it matters to me, and affects me, and though I am here to stay, it is incidental to my concerns as a writer. I do prefer a rural life — where it seems easier at times to apprehend (or, for a few moments: grasp at) another kind of "being." The sensual word as it presses against another — one that cannot be seen, cannot be touched, cannot be "known" but which suggests itself in ephemeral fragments — was of great interest to me when I wrote this group of poems.

Alyson Hagy

Alyson Hagy was raised on a farm in the Blue Ridge Mountains of Virginia. She is a graduate of Williams College and the University of Michigan and has taught at the University of Virginia, the University of Southern Maine, and the University of Michigan. She has published a novel, *Keeneland* and three collections of short stories, *Graveyard of the Atlantic, Madonna on Her Back,* and *Hardware River.* Her fiction has been awarded a Wyoming Arts Council fellowship, a National Endowment for the Arts fellowship, a Pushcart Prize, a Best American Short Story citation and been recorded for National Public Radio. Hagy teaches creative writing at the University of Wyoming. She lives in Laramie with her husband and son.

The Examiner

The sheriff found him at Minnie Koger's. He was in the back bedroom checking Miss Minnie's blood pressure, listening to her heart, going through motions both he and Minnie recognized. Adele answered the phone. She came to the door of the bedroom with a pink handkerchief twisted in her hands "It's a man says he's Sheriff Quentin on the phone," she sniffled. "Wants to speak to Doctor Pierce."

"Be right there." He slowed the urgency in his voice. "I need to talk a minute with your grandma."

Adele turned toward the kitchen, her shoulders resettled. She was a schoolteacher and had made dignity a quiet habit. But even with Adele out of the room, and Breenie and Joe on the porch sharing cigarettes, there was little privacy, no way he could speak without being overheard. He was sure this was how Miss Minnie wanted it. She'd lived in this tiny, paper-chinked house all her life. It had forever leaked family.

"My heart's give out, hadn't it?"

"Oh, your heart's still talking to me, Minnie." He laid two fingers across the bone-core of her wrist. "I don't like everything it's saying."

"Ninety-two years old, don't got much more to say. You just swear on that promise you made me, and I'll get along. I found peace with the Lord a long time before this." She coughed through her last words, a deep fluid wheeze that confirmed his diagnosis. Her lungs would fill in a day, maybe two. She'd struggle for breath until the end.

"I'm not going to call the ambulance. But Adele and them are worried. They fret after you."

"Adele does like I say." Minnie smiled, propped up against a bank of embroidered pillows. She still had her dentures in. Still had Breenie oiling her hair and braiding it to put under a black velvet cap. Minnie Koger had always made room for her vanity; it was part of the stories told about her and the babies she delivered for seventy years. Minnie Koger would come to a house day or night, and she'd stay every minute of a hard labor. But you'd better have a clean apron for her, maybe two, and you'd best not hurry her when she was putting on her face cream or lipstick, not even if that baby was crowning, or she'd make you wish you'd caught the child in your own ignorant hands.

He folded his stethoscope into his scuffed black bag. He could see the phone receiver lying on a freshly-wiped counter in the kitchen. The sheriff was waiting for him. The news wouldn't be good.

"One of my deputies found a burned-out car up at Shooting Creek. Says there's two bodies he can see. He's real upset." The sheriff spoke with the cadence of a man elected to portray calm. "I'm sorry to chase you down like this, Tom, but there's been some feuding up that way. I don't like how it sounds."

"Do I go past the mill?"

"My man is parked half a mile above the chapel."

"I'll get there."

He looked in on Minnie once more. She had fallen into a kind of sleep. The bright wool sweaters layering her chest obscured its flutter. Her parents had died in this house, and one of her own children. She didn't believe death deserved a commotion.

Adele and the others weren't talking when he stepped onto the porch, but he felt a silence descend over them just the same. Smoke ribboned the still air. It took Joe, a large man who worked on the line at DuPont, a moment to say his piece.

"How's she doing, doctor? Does she seem worse off to you, 'cause to me she seems about the same."

"About the same, that's true." He waited for Joe to look away as grieving men often did. "You want to keep her comfortable, and she is. But she's tired, I know she's told you that. She could pass along any time."

"But you saved her last time." Breenie Davis, a copper-skinned woman who ran her own beauty shop, tore at the neckline of her blouse. "This don't seem different."

"I didn't save her," he said. "Your grandma put up the fight. Said she wanted to see Easter again, as I recall. Something about tasting Adele's dumplings and pecan pie."

They laughed with him a little then, a murmur of good memory. Like most of his patients, they'd been raised poor and were familiar with the brisk hatchet blows of loss.

"I'll come back by after my last call if that's all right. To make sure the shortness of breath isn't worse. If it is, I might call to town for a tank of oxygen."

"She won't take it," said Adele. "She won't put that mask on her face."

"Maybe not, then." He worked his arms into his overcoat. "I'll come by just the same."

"Get you some pie if you're lucky, doctor. Adele done made two this morning." Joe shifted in the porch swing and framed his belly with his hands.

"I'm hurrying," he said as he stepped into the boot-worn yard. "Because if I don't, that pie will be gone. I can see that."

He'd been county medical examiner for more than a year, a post he'd taken because the pay was helpful. He was still fairly new in town, and his family was growing. He got an extra dose of disaster with the job — drownings at the lake, old folks who died alone and weren't discovered for days, farm accidents — but his internship in Richmond had prepared him for as much. His duties were minimal, part of the narrow public corridor toward death. He didn't think of himself as much of an official.

He took time to ease his Mustang down the rutted driveway. The car was impractical as hell on house calls. Old Dr. Jamison had told him he ought to have a truck for the roads around here. Of course Jamison had an opinion about everything. He gave financial advice; he cautioned his younger partner about being too casual in manner, preaching the importance of coat and tie and a Presbyterian demeanor. "We aren't supposed to fit in," Jamison said. "It's not for nothing that those witch doctors wear crazy keep-away masks." Jamison believed his patients paid for a dose of the extraordinary.

But he was a country boy himself, raised not two hours east. The deference good people showed him was difficult to accept, especially since he'd come to see what he practiced as more art than science. He'd always promised himself he'd know the quick flinch of humility, that he'd remember where he came from, and he managed the blind switchbacks of Shooting Creek Road with that thought in mind.

Just above the terraced clearing that held the Primitive Baptist chapel at Sweet Annie's Hollow he saw the frantic wink of red and blue lights through the trees. He crept by the strobed chaos until he passed the hulking tow truck from Tirey's Esso.

Deputy Prillaman was laying a new line of flares to alert traffic coming down the mountain. He was a thin man with an overcrowded mouth and the nervous, tensile walk of someone who has too much territory to cover. When Prillaman failed to quickstride over to give his version of the carnage, it was clear he'd been the one to find the car. It looked like it was all the deputy could do to keep his hands busy.

"Hey there, Larry, you recommend I change to my boots?" He kept his voice serious, but soft.

Prillaman looked down at his own heavy brown shoes which were clean. His head appeared to dangle from his neck. "Take your chances, Doc. Bobby Tirey's gonna have that mess up here soon anyway."

"Not until I've seen it, I guess. You find it?"

"Door handles melted right to the doors. You ever seen a thing like that?" Prillaman licked his lips as he spoke, like a man on the high cliff of nausea. Then he turned on the balls of his feet and went back to his spattering, hellish flares.

"Thomas." The sheriff was upon him with a handshake and a firm grip to the shoulder. "We pried the doors open and the Rescue Squad's got bags. I'll go down with you."

Sheriff Quentin was a short, trim man, a former state trooper who wore suits instead of a uniform. He thrived as a local anomaly, a Republican in a citadel of Democrats, a small man in a job where size was often equated with competence. Quentin was considered a survivor.

He could see the car now, a crumpled station wagon licked black by smoke and flame. If there were license plates, they weren't visible, but that was Quentin's job. His job was to make a few brisk observations, to state the obvious with neatness and clarity. It's done. These folks are gone. Like a priest, he thought, though without the elegant, beseeching sacraments. If there was a problem, the assistant state examiner would do the autopsies in Roanoke.

The hillside was steep and badly scarred by tire marks. He dug his heels into the cloak of slippery leaves. Quentin stayed behind him in a polite attempt to be deferential; he said he might put in a call to the ATF, depending on what they found. The local moonshiners had been crowding each other. "Jaybird Philpott wouldn't hesitate to kill a man who cut into his business. I hope that don't have a thing to do with this."

He used his eyes mostly. The smell was strong, but cool now, a mix of gasoline, rubber, the chemical tang of burnt upholstery. The interior had been reduced to flaking frame and coil. The windows had exploded from the heat.

"It was burning when it left the road." The sheriff circled the front end. "I hate to think somebody fired it up just to scorch these poor devils."

He could see them as well, two greasy stalks of spine and cinder leaning away from him. He covered his hand with a cloth offered by another of Quentin's deputies, Thurman he thought the man's name was, and pulled the driver's side door open. Black chunks of ash, or worse, spilled into his cuffs. An imagined blast of heat roared by his ears. He guessed he'd never know more than he did at just that moment. Two adults, one maybe smaller than the other. He couldn't tell whether they'd been alive when they burned, whether they were men or women. The gritty texture of the air made him want to sneeze. More than that, he resisted the scent of pit-blackened meat.

Thurman talked to the sheriff while they used a crowbar on the ruined tailgate. They were working on their theory of feuding and revenge, the recent shift from whiskey to marijuana in the hills. They didn't need him, not really. They weren't interested in witnessing death. What they wanted was a way to prosecute the loss of life. He made himself look again at the driver, steadily, thoughtfully, though it was hard to get beyond the seared white tonsure of the skull.

"Christ." It was Thurman sifting through the back.

"Godamighty, how'd we miss that." Quentin's voice lost its lubrication.

His own mouth went dry and spiky when he joined them. The body of a child, or what once qualified as one, was melted against a wheel well. He thought of the porousness of lava and bone. He thought of the bubbles in burned caramel.

"I don't like this," Thurman said. "Looks like maybe a propane bottle over here. Somebody might have used it to torch them. Sons-a-bitches could have burned themselves with it, though. Light a cigarette and boom."

"Tom?" The sheriff had recovered himself.

"They'll have to go to the state lab. Ask your boys to go easy, please. They'll break up when they're moved."

"You want to supervise?"

"No." He looked into the bare trees for something, flapping crows maybe. "I don't."

Night came as he gunned down the mountain. He didn't turn on the radio as he usually did, hoping to jacket himself in the voracious hum of the Mustang instead. As he drove too fast, edging over the yellow line on curves, he wondered what Jamison did in his damned giant pickup after a bad time. Did he drift off the asphalt to feel that high chassis wrench? Did he find a back road to run without lights? Maybe he did nothing, just let the gruesome and diseased pass through him like air through a syringe. And the mistakes? Did they breeze past the old man, too? There were mistakes, of course. He'd made a few himself. That was the hard reality of doctoring. Though that didn't explain why he felt so neutralized by what he'd seen in that car.   So hung and salted. There was nothing he could have done about it.

He saw the cat before it dashed into the road. Its eyes were green in his headlights, flat and fierce. It was a calico, just like his daughter had had once, a fact he registered as he crushed the brakes. The Mustang shimmied beneath him, but there was no thump. Was the animal as quick as it was arrogant? He hoped so. It was hunting, doing what it was made for. And it was easy to think of himself as the intruder.

He got out of the car then, a crazy thing. The engine had died, but the lights were still on, broadcasting false halos onto the scatter of a fallow field. He walked away from the car, not looking for the cat really, searching for the cool rapids of the wind instead, some real darkness, distance. If another car comes along, he thought, so be it. Let them be the ones surprised.

He took only a few steps, however, just until he could sense weeds underfoot and hear the multitude of oblivious crickets. He thought of Bobby Tirey winching the wreck up that tattered hill, shouting orders, mixing sweat and ash. Bobby would make a dinnertime tale out of what he'd seen and how he'd helped clean it up. So would the sheriff. And here he was shuffling blind and stump-fingered beneath the night, afraid of dark ends he hadn't even ushered in. Someone had made a terrible mistake, someone faceless now, a person he could never know, and he was the one suffering a fear. He'd always wanted a kind of power in the world, good power, healing hands. He'd sacrificed long years for that. And those trained hands felt chilled and grooved, no more useful than a failed mechanic's tools.

He drove to Miss Minnie's at an absolutely even speed. Breenie's Buick was gone, and Joe's muddy hound was in the

yard although he ignored its bristling growls. He couldn't begin
to imagine the territory as marked.

Adele met him at the door in a robe, her head covered
with a parrot green scarf. She didn't smile, and neither did he.
He went toward the back bedroom, drifting almost, his coat
melting from his tired shoulders, his bag settling quietly on the
braided rug in the front hall. He looked down at Minnie, his
neck bowed in its habitual, querying curve. She still breathed.
Her eyes had sunk into twin navel whorls above her ridged
cheeks. He heard Adele open the refrigerator, then close it. He
was grateful that she understood he wasn't hungry.

"I'll get you a chair," she said. "Most nights she likes me
to play a little gospel radio while I'm in the bath, but you'll like
it quiet." Then she was gone, and he was there alone, balancing,
peering, inhaling a bit slower than his patient, wondering just
which ugly blasted image he should call up to help him reach for
her bare, wasted palm.

Grits and Grittier:
Notes From a Regional Transplant

*"Art, though, is never the voice of a country; it is an
even more precious thing, the voice of the individual,
doing its best to speak, not comfort of any sort, indeed,
but truth."*
— Eudora Welty

I was raised in the South. On a farm. In the mountains.
And for a very long time I never doubted who I was. I was a
Southerner. You could hear it in the warm and lazy vowels of my
speech. It didn't matter that I went to college in New England or
spent most of my twenties in the Midwest. My writing, my
family, the most tangled knots of my identity were rooted in the
Blue Ridge. And if you ask me today where I'm from, I'll say
Virginia. Without hesitation.

The problem seems to come in my writing, for my fiction
is no longer always stained by the red clays of the South. This
bothers, or perplexes, or irritates the folk who like to categorize
writers. How can I be a Southern Writer (which is what people
used to call me) if I'm sketching out the lives of sailors on the
Great Lakes or archaeologists on the Continental Divide of
Wyoming?

How indeed?

And if I'm not a Southern writer — if the grits aren't
always burning on the stove — then who, or what, am I? Does it
matter? Is regional identification important to art in any way?
Should I be pacing the floor to the banjo clang of my Bill Monroe
tapes? Should I be calling my brother in Richmond to retool my
accent?

I should admit that I have painted myself into my own

corner. I have tried to infuse my writing with a deep affection for landscape, whether barrier island or basin and range. I ask readers to try to live in the worlds I create, so it is little wonder that some of them want to know the definite boundaries of those worlds. Where are your stories *from*, I'm asked? How do you *know* those places? It is understandable — perhaps even flattering — that readers want me to be identifiably part of the landscapes I describe. Many of us crave literal "authority;" we want to be sure our writers know what they are talking about. I am the sort of writer, however, who puts more stock in the instincts of her imagination than in any hard-won knowledge of archaeology, or shark fishing, or the navigation of freighters I might have acquired during my scurry for stories. Don't get me wrong. Research in science, history, and natural history has been crucial to my work. Still, I have learned to trust intuition. I don't have to *be* my characters; I only have to *know* them. This allows me to be an impassioned sojourner to each fictive landscape I create, since I cannot always be a native. I often write beyond my homeland, beyond my gender, race, class, and sometimes I am successful at it. When I think about it at all, I think of myself as an American writer because I am particularly drawn to the hardscrabble margins of our nation, places like my Virginia home, like the Outer Banks of North Carolina, the upper peninsula of Michigan, the plains and mountains of Wyoming — all settings for my fiction, all places that seem to me essentially American. Yet it would be more honest for me to claim no other honorific than *writer*. That is responsibility enough.

The ferocity with which many of us cling to an identifiable region — its land forms, cultures, and histories — is often admirable. I doubt most artists would come into being without ferocity. Still, I believe it is one role of the writer to explore every manifestation of human community he or she can find. Our explorations should not be sentimental, defensive, romantic, nor too drenched in nostalgia (though that is a tall order for a Southerner). Flannery O'Connor, an important early influence in my development as a writer, might disagree with me here. O'Connor insisted that "the best American fiction has always been regional wherever there has been a shared past, a sense of alikeness,." Yet even O'Connor, who drew her artistic strength from her Catholicism and her close-to-the-bone knowledge of rural Georgia, noted that what regional identity gives us is "the possibility of reading a small history in a universal light." That's the point, isn't it? To find the "universal light." Like Wallace Stegner, I would say that the best writer is a "lover but not much of a booster." Our role is to imagine, analyze, recast, and reforge more than to preserve. Stegner was correct, I think, when he asserted that a regional identity, which he clearly possessed, was best used "as a springboard or a launching pad instead of a prison." Westerners, like Southerners, are a proud, sometimes embattled folk, yet they are also inextricably American, and citizens of the wider world. It does us little good to wall ourselves off. For a writer, constructing such a wall risks damming the most powerful currents of art.

I have been in Wyoming a relatively short time. I have only begun to write about the state — tentatively, with curiosity. I can't yet say whether that work will be good by my standards or anyone else's. I recall Stegner's wry declaration that migrants to the West historically "carr[ied] habits that were often inappropriate and expectations that were surely excessive." I hope I won't make the obvious greenhorn mistakes. It helps me to keep a few of Eudora Welty's wiser words in mind. Welty is eminently Southern, of course. And she is importantly American, supremely human. "The challenge of writers today," Welty tells us, "is not to disown any part of our heritage. Whatever our place, it has been visited by the stranger, it will never be new again. It is only the vision that can be new; but that is enough."

Mark Jenkins

Mark Jenkins is the author of *Off the Map*, *To Timbuktu* and *The Hard Way*. *To Timbuktu* was chosen by the L.A. Times Book Review as one of the Best 100 Books of 1997. In the magazine world, Jenkins is an adventure columnist for *Outside*. His column, "The Hard Way," explores the meaning and joy of the physical, outdoor life — from clandestine journeys across Tibet to mountaineering in Bolivia. Jenkins grew up in Laramie and continues to live there with his wife, Sue Ibarra, and two daughters, Addi and Teal.

From *To Timbuktu*

Part III: The River

When we first see the bridge it is so far away it doesn't seem real. It is like a mirage. We keep paddling and it doesn't disappear.

It is a quarter-mile long cage set forty feet above the water. Monuments of concrete divide the river into equal parts. On shore, in the shade beneath the bridge, we can see naked boys. They are striking the water with sticks and splashing each other. One boy spots us. When he points, the others stop what they are doing and stare, holding their sticks on their heads like spears.

When we finally come close, they leap into the river and struggle out to us, the brown water up to their chests.

It was already decided that when we reached Kouroussa, Mike and Rick and John would go into town for food and I would stay with the boats. I help them drag their kayaks up the bank. They get out their daypacks and money and go off and I'm left with the boys.

The boys are wildly inquisitive. Rolling their eyes and jabbering, their small hard hands touching everything. As if boys emit a smell, like winged insects, new boys eager and reckless come tripping over themselves flying down the bank. I must make it clear that they can't mess with the three beached boats. They are disappointed, instead they surround mine. They touch it, feel the ribs under the skin, fiddle with the deck lines and the rudder, knock heads peering inside the cockpit. They are mechanically-minded. They want to know how it works.

I was a boy once. It is a bright day and I have a long wait. I take up my paddle and slip back into my boat. I maneuver through the crowd in the water and paddle back out into the openness of the river. I make two small circles and then glide back in.

I hold out my paddle as I pierce the mob. A dozen pairs of hands grab it. I sit in the boat and look at all the boys pressed against the hull. They are so excited they're hostile. Eyes and elbows and fists, shouldering and twisting and fighting. I choose a small boy. All I can see is his head at water level between the legs of other boys. He squeezes through and I lift him into the boat onto my lap.

I stroke the boat around in a small circle near the shore. The boy is so proud. He keeps looking back at his friends and shouting to them and waving his arms. I let him hold the paddle with me but he is not paying attention to the movement of the paddle. He doesn't notice the movement of the boat or the movement of the water. He is on stage, like a dancer, his eyes on his audience and his head held in place until his neck can twist no more and he must spin it around, losing eye contact for a split second.

I don't know whether I have done the right thing or not. I paddle the boat back into the gang of boys. They are insolent with envy and desire. I choose another child, lift him in, backpaddle out. I give rides for an hour. All the boys are beside themselves with pride and power and happiness.

Circling back in with what I have decided is my last passenger I see a girl coming down to the river. The bank is steep and slick. She is careful, stepping through the web of tree roots as if they were big hands that might grab her. On her head she is balancing an enormous basin.

When I lift the last boy out others are fighting to get in. I push the mob back and step out of the boat and stand on a rock. Several boys start to get into my boat and I yell at them. One ignores me and climbs into the cockpit and I am forced to haul him out. He is indignant and tries to hurt me with his eyes.

I am watching the girl. Perhaps she is eight years old. She is walking with her neck. Her neck is lean and tall. Her shoulders are narrow and square and her head does not turn. The basin floats through the air. Her grace is effortless and shocking.

As she descends the slope I see two feet protruding from the sides of her waist. By her walk and her shoulders it is plain she has been carrying this child since he was born. Perhaps this child is her brother, perhaps her cousin. It doesn't matter.

Cinched high around her tiny waist is a piece of twine. A gourd, split in half, is attached to the twine by a thong.

She ignores the crowd of boys and walks past us, away from us, down along the bank. Her bare feet sink into the mud. The child she is carrying is asleep, his head sideways between her shoulder blades.

The boys are pulling at me, grabbing my arms to get my attention.

She wades into the river, the basin solid upon her head as if it were permanently connected. The dark water stains her sarong. She moves into the liquid, sinking with every step. She continues out into the river until the water is above her waist and the child's sleeping feet tap the surface.

Her sarong is floating in folds against her, the gourd resting on the water. She unties the gourd from the twine and begins to scoop up cups of brown river. It is a smooth motion. She dips the gourd, gently raises it above her head out over the lip of the basin, and empties it. She cannot see where she is pouring the water. It is somewhere above her head, only her hand knows where. Nothing moves on her body but one arm. She repeats the motion again and again. It is a very large basin and the gourd is small.

I have to drag two boys out of the boat, one with each hand.

The basin is levitating above the river on her head. She cannot see how full the basin is. She feels it. The weight of it.

The boys are pushing and provoking all around me.

She is done. Her arm stops its swiftsmooth motion. She ties the gourd back onto the twine around her waist. She slowly twists and begins to wade back to shore, walking even more with her neck, the folds of her sarong clinging to her little body. She rises out of the water and her sarong is stained the color of the river.

She sees the boys out of the corner of her eye. Then she sees me. She is walking carefully along the bank through the mud without stopping but she sees me coming toward her.

I am talking to her and pointing to my boat. She is wary and keeps walking, pretending not to see me for she has her task and that is all. But I can see it. She is still a child. She is curious. I know she doesn't comprehend my words but she knows what I am saying. Her eyes give her away and she stops. I turn around and start to return to the boat and look back over my shoulder to see if she is following.

She has not moved. She is gazing at me, standing very still with the basin on her head, water dripping down her legs, the child's feet poking out along her waist.

I walk back to her. Standing beside her I realize how small she is. I can see into her basin. The river water is motionless. I grasp the sides of the basin and lift. I can barely move it. She doesn't duck. She waits to see if I can raise the basin off her head. I step backward and the water sloshes and I slip in the mud and the basin tips and water pours out and my face burns and she is laughing. I set the basin down in the mud. Half the water is gone.

She follows me to the boat. I try to take her hand to step across the stones but she lets go. She walks behind me through the crowd of boys. They are shouting at me. I have betrayed them. They are shouting at her. She doesn't hear them.

I seat myself in the boat and then lift her in on my lap.

The child is on her back but I am surprised how light she is. Were it not for the weight of the human she is carrying I believe she would weigh nothing. She would be so buoyant she would simply float into the air above the brown river.

The boys are upset and contemptuous but I wrench the paddle from them and push out. They grab the boat and try to stop it and I have to hit their hands with the blade.

We glide backward. She is sitting on my lap and the child is resting against my chest. We slip away from the shore, away from the crowd of boys and the noise they are making. I let the current turn us. I hold the paddle high and begin to stroke side to side above her head. She places her hands in front of her on the soft skin of the boat.

She is feeling the boat gliding through the water. Her head does not turn, as if the basin of river water were still upon her. She is feeling the water going around the boat. It is the same water that stained her sarong but now she is in it and protected from it. She feels the water going down the sides of the boat, under the boat.

Her hands are flat on the hull but then she lifts them and gently drops her arms to either side of the boat and touches the water. She feels the water moving through her fingers.

I take her far out into the river. The boys on the shore grow tiny and insect-like, but she does not look back.

We make a circle so large it doesn't seem like a circle. A circle so wide and long and open we almost reach the other shore.

On the other shore there are women standing in the water washing clothes and singing. They have spread bright clothes on the bushes and rocks to dry. They wave at us.

When I paddle back many of the boys have dispersed. They are playing somewhere else. I slide into shore and help her up. She steps into the brown water. The weight of the child is hers again.

I follow her up the bank to the basin. She looks down into it but there is no reflection. I lift the basin onto her head.

She walks back down the bank, wades into the water up

to her ribs, unties the thong holding the gourd and begins again, catching the river.

Back when we were searching for a put-in, near the village of Mamouria, Sori took me to the hut of a distinguished chief. I had a question and he said this chief was very wise and could answer it.

Sori went into the hut first. He was inside several minutes before stepping out. He said I could go in now, he would wait outside. I ducked my head and entered, exchanging blazing light for penumbral shade.

"Welcome."

The chief was very old and very tall. He stooped like all men who are that tall. He was in a tattered hide skirt. His skin sagged around his knees and elbows.

He was folding an envelope and placing it on a shelf pegged into the wall. He said it was his military disability check from France. The check would be carried by foot to a bank in a small town, cashed, then the money passed back through the jungle. It was a small amount. It helped support his village.

The French had conscripted him in 1940. He was in the Free French forces and fought the Italians at the Kufra Oasis. Then they put him on a ship to England and it was blown apart by the Germans near Malta. Only he and seven other men survived. They were picked off the ocean by a Spanish gunship. Afterward, after he survived the operations, he was sent to a hospital in England to learn how to walk again. He stayed in England for nine years. That is where he learned how to speak English.

When he came back to his village he was an important man. He went away a rickety tall boy with knobby dry knees and came back with scars and money.

"But that is not what you wanted to talk about."

"No."

"You wish to know why our women are cut."

"I do."

"That is simple. Because otherwise one man could never satisfy a woman. A woman would need many men."

"I don't believe that."

He laughed. "Yes, of course. You could not."

I wasn't sure whether he was insulting me.

"Well then, I shall just say it is our custom."

"It is a barbaric custom."

"Please," a sneer passed briefly across his face, "do not speak to me of barbarism."

"Are your own wives *cut*?"

"It is not possible for a woman to marry if she has not been circumcised."

"It is not circumcision. It is castration."

He sighed.

"But why? You have seen the outside world."

"Yes, I have."

"And it is still done here, in your village?"

"Yes."

"To all of them?"

"Yes, at age seven."

He was not offended. I could ask him anything.

"How is it done?"

"It used to be done with a knife. A small knife, very sharp. Now it is sometimes done with a razor blade."

"Who does it?"

"The old women of the village."

"They hold them down."

"I have not seen it."

But I was seeing it. A little girl screaming and convulsing with fear and they sit on her arms and spread her legs and sit on her little knees and her stomach is quivering and they spread her labium and begin cutting and the blood is warm flowing off her into the dirt and the little girl's mouth is open and she cannot scream now her eyes brilliant from the horror because she believes she is dying.

"It will not continue."

"Perhaps."

"It is unspeakable."

"Yes, we do not speak of it."

"It should be spoken of. Everyone should speak about it."

"There would be problems."

"There should be problems."

He smiled wearily.

On the trail gliding through the high grass where long ago we could have been killed by a lion but now there are none, I had asked Sori if he believed in this practice.

"Is not in Koran."

"Then you do not do it."

"No."

"Then your daughters cannot be married?"

"They marry."

"Sori, what if it were in the Koran."

"Then I do it."

And we had kept on quietly and easily through the high grass where once there were lions.

The chief seated himself on a low stool, slowly leaned his back against the mud wall, and crossed his legs under his skirt.

"May I tell you something?"

"All right."

"Do you know what all white people fear most?"

"I do not know all white people."

"White people fear the fear of pain."

"And black people don't?"

"Yes. But it is not the same. We believe pain is necessary. We accept it. It is part of everything. We even celebrate it."

"Nonsense. You live with it."

"Yes. Yes, exactly. We don't run from it. "

"You misjudge me. It is not just the pain, it is the loss."

"Ah, but it is a gain. Freedom from desire."

"And men do not require such freedom?"

"A man without desire is not a man."

"And a woman?"

"She is a wife and a mother. A better wife. A better mother."

"I do not believe this."

"Yes, of course."

He offered me the stool beside him and began to clean his fingernails with a sharp stick.

"When I was in England I learned many things. I was a boarder at Mrs. Rollins' residence on High Chatfield Road. She was very kind to me. She called me Meto because she could not pronounce my name. Many times she said to me, 'Never mind Meto, underneath we are all the same.'"

He paused for my reaction. I had none.

"Do you know what I think? I think Mrs. Rollins needed to believe this. I think all white people need to believe this. I don't know why. It is not true. We are not the same."

"I do not believe this either."

"Yes, of course. But you do see then?"

"No. See what?"

He clasped his hands and took a long breath through his nose. He was waiting. Allowing me time to think about what he had said.

"Do you know what your guide Sori Keita told me?"

I shook my head.

"He said you could walk like a Malinki. That is why I agreed to speak with you. He said you could walk like we black men walk, that inside, you were a black man. This concerned me very much. But now I have spoken with you and I am relieved. You are white. Inside and out."

He raised his hand cutting me off.

"I know. You don't believe this."

"I don't."

"Now you must see?"

"I don't."

The chief wore an expression of complacent exasperation.

"We, you and I, we don't believe in the same things. How could we possibly be the same?"

Sori's head came into the hut below the beam.

"We must go now."

I stood up. The chief stood up. I shook his hand.

"Thank you for the conversation."
"Not at all. Farewell, white man."

Growing Up in Wyoming

I grew up outdoors, in Wyoming. Bicycling with my brothers across the prairie through the long summer days. Dusk soaking into the red dirt hills, the smell of sage rushing up our nostrils. In winter, mining a snowcave from the largest drift we could find, so frozen our lips wouldn't form words. Using my jacknife to cut forked willows down by a hundred creeks and carving them into hotdog-marshmallow-stab-the-coals stick for a hundred campfires. Lying in the dark in a tent in the woods listening. Killing animals with a rifle. Climbing mountains. Singing through all conditions — in the old station wagon, in a fearsome pew, around the campfire, in a whiteout.

Had I been raised indoors it wouldn't have mattered that I was in Wyoming. White middle class indoors look the same in Ohio. Either way, brought up in painted wood boxes or out under the sky, the geography of your childhood is a sliver broken off in your foot. Over the years it travels up through your body and into your heart.

I got a degree in philosophy from the University of Wyoming and was shocked to find that the job market for philosophers was bleak. I interviewed with the Associated Press expecting a posting in Ethiopia or Afghanistan. They smiled. In the fall I moved into a tiny cabin at 10,000 feet with a typewriter and a beautiful woman. No running water, no bathroom, a bed piled high with down sleeping bags. The door opened inward so we could dig ourselves out after each storm. Writing all morning, cross-country skiing all afternoon.

The first story I sold was about mountaineering, the second was on using a map and compass. What else? These were subjects I knew well enough to write about. I was living a physical life. I still am. I wrote nonfiction because it fit my life — and because I could sell it. I still do. My first book, *Off the Map*, is about bicycling across Siberia. My second book,

To Timbuktu, is about kayaking the Niger river in West Africa. My third book is a collection of my "Hard Way" columns from *Outside* magazine.

I sense the landscape of my homeland has influenced my language. Wyoming geography is spare, elegant and durable, three characteristics I strive for in my writing. There is little that is florid, mushy, profuse or pretentious in Wyoming and I work to expunge such features from my prose. Wind and cold and sun have shaved Wyoming with Occam's razor and I use the same blade in my craft. My best words are small and nimble as a brookie. My best lines lean and straight as a lodgepole pine. If I have done my work well, the story should be limpid as a tarn in the Wind Rivers.

I think the notion of "regionalism in literature" is nonsense, a contradiction of terms. Great writing — literature — always, by definition, transcends its region. Great writing reveals the universal in mankind. This is not profound. It is why a Texan can revel in Tolstoy, why a Russian can read Nadine Gordimer with a grimace and a nod, why a Kenyan can read Gunter Grass and laugh. All writers come from somewhere. They grew up somewhere, they live somewhere. Experiences, environments and imagination are just the raw materials — it is the magic of the act of writing that transforms them into a story.

Was Shakespeare a "regional" writer? Was Kafka? To me the question is absurd — perhaps the invention of some sour academic searching for another artifice with which to pigeonhole writers and maintain tenure. Was Gauguin a "regional" painter? Was Francis Bacon? Was Giacometti a "regional" sculptor? Or Rodin? To ask this question is to fail to understand the most fundamental inspiration for great art of any kind.

I suggest that when critics use the word "regional" to describe the work of a writer, they are behaving cowardly. They are attempting to conceal their disparagement in professorial sophism. Just swap the word "provincial" for "regional" and you'll cut to the chase. Provincial writing fails to transcend its environment and thus fails to illuminate the universal. Consequently, provincial writing is not literature.

Tim Sandlin

Tim Sandlin was born in Duncan, Oklahoma, and lived in Wyoming seasonally from 1960 until establishing permanent residency in 1975. Sandlin has a B.A. from the University of Oklahoma and an M.F.A. from the University of North Carolina at Greensboro. As a writer he has published six novels, a book of columns and ten screenplays for hire. Currently, Sandlin is working as a screenwriter.

Journal 4/7/97

The spring '97 Grovont Trilogy book tour began with a 500-mile drive across Wyoming on a beautiful Sunday afternoon. There's an ice cream shop at the Farson junction that is the closest thing the high plains desert has to an oasis. I ordered a small vanilla and they piled as much ice cream as can humanly be piled on a cone. At least a pint. I've never seen anyone order a medium or large. The mind boggles at the thought.

Monday I did a Cheyenne local live-at-noon TV show. My three minutes came between the cooking tip and the weather. The weatherman stood in front of a blank blue wall pretending to point at a cold front that has been chasing me for six days.

That night's reading was opposite the NCAA basketball national championship. Every few minutes the events coordinator, who was from Kentucky, slipped away to check the score. While I was answering "Where do you get your ideas?" she signaled updates from the back of the crowd. I've been asked that question hundreds of times and I still can't think of an answer that isn't smart-ass, new age, or a lie.

Tuesday, I had two scheduled radio shows fall through. Long stories for both. My hotel room in Boulder had two TVs and three phones (including one in the bathroom.) Ten years ago

I didn't have any TVs or phones (or a bathroom for that matter) so this opulence thing still felt weird. I kept expecting the police to break down the door and arrest me.

The Boulder Book Store has one of the most beautiful places for readings around. It used to be a Buddhist chant room. Forty people showed up, which is a crowd for me, and many of them knew my books better than I do. The night made up for the busted radio interviews. Afterwards some of us went to a wine/espresso bar where the waitress wore nothing but underwear.

Wednesday I did a radio interview at a college station in Fort Collins with a kid who looked fifteen and said he normally didn't read but my book is cool. He asked "Where do get your ideas?" and I said they come from a secret Web site that only published novelists can access. I couldn't help it. The kids following my show were broadcasting on-air body piercing. I didn't stay for it, but they looked interesting.

After the reading at Stone Lion Books that night, a shy guy presented a copy of *Sorrow Floats* and asked me to sign it to the girl who'd left him. "Tell her to come back to me. If you tell her, she'll listen." Another guy told me he was getting a divorce because of something I wrote in the acknowledgments of *Skipped Parts*.

Thursday my girlfriend Carol caught up with the tour, and we did Tattered Cover in Denver. For a writer on tour, the Tattered Cover is Broadway. If you've made it there, you've made it everywhere. I've heard folks say they won't let you in the Author's Guild if you haven't read at Elliot Bay in Seattle, and Elliot Bay is a wonderful store, but for me, the Tattered Cover is Mecca. Colin Powell signed 2,467 books for fans there, and when the T.C. employees cut off the end of the line, there was a near riot. I signed twenty-eight books, plus stock, Thursday night, and it was the thrill of a lifetime of lonely typing.

Friday, I taught a class at Aurora Community College. Nice folks. One woman asked how I made my characters feel real and I told her about the Christmas I was alone and my characters all exchanged presents. There were eight of us around the tree. The teacher told me I was scaring the students.

Then we drove to Colorado Springs for some drive-by signings and on to Taos, through a ground blizzard, for a weekend with our friend, John Nichols, whose writing and life taught me a high percentage of all I know, and now we're headed for Santa Fe and more fun.

Whenever two or more authors get together, here is what they talk about: 1) money, 2) sports, and 3) horror stories of the book tour. I've driven five hundred miles to do a reading where only three people showed up. In Nashville the contact person had gone on vacation and no one could locate any of my books. A radio interviewer in Kansas City asked me what kind of music I write. It only takes a couple of humiliations to realize the worst that can possibly happen really isn't that bad. So you sit behind a table for two hours watching shoppers avert their eyes as if you're a street beggar. It still beats work.

Journal 4/8/97

The Laughing Horse Inn in Taos is one of the truly cool literary hotels in America. The coffee cups read D.H. LAWRENCE MAY HAVE SLEPT HERE and at the communal breakfast table this morning I mentioned Allen Ginsberg's death and everyone there knew who I was talking about. Taos is the capital of old guys with grey pony tails. The first time I went to the Taos Inn, I thought they were holding a Georgia O'Keefe look-alike contest. If you're into harmonics, convergences, fine art, and beautiful country, Taos, New Mexico, is the place to be.

Interesting quotes from the last week of book signing: "Sign it to Lorrie. Make it sound as if the two of you have a torrid sexual history." "Can you get me an agent?" "I'm buying this for my father; he'll hate it." "I've had the most bizarre life. All my friends say I should be a writer."

That last one always amazes me. Why do people think that because they've had interesting lives they would be good writers, if they only had the time to type up the story? I mean, victim memoirs are big now, but that's nonfiction; these people seem to think they'd be John Grisham if only they had his free time. I still get calls from people offering to tell me their story and I can write it and together we'll split the money.

Let's talk about the purpose of the book tour. The Writers on the Road Web site lists 255 writers crossing the country this spring, reading, signing, fighting for media time and space, and guzzling enough coffee to kill a lab rat. And from what I can see, 255 is but a small percentage of those of us actually out here. So why are we doing this? I'll wager not more than five sell enough books to pay the traveling expenses. Most writers at least claim to be quite uncomfortable with promotion. The personality type that enjoys sitting in a room alone for two years writing a novel does not enjoy tap dancing in front of a crowd and screaming, "Look at me!"

As I see it, the whole deal is a matter of name recognition. People do not plop down $22.50 for a book by someone they've never heard of. Which is why first novels rarely sell worth squat. Every season brings on one media darling and roughly three hundred disappointed first novelists. So we fight for that necessary evil — fame. The publishers send us out for that poster in the bookstore window, or the flyer they send to the store mailing lists, or the one sentence announcement in the Community Calendar section of the alternative newspaper. Fifty people and a feature in the Sunday arts supplement are to be killed for, but even a reading attended by four people who don't buy books isn't the Godawful failure the writer thinks it is. Not that you don't feel like gum under a desk at least once each tour.

There are many types of tours, ranging from the best seller ensconced in a hotel room, granting a half hour apiece to hordes of journalists and photographers lined up in the hall, to the self-published poet with six cases of books in the trunk of his car, driving from store to store, begging managers to stock a couple of copies on their Signed by the Author shelf. Tony Hillerman did a small libraries of the West tour about ten years ago, where at the end of each talk he asked the crowd if anyone would give him a ride to the next town. My friend Win Blevins does tours where he shows up at the wholesaler warehouse loading docks at four a.m. with coffee and donuts for the truck drivers. Truck driver schmoozing isn't so much about numbers as placement on the racks. After all, the shelf life of a paperback book in a grocery store is exactly the same as yogurt, and books at chest level outsell ankle-biters by a tremendous margin. It's worth passing out donuts at dawn.

The GroVont spring of '97 tour is my fourth book trip, the second by car. When *Sorrow Floats* came out in 1992, or so, I drove around the South and Midwest for eight weeks, flogging myself and books. That was a dues payer. A humility machine by any standards, although I met some terrific people and saw some beautiful stores. I've never had a bad meal in a bookstore.

By comparison, the *Social Blunders* hardback tour was a luxury item involving airplanes and media escorts. The media escort is not the vanity extra I always thought. They call all these bookstores, other than the one where you make your primary appearance, and set up what are called drive-by signings — meet the staff, sign stock, hobnob with whomever is around. With an escort, the traveling writer can visit ten or more bookstores in a city instead of one. There's a woman in Portland who claims she can hit sixty stores in a day. I've met her and I believe.

Journal 4/9/97

Back in junior high, my English teacher made us do a book report on a nonfiction book — any nonfiction book. I was no more interested in nonfiction then than I am now, so I chose the shortest nonfiction book in the Duncan Junior High library. *Romance and Drama of the Rubber Industry* by B.F. Goodrich, Jr. Actually that book may be why I'm such a poor nonfiction reader today. Anyhow, here's a report on "The Romance and Drama of the Author Tour," for April 7, 1997.

7:30 a.m. — Wake up and start choking down coffee as quickly as possible in hopes of being awake for my

8 00 a.m. — Phone interview with Crazy Dave on "The Crazy Dave Show" on KNYN-FM, Santa Fe. It's a country-western station and Dave was a lot more awake than I was.

8:30 a.m. — Talk to my publicist at Riverhead. We're going to Phoenix Wednesday instead of Las Cruces, for a radio show, then a phone radio show with the guy in Tucson who canceled on me last Monday, then I drive to Tucson and turn around and drive back to Phoenix. The trip itinerary started as a twenty-five page fax and has averaged nine pages of changes per day.

9:00 a.m. — Check out of the Laughing Horse. Go find a place called Word Crafter for a computer that can print my AOL journal and fax it to the woman in New York or someplace.

10:00 a.m. — Back to the Laughing Horse for things we forgot the first time out.

11:00 a.m. — Drive to Santa Fe. Carol drives so I can write my AOL journal entry for tomorrow. I finish about two-thirds of a rough draft, but, let's face it, these people are writers, I can't send in a rough draft.

1 :00p.m. — Arrive at the Hampton Inn. The nice woman at the desk says we can't check in till three.

1:15 p.m. — Double back into town to locate the radio station and bookstore for tonight's gigs. This is fairly crucial because you can't be late for live radio.

2:00 p.m. — Dynamite lunch at Tomasita's, which is a converted railroad station. Every railroad station in the country must have been turned into a restaurant by now. Are there any real stations left?

3:00 p.m. — They let us check in. Carol goes to work out while I finish the AOL journal. I decide to hell with it; this is a journal, they can have a rough draft.

3:30 p.m. — My publicist calls again. Friday is supposed to be a day off, but, as luck would have it, the Putnam/Berkley sales conference is in Scottsdale while I'm in Phoenix. Looks like I'm in for a schmoozing frenzy. This is important. If the sales force isn't enthusiastic, the books won't be in the stores and if the books aren't in the stores I'll be back rolling egg rolls by summer.

3:45 p.m. — Talk to my agent in L.A. He's set up five meetings while I'm doing book promotion in L.A. next week. He wants me to come up with a "high concept pitch" before my meetings. This means an all new plot and set of characters by Monday. As if I don't have anything else to do.

4:00 p.m. — Phone call from the head of development for Alliance Pictures in Toronto. She's faxing first draft notes on my *Sex and Sunsets* screenplay from the guy who owns the company. It doesn't seem to matter that I started the second draft over a month ago and it's pretty much done. The new set of notes will have to be "incorporated."

4:15 p.m — Start typing tomorrow's AOL journal onto my laptop with the R that sticks. I may have to learn to write without using R's.

4:30 p.m. — Get ready for tonight's activities.

5:00 p.m. — Interview on "Sunset Salute" on KVSF-AM with C.R. Power and a woman named Snow. They're old pros at talk radio — didn't know a thing about me until the commercial before we went on, yet they were fun and entertaining. I showed them my Fargo snow globe with the overturned car, dead body, and pregnant sheriff. It's cool, but you almost have to see it.

6:30 p.m. — Arrived at Old Santa Fe Trail Books and met the

Lefflers, friends from my grade school days, then a reporter who wrote a good review of my books, then some old friends from Wyoming. One problem with readings on the road is quite often several sets of people you haven't seen in years and want to spend time with show up all at the same time.

7:00 p.m. — Real nice reading. Lots of people. Lots of questions. Lady in front who laughed at everything I said whether it was supposed to be funny or not.

8:45 p.m. — Interview with two kids from "The Independent," a student newspaper for the College of Santa Fe. Great kids. They couldn't believe how old I am.

9:45 p.m. — Back to the hotel. Finish typing tomorrow's AOL journal.

10:15 p.m. — Locate a Kinko's in the phone book where I can print and fax in the morning.

10:30 p.m. — Find the address and location of a Border's where I'm supposed to sign stock in the morning.

11:00 p.m. — The fax from Toronto comes in. They want the first draft changed in a completely different direction than I spent the last month changing it.

11:30 p.m. — Figure out on the map where I go for tomorrow's noon radio interview in Albuquerque.

Midnight — Read Anne Lamott's new book until I fall asleep.

Journal 4/10/97

Jottings along the eight-hour drive from Albuquerque to Phoenix through the wind storm from hell:

We met Tony Hillerman in person this morning — high point of the tour, so far. Tony is proof that nice guys can lead the pack. And Tony is nice to an amazing degree. We swapped stories for a couple of hours. He told us about the University of Oklahoma writing program after World War II (he wasn't good enough to get into the fiction classes) and his own horror stories of authors on the road. Being a best seller, his stories aren't the "I drove 500 miles through a blizzard and no one showed up" variety. His are more along the lines of being dragged from city to city from six in the morning till two the next morning — three plane flights in a single day, no food for forty-eight hours because there wasn't time, having six cases of books brought to his hotel room at midnight that must be signed before he can go to bed. The sort of challenge most of us never worry about.

I used to review books fairly often for the *New York Times Book Review*, and one of the last books I did was David Bowman's *Let the Dog Drive*. I gave it a rave. (In technical terms, all reviews fall into rave, mixed, or trash jobs). A year or so after my review ran, a letter arrived from a guy who bought the Bowman book because of my recommendation, and he hated it. He wanted his money back — from me. The guy actually billed me $22.90. Needless to say, the letter went into my nut file and I didn't pay the guy's bill. So now, another year later, this guy shows up at my reading last night at Page One Books in Albuquerque. He still wants his money. I offered to send him Bowman's address but he wasn't interested. He bought the book because of me, so I owe him the refund. We wound up having coffee while he told me the details of his ongoing third divorce.

A bunch of us writer types went to dinner after the Cleveland State University writers conference last summer, and Karen Joy Fowler (*Sarah Canary, Sweetheart Season*) had us each tell our most horrific book tour story. Most of them didn't seem so horrible to me — one woman had a member of the audience die during a reading, but that can happen anywhere. Famous Unnamed Author arrived at a chain bookstore and saw there were no posters about the signing, no piles of books. He asked to speak to his contact person. They led him to an office in back.

He said, "Hi, I'm Famous Author's Name." The contact looked at him and said, "Did you bring a resumé?"

I did a reading at the Hungry Mind in Minneapolis where most of the audience didn't speak English. They'd been bused in to learn about typical American culture (which, if you've read my books, is a frightening thought). They sat there stone-faced, not understanding a word, until halfway through the reading when their bus pulled up and they all left.

One last story and I'll quit:

Writers are treated like rock stars in Iowa City, Iowa, so much so that Prairie Lights Bookstore broadcasts its events on a live one-hour radio show four or five nights a week. William Least Heat Moon was scheduled the night after my reading, so I stayed an extra day to hear him. Time came for the appearance, three hundred people sat in an auditorium, and no William. He arrived, from Wisconsin, with less than a minute to spare and no idea he was going on live radio in front of 300 people. And he had to pee. Fat chance. The radio woman grabbed his hand, dragged him on stage, and the show went on the air. I learned a lot in the next hour. 1) Never let anyone at the gig know you've arrived until you use the facilities, and 2) the show must go on. William was fascinating. Professional. A great speaker except he kept tapping one foot. After the talk, over 100 people lined up to have him sign books and tell him anecdotes about how he affected their lives and he didn't even take a break. I like to think I'm a professional, but I would have taken a break.

P.S. Overheard just now at a pay phone at the Holbrook Truck Stop, a woman is talking: "I parked by the water and he jumped out the window and an alligator ate him."

Journal 4/11/97

"Registered nurses in California received credit for participating in classes on crystal healing." *Glance* magazine.

The article goes on to say "When touched, the crystal vibrates at a frequency that is in harmony with your own, so there is an increased awareness enabling you to create your own reality."

Create your own reality. That's the goal of every novelist, so it shouldn't be so weird to do it by gluing rocks to chakras. That's got to be easier than a fourth draft. Speaking of creating your own reality, we were driving through a desert hurricane of a windstorm on the New Mexico-Arizona border yesterday — those orange barrels the highway department closes lanes with were blowing across the interstate like tumbleweeds — when the car phone rang (so sue me; I have a car phone for the trip) and it's some producer from Hollywood who wants me to write a movie. Only in America can a survival situation be interrupted by a movie deal.

Working with the folks in Hollywood is a lot of fun once you realize they're speaking a different language than everyone else. They take meetings, do lunch, pitch ideas they want turned into concepts. Life is arcs and beats. Without sexual or sports metaphors the town would shrivel up and die. The person who "loves" your work and is "deeply committed" to it, probably hasn't read it. An agent will say, "I have a relationship with Such-and-So at Fox." My theory is that when the relationship becomes the primary business tool you have a tainted situation. The challenge is to avoid cynicism. You must remember that love and courage are real, not just story elements. I've handled this by only working with people I like. A lot. My outhouse is paid for, I don't have to deal with mean people.

More disconnected ramblings on the last day of my AOL journal: mountains in Arizona look like you're looking at them through binoculars. Must be the air. It is possible to live on a macrobiotic diet of Pepcid and coffee.

A man said to me the other night, "I could be famous if I lowered myself to writing sex scenes, the way you do."

A Tucson radio interviewer could not understand why I washed dishes for a living all those years. He said, "You had a degree, didn't you?" I said I wanted to write. "But why didn't you get a real job?" I didn't tell him about turning thirty-five while living in a tent.

I suspected another interviewer of having her own agenda. She asked me if I was a vegetarian and what I thought of people who used lactose. It was a trick bringing those questions back around to my books.

On a completely different subject —

Writing fiction involves a lot of tragedy rehearsal. You say to yourself, "If I had a brother and if he committed suicide, how would I feel?" then you feel that way for a while and write about it. This is one reason it's hard to be married to a writer. Their moods bear no connection to circumstances. I like to think I'm feeling the true depths of emotions, but then the mail arrives. Often — quite often — letters come in that start with "I feel like I'm a character in one of your books," then they go on to say their sister is in prison for manslaughter, their boyfriend is a heroin addict, and their child died last year. That's when I realize that to actually live is so much more intense than to create life. I also realize all comedy, from I Love Lucy to Liar, Liar would be tragic if it were true. The letters end with thanking me for showing them they aren't alone and with humor and love they can make it through. Makes me feel like a total fake, drinking lattés and talking on the car phone to women in power suits. What do I know about the lives I write about?

Old people write me and send photos of their cats named after my characters — "This is Maurey, she's a Siamese-Manx." Guys break up with their girlfriends and because they're too embarrassed to talk to other guys, they write me fifteen-page letters — drunk, two a.m. — telling me how much it hurts. Women write to explain, in detail, how their boyfriends are in bed. This is a true quote: "I don't like him at all but he's so good at oral sex I don't want to break up." I send back a postcard saying, "Thanks for your support."

What I never get is what I fantasized all those lonely years of typing through the long Wyoming winter — offers of marriage, or let-me-have-your-baby. Which is for the best now because I have a fine girlfriend who drives me around while I promote myself, but you can't help but wonder, if this author cliché is a lie, maybe they all are.

Anyhow, this is your fifth and final installment of Tim Sandlin on Tour. I still have three weeks of wandering the countryside, begging people to listen to me, so if you're anywhere on the route, come on out, I'll show you my Fargo snow globe.

So long from Tucson. Or Phoenix. I forget.

How Place Affects
My Subject Matter

A Montana woman asked William Faulkner why his fiction was so much better than that of the writers in her home state. She claimed that Montana writers loved Montana as much as Faulkner loved Mississippi, therefore their fiction should be just as powerful as his. Here is Faulkner's answer: "Madame, I *hate* Mississippi."

Therein lies what has always struck me as a major obstacle, or maybe we should call it disadvantage, to being a writer in the Rocky Mountains. We are too damn satisfied with where we live. Wyoming is paradise, at least for those who live here, and paradise makes for boring fiction. A story needs anger and depression; peace of mind is great for those who have it, but no one wants to read about a nice place. We should learn the lesson of Dante. He was the first to show us heaven is a fine place to live, but hell makes for a more interesting poem.

So, fairly early in my scribbling career I put aside the need to find a new way of describing the sunset. There isn't a new way. Instead, I chose to write about the West as I saw it, which was the view from behind the Hobart dish machine at Cache Creek Station restaurant, then, later, a saddle bar stool in the Million Dollar Cowboy Bar. I live in a town where a stagecoach circles from morning to nightfall all summer, endlessly hauling displaced children who wave rubber tomahawks and shout "This sucks." Many of these children have never seen horse poop. Some have never seen stars. Their idea of a cowboy is formed by the grown men who shoot each other with blanks every evening at seven in the intersection in front of the Gap outlet store. Their elk are behind a fence. Their bears have names like Boo-Boo.

John   Rember   calls   my   homeland   "The   Lycra

Archipelago." The larger islands in the chain are Sun Valley, Idaho; Jackson, Wyoming; Steamboat Springs, Colorado; Taos, New Mexico; Moab, Utah. We are the towns where the citizenry's primary directive is to perfect their bodies. Outsiders will tell you we are money driven, but that isn't true — we are driven by the insatiable need for vigor. Health comes first, then real estate, then an obsession with keeping things the way they were last week. Realtors are the gold diggers and bordello queens of the 90s; lawyers are the carnivores; tourists, the buffalo. Our homeless street people can tell you what wine goes well with a hummus pita. Our mantra is, "If we let that development come in here, why, we're no better than Aspen."

But, it's not all silly California yuppie scum buying custom-made cowboy hats to wear in the ski lodge. There are those who see the battle of the New West as a matter of real survival.

"Happy families are all alike; every unhappy family is unhappy in its own way." The same goes for cowboys.

Like basically everything else in Wyoming, the explanation is found in *Shane*. Besides being the greatest movie ever made, *Shane* is the archetypal story of Jackson Hole. It is the story that started when colonists displaced the Iroquois who displaced the Cheyenne who came here searching for someone they could displace, and still goes on today with the billionaires running the millionaires out of the valley.

On one side we have the cattleman, Rufus Ryker, who has suffered, fought, and survived fifty Wyoming winters to carve out an empire for himself and his people; and, on the other side, we have the Staretts, Shipsteads and Torreys, immigrants into the West, families who only need room to start a new life where their dreams can become reality. Into this, we throw Shane, the tourist who only wants to be left alone, but ultimately no one is neutral, no one can escape the land development issue.

Today, instead of ranchers against homesteaders, we have those who worked for the Western way of life against those who would buy it. The old-timers who suffered through winters before cable TV, Federal Express, and plowed highways, are being run over by stock brokers driving Range Rovers with vanity plates and Trout Unlimited bumper stickers; men and women who think daily jet service to L.A. is an inalienable right; newcomers who not only don't eat the fish they catch, but consider anyone who does as scum. Leash laws, smoking regulations, land use codes — these are the wellsprings of resentment. It is not enough for the new people to live the way they want, everyone else has to live that way.

Resentment breeds envy, anger, substance abuse, and road rage. Now, we have the raw materials for fiction as good as Faulkner's.

This is the West I am interested in writing about and these are my themes: the struggle to stay forever young; the never-ending battle between those who would make money by destroying paradise and those who want to keep it the way it was when they got here, even if that was last week; and *Shane*.

Other books by the authors
and acknowledgments of
previously published work

Annie Proulx

1988   *Heart Songs and Other Stories*, Scribner, New York, N.Y.

1992   *Postcards*, Scribner, New York, N.Y

1993   *The Shipping News*, Scribner, New York, N.Y

1996   *Accordion Crimes*, Scribner, New York, N.Y

1997   Editor, *Best American Short Stories of 1997*,
       Houghton Mifflin Co., Boston, Massachusetts

1999   *Close Range: Wyoming Stories*, Scribner, New York, N.Y

2003   *That Old Ace in the Hole*, Scribner, New York, N.Y

David Romtvedt

1984   *Moon*, Bieler Press, St. Paul, Minnesota

1984   *Free and Compulsory For All:*,
       Graywolf Press, St. Paul, Minnesota

1987   *Black Beauty, A Praise and Kiev, the Ukraine:*,
       Blue Begonia Press, Yakima, Washington

1988   *Letters from Mexico*, Kutenai Press, Missoula, Montana

1988   *How Many Horses*, Ion Books, Memphis, Tennessee

1991   *Yip, a Cowboy's Howl*,
       Holocene Books, Spartanburg, South Carolina

1992   *A Flower Whose Name I Do Not Know,*

        Copper Canyon Press, Port Townsend, Washington

1993   *Crossing Wyoming*, White Pine Press, Buffalo, N.Y.

1995   *Buffalotarrak: An Anthology of the Basque people of Buffalo, Wyoming*, Red Hills Publications, Buffalo, Wyoming

1996   *Certainty*, White Pine Press, Buffalo, N.Y.

1997   *Windmill: Essays From Four-Mile Ranch*, Red Crane Books, Santa Fe, New Mexico

Linda M. Hasselstrom

1984   *Journal of a Mountain Man: Clyman, James, 1792-1881*; Editor, Linda M. Hasselstrom, Mountain Press Pub. Co, Missoula, Montana

1984   *Caught By One Wing: poems*, J.D. Holcomb, San Francisco, California

1987   *Windbreak: A Woman Rancher On the Northern Plains*, Barn Owl Books, Berkeley, California

1987   *Roadkill*, Spoon River Poetry Press, Peoria, Illinois

1987   *Going Over East: Reflections of a Woman Rancher*, Fulcrum, Golden, Colorado, Revised edition: 2001

1991   *Land Circle: Writings Collected From the Land*, Fulcrum, Golden, Colorado

1993   *Dakota Bones: Collected Poems of Linda Hasselstrom*, Spoon River Poetry Press, Granite Falls, Minnesota

1994   *A Roadside History of South Dakota*, Mountain Press Pub., Missoula, Montana

1997   *Leaning Into the Wind: Women Write From the Heart of the West* Editors: Linda M. Hasselstrom, Gaydell Collier, Nancy Curtis Houghton Mifflin, Boston, Massachusetts

1998   *Bison: Monarch of the Plains*, David Fitzgerald, Linda M. Hasselstrom, Graphic Arts Center Pubs, Portland, Oregon

1999   *Feels Like Far: A Rancher's Life on the Great Plains*, Lyons Press, New York, N.Y.

2001   *Bitter Creek Junction*, High Plains Press, Glendo, Wyoming

2001   *Woven on the Wind: Women Write About Friendship in the Sagebrush West. Editors:* Linda M. Hasselstrom, Gaydell Collier and Nancy Curtis.
Houghton Mifflin, Boston, Massachusetts

2002   *Between Grass and Sky: Where I Live and Work,* Linda M. Hasselstrom University of Nevada Press, Reno, Nevada

Jon Billman

1999   *When We Were Wolves,* Random House, New York, N.Y.

John D. Nesbitt

1990   *Lesser-known Works of Wyoming Fiction,* John D. Nesbitt, Eastern Wyoming College, Torrington, Wyoming

1991   *Adventures of the Ramrod Rider: A Trio of Gripping Tales,* Wild Rose and Cedar Press, Torrington, Wyoming

1994,   *One-Eyed Cowboy Wild,* Walker and Co., New York, N.Y.

1995,   *One Foot In the Stirrup: Western Stories,*
RR Productions, 1995, Torrington, Wyoming

1995   *Twin Rivers,* Walker and Co., New York, N.Y.

1996   *I'll Tell You What: Fiction With Voice,*
RR Productions, Torrington, Wyoming

1997   *Wild Rose of Ruby Canyon,* Walker and Co., New York, N.Y.

1997   *Antelope Sky: Stories of the Modern West,*
RR Productions, Torrington, Wyoming

1998   *Keep the Wind in Your Face,* Endeavor Books, Casper, Wyoming

1998   *Seasons In the Fields: Stories of a Golden West,*
RR Productions, Torrington, Wyoming

1998   *Black Diamond Rendezvous,* Leisure Books, New York, N.Y.

1999   *A Good Man to Have in Camp,*
Endeavor Books, Casper, Wyoming

1999   *Blue Book to Basic Writing,* Endeavor Books, Casper, Wyoming

1999   *Adventures of the Ramrod Rider: Gripping Tales, Augmented and Revised by the Author,* Endeavor Books, Casper, Wyoming

2000   *Writing for Real,* Endeavor Books, Casper, Wyoming

2000   *North of Cheyenne,* Leisure Books, New York, N.Y.

2000   *Coyote Trail,* Leisure Books, New York, N.Y.

2001   *Man from Wolf River,* Leisure Books, New York, N.Y.

2002   *For the Norden Boys,* Leisure Books, New York, N.Y.

2003   *Black Hat Butte,* Leisure Books, New York, N.Y.

Robert Roripaugh

1961   *A Fever for Living,* Morrow, New York, N.Y.;

1963   *Honor Thy Father,* Morrow, New York, N.Y.

1975   *"The Legend of Billy Jenks"* (pp 138-163), *The Far Side of the Storm: New Ranges of Western Fiction,* Editor: Gary Elder, San Marcos Press, 1975, Los Cerrillos, New Mexico

1976   *Learn to Love the Haze,* Spirit Mound Press, Vermillion, South Dakota

1986   *"Wyoming Ranch Life Thirty Years Ago"* (pp 77-91) *Historic Ranches of Wyoming* By Judith Hancock Sandoval, Nicolaysen Art Museum, Casper, Wyoming

1992   *Foreword. (pp xv-xx), LandMarked: Stories of Peggy Simson Curry* Editor: Mary Alice Gunderson, High Plains Press, Glendo, Wyoming

1993   *"Leave's End"* (pp 49-66), *Higher Elevations: Stories from the West,* Editor: Alexander Blackburn and C. Kenneth Pellow, Swallow Press/Ohio University Press, Athens, Ohio

2001   *The Ranch: Wyoming Poetry,* University of Wyoming, Laramie, Wyoming

Page Lambert

1995   *Tumblewords: Writers Reading the West* (Western Literature Series), Contributor: Page Lambert, essay "Homefires" Editor: William L. Fox, University of Nevada Press, Reno, Nevada

1995   *The Stories that Shape Us: Women Write About the West: An Anthology*; Editors: Teresa Jordan, James Hepworth, Contributor: Page Lambert, essay " Porcupine Dusk," W.W. Norton and Co., New York, N.Y.

1996   *Chicken Soup for the Woman's Soul*, Contributor: Page Lambert, essay "Gifts," Editors: Jack Canfield, Mark Victor Hansen, Marci Shimoff, Jennifer Howthorne, Health Communications, Inc., Deerfield Beach, Florida

1996   *Chicken Soup for the Cat and Dog Lover's Soul*, Contributor: Page Lambert, essay "Hondo," Editors: Jack Canfield, Mark Victor Hansen, Carol Kline, Marty Becker, D.V.M.

1996   *In Search of Kinship: Modern Pioneering on the Western
        Landscape,* Fulcrum Publishing, Golden, Colorado

1997   *Leaning into the Wind: Women Write from the Heart of the West,*
        Contributor: Page Lambert, essay 1998 *"Redy's Foal,"*
        Editors: Linda Hasselstrom, Gaydell Collier, Nancy Curtis,
        Houghton Mifflin Co., NewYork, N.Y.

1997   *Shifting Stars: a Novel of the West,* Forge, New York, N.Y.

1998   *Writing Down the River: Into the Heart of the Grand Canyon,*
        Contributor: Page Lambert, essay *"Faces of the Canyon,"*
        Editor: Kathleen Ryan, Northland Publishing, Flagstaff, Arizona

2001   *Woven on the Wind: Women Write about Friendship in the
        Sagebrush West,* Contributor: Page Lambert, essay, *"Backbeat"*
        Editors: Linda Hasselstrom, Gaydell Collier, Nancy Curtis

2002   *Ranching west of the 100th Meridian: Culture, Ecology, and
        Economics;* Contributor: Page Lambert, chapter *"An Intimate
        Look at the Heart of the Radical Center,"* Editors: Richard L.
        Knight, Wendell C. Gilgert, Ed Marston,
        Island Press, Washington, D.C.

2003   *Heart Shots,* Contributor: Page Lambert, "Deerstalking,"
        Editor: Mary Strange, Stackpole Press, Pennsylvania

Barbara Smith

Poetry published in the following collections

1984   *Wyoming Promises,* Editor: Nancy Curtis,
        High Plains Press, Glendo, Wyoming

1988   *The Last Best Place,* Editors: William Kittredge and Annick
        Smith, Montana Historical Society, Helena, Montana

1991   *Letter from Wyoming,* Editor: Jean Hanson,
        Wyoming Arts Council, Cheyenne, Wyoming

1992   *Ucross: The First Ten Years,* Editor: Charles Levendosky,
        Ucross, Wyoming

1994   *Drive, He Said,* Editor: Kurt Brown,
        Milkweed, Minneapolis, Minnesota

1997   *Leaning into the Wind*, Editors: Linda Hasselstrom, Gaydell
         Collier, and Nancy Curtis,
         Houghton Mifflin Co., New York, N.Y.

2001   *Woven on the Wind*, Editors: Linda Hasselstrom, Gaydell
         Collier, and Nancy Curtis,
         Houghton Mifflin Co., New York, N.Y.

Geoffrey O'Gara

1983   *The Western ABC*, Geoffrey O'Gara, Sylvia Long,
         Trotevale, Lander, Wyoming

1989   *A Long Road Home: Journeys Through America's Present in
         Search of America's Past* , Norton, New York, N.Y.;
         paperback edition: Houghton-Mifflin, New York, N.Y.

1997   *Great Lakes*, National Geographic Society, Washington, D.C.

2000   *What You See in Clear Water: Life on the Wind River
         Reservation*, Alfred Knopf, New York, N.Y., Vintage paperback

2000   *Ring of Fire: Writers of the Yellowstone Region* Author: William
         Hoagland, Geoffrey O'Gara, and others,
         Rocky Mountain Press, Cody, Wyoming

2000   *Frommer's Yellowstone and Grand Teton National Parks*,
         IDG Books Worldwide, Inc., Foster City, California

2000   *Yellowstone and Grand Tetons National Parks*,
         Frommers/Transworld, London

2000   *Far West: Guide to America's outdoors*, Author: Geoffrey
         O'Gara; Phil Schermeister, National Geographic,
         Washington, D.C.

2001   *National Geographic Guide to America's Outdoors Far West*,
         Geoffrey O'Gara, Phil Schermeister, National Geographic
         Society Hi Marketing, Washington, D.C., London

2002   *Frommer's Montana and Wyoming*,
         IDG Books Worldwide, Inc.,Foster City, California

2002   *Yellowstone and Grand Teton National Parks*, Eric Peterson;
         Geoffrey O'Gara, Frommers/Transworld, London

Charles Levendosky

1970   *Perimeters,* Wesleyan University Press, Middletown, Connecticut

1974   *Small Town America,* Boxwood Press, Statesboro, Georgia

1974   *From Hell to Breakfast* (multimedia piece)with Wendel Logan as composer, Oberlin Conservatory of Music

1975   *Words & Fonts,* Georgia Arts Council and Boxwood Press

1978   *Aspects of the Vertical,* Point Riders Press, Norman, Oklahoma

1980   *Distances,* Dooryard Press, Story, Wyoming

1981   *Wyoming Fragments,* Buffalo Point Press, Cody, Wyoming

1982   *Nocturnes,* Dooryard Press, Story, Wyoming

1986   *Hands and Other Poems,* Point Riders Press, Norman, Oklahoma

1995   *Circle of Light,* High Plains Press, Glendo, Wyoming

2003   *The Peeping Tom Poems,* Clark City Press, Livingston, Montana

Poetry included in these anthologies:

1972   *Breakthrough Fictioneers,* Editor: Richard Kostelanetz, Something Else Press, New York, N.Y.

1975   *Words Wyoming,* Editor: Paul Dilsaver, *Rocky Mountain Creative Arts Journal*

1977   *Traveling America with Today's Poets,* Editor: David Kherdian, Macmillan, New York, N.Y.

1977   *Joys of Fantasy,* Editor: Siv Cedering Fox, Scarborough Press, New York, N.Y.

1980   *Text-Sound Texts: North America,* Editor: Richard Kostelanetz, Something Else Press, New York, N.Y.

1980   *The Windflower Almanac,* Editors: Ted Kooser,Wildflower Press

1981   *70 on the '70s: A Decade of History in Verse,* Editors: McGovern and Snyder, Ashland Press, Ashland, Ohio

1981   *Point Riders Press Anthology of Great Plains Poetry,* Editors: Henderson and Parman, Point Riders Press, Norman, Oklahoma

1982   *48 Younger American Poets,* Editors: Carr, Ferrarie and Olson, Four Zoas Press

2002   *Perfect in Their Art: Poems on Boxing from Homer to Ali,* Editors:
         Hedlin, Robert and Waters Southern Illinois University Press

2002   New Century North American Poets, Editors

Warren Adler

Warren Adler Novels:

> *The War of the Roses – the Children (forthcoming, spring 2004)*
> *The War of the Roses*
> *Random Hearts*
> *Trans-Siberian Express*
> *Mourning Glory*
> *Cult*
> *The Casanova Embrace*
> *Blood Ties*
> *Natural Enemies*
> *Banquet Before Dawn*
> *The Housewife Blues*
> *Madeline's Miracles*
> *We Are Holding the President Hostage*
> *Private Lies*
> *Twilight Child*
> *The Henderson Equation*
> *Undertow*

The Fiona Fitzgerald Mysteries

> *American Quartet*
> *American Sextet*
> *Senator Love*

Immaculate Deception
The Witch of Watergate
The Ties That Bind

Short Stories

The Sunset Gang
Never Too Late for Love
Jackson Hole, Uneasy Eden

Tom Rea

1977   *Man in a Rowboat,*
        Copper Canyon Press, Port Townsend, Washington
1985   *Smith and Other Poems,* Dooryard Press, Story, Wyoming
2001   *Bone Wars: The Excavation and Celebrity of Andrew Carnegie's
        Dinosaur,* University of Pittsburgh Press, Pittsburgh, Pennsylvania

B.J. Buckley

1987   *Artifacts: Poems,* Willow Bee Publishing, Saratoga, Wyoming
        "Living in Another World," Northern Lights
        "Bear in a Tree with Apples," Northern Lights
        "Grace," InterMountain Woman
        "Mad Alyce in October," The Cumberland Poetry Review

C.L. Rawlins

Poetry in journals:

"Eleison," *Petroglyph*

"In Rock Springs there will be a reading," *Camas*

"Drinking in the Space," *Sequoia*

"Grace," *Owen Wister Review*

"Solvay Trona Mine, June 30, 1994," *Poetry Wales*

"Enter My Dreams, Love," *Poetry Ireland Review*

Books:

1985   *Ceremony on Bare Ground: Poems.*
         Compost Press, Salt Lake City, Utah

1993   *Witness: A Year in the Wind River Range.*
         Henry Holt, New York, N.Y.

1996   *Broken Country: Mountains & Memory.*
         Henry Holt, New York, N.Y.

1998   *In Gravity National Park.*
         University of Nevada Press, Reno, Nevada

2002   *The Complete Walker IV, with Colin Fletcher.*
         Alfred A. Knopf, New York, N.Y.

Vicki Lindner

1982   *Outlaw Games,* Dial Press

1987   *Unbalanced Accounts: Why Women are Still Afraid of Money*
         Annette Lieberman and Vicki Lindner, The Atlantic Monthly
         Press, 1987, Viking/Penguin, 1988, reprinted in a revised,
         updated edition as *The Money Mirror: How Money Reflects
         Women's Dreams, Fears, and Desires* by Allworth Press in 1996.

Dainis Hazners

1999   limited edition chapbook

Alyson Hagy

1986   *Madonna on Her Back: stories,*
        Stuart Wright, Winston-Salem, North Carolina
1991   *Hardware River: stories,* Poseidon Press, NewYork, N.Y.
2000   *Keeneland,* Simon & Schuster, New York, N.Y.
2000   *Graveyard of the Atlantic: stories,*
        Graywolf Press, Saint Paul, Minnesota

Mark Jenkins

1992   *Off The Map: Bicycling Across Siberia,*
        William Morrow, New York, N.Y.
1997   *To Timbuktu,* William Morrow, New York, N.Y.
2002   *The Hard Way,* Simon and Schuster, New York, N.Y.

Tim Sandlin

1987   *Sex and Sunsets,* Henry Holt, New York, N.Y
1988   *Western Swing,* Henry Holt, New York, N.Y.
1991,   *The Pyms: Unauthorized Tales of Jackson Hole,* Tim Sandlin and
        Diane Kaup-Benefiel, Oothoon Press, Jackson Hole, Wyoming
1991   *Skipped Parts,* Henry Holt, New York, N.Y.
1992   *Sorrow Floats,* Henry Holt, New York, N.Y.
1995   *Social Blunders,* Henry Holt, New York, N.Y.

1998   Screenplay for *Floating Away*, Showtime Productions
2001   Screenplay for *Skipped Parts*, Trimark Productions
2003   *Honey Don't*, Putnam Books, New York, N.Y.

For Further Reading

The editors acknowledge that the writers featured in this volume represent just a smidgen of those novelists, short-story writers, essayists, and poets in Wyoming. So we offer a list that points to "further reading" by writers who live in Wyoming, who once lived in Wyoming but have moved on to greener (but not necessarily more interesting) pastures, and those writers who have died. It also is an attempt to list those notable books that have been published since the Wyoming Center for the Book began this project five long years ago. In some cases, we have listed multiple books because the authors are so prolific. Still, it's best to consider this list a sampler of work by writers with ties to Wyoming.

For a much more complete look at books about Wyoming, go to the Wyoming State Library's catalog at:

http://wyld.state.wy.us

or view authors database at

http://www-wsl.state.wy.us/slpub/cenbook/index.html

Here's the list:

Renee Askins
    Shadow Mountain, Doubleday, New York, N.Y.

Julene Bair
    One Degree West: Reflections of a Plainsdaughter,
    Mid-List Press, Minneapolis, Minnesota

Barbara Allen Bogart
    *In Place: Stories of Landscape and Identity from the
    American West*, High Plains Press, Glendo,Wyoming

C.J. Box
    Open Season and *Savage Run*,
    C.J. Putnam's Sons, New York, N.Y.

Burt Bradley
    Translating Goias,
    Federal University of Goias, Goiania, Goias, Brazil

Bobby Bridger
    Buffalo Bill and Sitting Bull: Inventing the West,
    University of Texas Press, Austin, Texas

Larry Brown
    Coyotes and Canaries,
    High Plains Press, Glendo, Wyoming

Ed Bryant
    Wyoming Sun, Jelm Mountain Press, Laramie, Wyoming

Lily Burana
    Strip City, a Stripper's Farewell Journey Across America,
    Hyperion, New York, N.Y.

Struthers Burt
Powder River Let 'Er Buck, Rinehart, New York, N.Y.

Chip Carlson,
Tom Horn: Blood on the Moon,
High Plains Press, Glendo, Wyoming

Annette Chaudet
Montana Spring writing as Richard Magniet
as editor & contributor: *Hard Ground III: Writing the Rockies*,
and other anthologoies, Pronghorn Press

Bob Cherry
West of Empty, One-Eyed Press, Cody, Wyoming
Spirit of the Raven:An Alaskan Novel
One-Eyed Press, Cody, Wyoming
Inua, One-Eyed Press, Cody, Wyoming
Little Rains, One-Eyed Press, Cody, Wyoming

Gaydell Collier, Nancy Curtis, and Linda Hasselstrom, editors,
*Leaning Into the Wind: Women Write from
the Heart of the West*
Houghton Mifflin, Boston, Massachusetts
*Woven on the Wind: Women Write About Friendship
in the Sagebrush West*
Houghton Mifflin, Boston, Massachusetts

John Byrne Cooke
The Snowblind Moon, Tor, New York, N.Y.

Peggy Simson Curry
Summer Range, Dooryard Press, Story Wyoming
Landmarked: Stories of Peggy Simson Curry,
High Plains Press, Glendo, Wyoming

Lyn Dalebout
> *Out of the Flames*, Blue Bison Press, Moose, Wyoming

Gretel Ehrlich
> *The Solace of Open Spaces* and *Heart Mountain*,
> Viking Penguin, New York, N.Y.

Ron Franscell
> *Angel Fire,*
> Laughing Owl Publishing, Grand Bay, Alabama

Alexandra Fuller
> *Don't Let's Go to the Dogs Tonight*,
> Random House, New York, N.Y.

James Galvin
> *The Meadow* and *Fencing the Sky,*
> Henry Holt & Co., New York, N.Y.

Jim Garry
> *This Ol' Drought Ain't Broke Us Yet*,
> Orion Books, New York, N.Y.

Kathleen O'Neal and W. Michael Gear
> More than 30 novels individually and together including:
> *Bone Walker: An Anasazi Mystery,* Forge, New York, N.Y.
> *People of the Owl, Forge,* New York, N.Y.
> *Thin Moon and Cold Mist*, Forge, New York, N.Y.
> *Long Ride Home*, Tor, New York, N.Y.

Mary Alice Gunderson
> *Devils Tower: Stories in Stone,*
> High Plains Press, Glendo, Wyoming

Janell Hanson
> *The Side-Effects Kid*, Partae Press, Laramie, Wyoming

Hannah Hinchman
>   *A Life in Hand: Creating the Illuminated Journal*,
>   Gibbs Smith, Publisher, Layton, Utah

J. Royal Horton
>   *Murder in Jackson Hole* and *Murder in Mixteca*,
>   Sunlight Publishing, Colorado Springs, Colorado

Donald Hough
>   *The Cocktail Hour in Jackson Hole*,
>   W.W. Norton & Co., New York, N.Y.

Teresa Jordan
>   *Riding the White Horse Home*, Pantheon, New York, N.Y.

Ted Kerasote
>   *Heart of Home: People, Wildlife, Place*,
>   Villard, New York, N.Y.

T.A. Larson
>   *History of Wyoming*,
>   University of Nebraska Press, Lincoln, Nebraska

Jeff Lockwood
>   *Grasshoppers Dreaming: Reflections on Killing and Looking*,
>   Skinner House Books, Boston, Massachusetts

Joe Marshall III
>   *In the Dance House: Stories from Rosebud*,
>   Red Crane, Santa Fe, New Mexico

Ann McCutchan
>   *The Muse that Sings: Composers Speak about
>   the Creative Process*,
>   Oxford University Press, New York, N.Y.

Michael McIrvin
>*Déjà vu and the Phone Sex Queen,*
>J-Press Publishing, White Bear Lake, Minnesota,
>*Optimism Blues: Poems Selected and New,*
>Cedar Hill Publications, San Diego, California

Clinton McKinzie
>*Edge of Justice*, Delacorte, New York, N.Y.

Candy Moulton
>*The Grand Encampment: Settling the High Country,*
>High Plains Press, Glendo, Wyoming
>Candy Moulton and Max Evans, editors,
>*Hot Biscuits: Eighteen Stories by Women and Men of
>the Ranching West*, University of New Mexico Press,
>Albuquerque, New Mexico

Mardy and Olaus Murie
>*Wapiti Wilderness*, Alfred A. Knopf, New York, N.Y.

Martin Murie
>*Windswept*, Homestead Publishing, Moose, Wyoming

Bill Nye
>*His Own Life Story,*
>Books for Libraries Press,Freeport, N.Y.

Mary O'Hara
>*My Friend Flicka*, Perennial Library, New York, N.Y.

Geoff Peterson
>*Bad Trades,* Creative Arts Book Co, Berkley, California;
>*Medicine Dog,* St. Martin's Press,New York, N.Y.

Michael Punke
>*The Revenant*, Carroll & Graf, New York, N.Y.

A.K. Pyatt
> *The Women of Eden*,
> M-O-T-H-E-R Publishing, Rock Springs, Wyoming

Paisley Reckdal
> *Six Girls Without Pants: Poems* Eastern
> Washington University Press, Cheney, Washington
> *The Night My Mother Met Bruce Lee: Observations
> on Not Fitting In*, Pantheon, New York, N.Y.

Shelly Ritthaler
> *The Ginger Jar*, Raven Creek Press, Upton, Wyoming

Lee Ann Roripaugh
> *Beyond Heart Mountain*, Penguin, New York, N.Y.

Jack Shaefer
> *Shane*, Houghton-Mifflin, New York, N.Y.

Tom Shakespeare
> *The Sky People*, Vantage, New York, N.Y.

Mark Spragg
> *Where Rivers Change Direction*,
> University of Utah Press, Salt Lake City, Utah
> *Fruit of Stone*, Riverhead Books, New York, N.Y.

Rupert Weeks
> *Pachee Goyo, the Bald One*, Vantage, New York, N.Y.

Nancy Weidel,
> *Sheepwagon: Home on the Range*, High Plains Press

Sam Western,
> *Pushed Off the Mountain, Sold Down the River:
> Wyoming's Search for Its Soul*, Homestead Publishing

Eva Floy Wheeler
> *A History of Wyoming Writers*, self-published

Owen Wister
> *The Virginian, A Horseman of the Plains*,
> Dodd, Mead & Co., New York, N.Y.

David Zoby (with David Wright),
> *Fire on the Beach*, Scribner, New York, N.Y.

Printed in the United States
24961LVS00002B/388-390

9 780971 472570